Community-Centered Journalism

Community-Centered Journalism

Engaging People, Exploring Solutions, and Building Trust

ANDREA WENZEL

UNIVERSITY OF
ILLINOIS PRESS
Urbana, Chicago, and Springfield

© 2020 by the Board of Trustees
of the University of Illinois
All rights reserved
1 2 3 4 5 C P 5 4 3 2 1
♾ This book is printed on acid-free paper.

Library of Congress Cataloging-in-Publication Data
Names: Wenzel, Andrea, 1977– author.
Title: Community-centered journalism: engaging people,
exploring solutions, and building trust / Andrea Wenzel.
Description: Urbana: University of Illinois Press, [2020] |
Includes bibliographical references and index. |
Identifiers: LCCN 2020001593 (print) | LCCN 2020001594 (ebook)
|ISBN 9780252043307 (cloth) | ISBN 9780252085222 (paperback)
| ISBN 9780252052187 (ebook)
Subjects: LCSH: Journalism, Regional. | Local mass media. |
Journalism—Social aspects.
Classification: LCC PN4784.R29 W46 2020 (print) | LCC PN4784.
R29 (ebook) | DDC 070.4/33—dc23
LC record available at https://lccn.loc.gov/2020001593
LC ebook record available at https://lccn.loc.gov/2020001594

Contents

Preface   vii

Acknowledgments   ix

Introduction: The Case for Shared Community Stories   1

1 Shifting Stories with Solutions Journalism   23

2 Connecting Journalists and Community Members   47

3 Developing an Intervention: Building a Public Sphere in Polarized Places   75

4 The Process Is Portable: Toward a Community-Driven Intervention   105

5 A New Kind of Journalist? Competencies for Community-Centered Journalism   125

Conclusion: To Repair, or to Burn It Down?   158

Appendix: Methods for a Process Model   165

Notes   173

Bibliography   193

Index   201

Preface

One of the most remarkable stories I have heard about community engagement came from a colleague of mine in Afghanistan. After almost a decade-long stint in U.S. public radio, I found myself in Afghanistan from 2008 to 2010, working with Afghan associates to develop and manage media projects in local languages for Afghan audiences. The encounter in question happened to my colleague years earlier, before the Taliban's government fell in 2001. He was working with what at the time was the BBC's Afghan Education Project (AEP).[1] AEP, which was Afghan-run, produced documentary feature programs, but it was most famous for its radio soap opera, *New Home, New Life*. The program tackled serious and sensitive issues like health or education for girls but did so through entertaining storylines. AEP even had a cartoon magazine to go along with the radio program.

Rather than start with journalists and editors to develop story ideas and then go out and report them, as is the norm in many newsrooms, each project began with a needs assessment. AEP researchers went to villages around the country to hear about challenges or concerns residents had about a range of issues. They'd also ask how local knowledge was used to find solutions to health or agriculture issues or to resolve conflicts. They noted what local assets or organizations people in these communities had access to and documented the turns of phrase people used to talk about issues. These findings were then discussed with organizations and others considered to have subject matter expertise on the issues along with the editors and producers. This informed the development of all of AEP's programming ideas.

Before the Taliban fell in 2001, AEP was based in Pakistan (it was started as a project staffed by Afghan refugees during the civil war). But while in Pakistan, the organization's workers would still go into Afghanistan to do their needs assessments. When driving back from one of these needs assessments, my colleague noticed in the rearview mirror that his vehicle was being chased by members of the Taliban. When he and his associates realized they couldn't get away, they pulled over, fearing the worst. While AEP programs had not been banned by the Taliban, it was still risky to be caught working with an international media outlet. The Talib walked up to my colleague's window, demanding to know if he and his team were indeed with the BBC's AEP. When they admitted they were, he declared that he had heard that they were giving away cartoon magazines in the village they were just visiting. He wanted some for himself. He was a fan.

This was not the only story I heard about the Taliban or others in conservative areas of Afghanistan being loyal listeners to AEP programs. My colleagues attributed this to their efforts to be culturally sensitive and politically neutral. But this phenomenon also illustrated to me the power of their research-based approach to developing programs, which made such sensitivity possible.

During the time I worked with the project I saw more examples of how AEP's approach centered the experiences of community members. For example, AEP staffers might collaborate with local radio stations and community-based organizations to host listening sessions and discussions about issues raised in the radio programs. They aimed to hold each in a location where residents would feel comfortable gathering and talking. For some projects with Afghan women, this might mean over tea in private homes. Other programs attempted what we might now call crowdsourcing—inviting listeners to share local problems and following up to report on how they could be addressed. Programs also highlighted examples of how a problem was solved—like getting access to electricity in a rural village, or how a woman became a provincial council representative with the support of her family.

It would be several more years before I heard the terms "solutions journalism" or "engaged journalism," let alone "communication infrastructure theory."[2] But the experience planted a seed, as well as questions, about how journalism processes can be reimagined, even in the face of daunting circumstances, and how the needs and agency of communities may be centered to open pathways for journalism to be a means to larger ends of connection and problem solving.

Acknowledgments

As someone who has almost always worked on projects in teams, it is perhaps not surprising that I have managed to impose upon a great many people (more than I can mention by name here) to gather input and feedback over the course of writing this book—and even before I ever conceived of writing it.

I would never have gotten interested in the realm of solutions journalism or engaged journalism had I not been given a chance to experiment in these realms as a practitioner (before those terms were in fashion). I am especially grateful to the long-running WBEZ radio show *Worldview* for taking a chance on me and giving me the latitude to try new things. Over my fifteen years in public radio and international media development, I learned invaluable lessons from colleagues and from the communities we sought to connect with, whether they were in Chicago, DC, or Kabul.

Once I crossed over into the world of academia, I had the great fortune of connecting with the Metamorphosis Project at the University of Southern California, led by my brilliant adviser Sandra Ball-Rokeach. Through her guidance and the generous support of fellow team members and Meta alums, I learned that academic work could be change-oriented, collaborative, and engaged. In addition to gaining training in the theoretical frameworks that continue to guide me, I collaborated with Metamorphosis colleagues on the Los Angeles–based work in this book.

The case studies explored in this book would not have been possible without the support of the Tow Center for Digital Journalism at Columbia University.

As a fellow, I have benefited greatly from the backing and input of Tow colleagues past and present, especially Emily Bell, Pete Brown, Katie Johnston, Claire Wardle (now of First Draft), and Kathy Zhang. I have also appreciated the opportunity to collaborate on these cases with other fellows including Sam Ford, Anthony Nadler, and Melissa Valle.

My colleagues at Temple University have been tremendously supportive of me, and several offered thoughtful input on early drafts of chapters, including Brian Creech, Marc Lamont Hill, Magda Konieczna, Logan Molyneux, and Soomin Seo. I'm incredibly grateful for the valuable feedback I received on the manuscript from Jake Batsell, Letrell Crittenden, Jacob Nelson, and Sue Robinson. I would like to thank Daniel Nasset and the University of Illinois Press team. And I of course owe much gratitude to the support and encouragement I've received both from my family and my very dear network of friends who have helped me to stay grounded, even as the ground I am rooted in has shifted over countless moves and career twists.

This book is dedicated to the many community members and journalists who have joined me in trying to imagine what a better relationship between news media and publics could look like—both those I have spoken with for this book and friends who have indulged me in numerous conversations on this subject in recent years. Their willingness to candidly reflect on the harm caused by historically inequitable systems and at the same time to be open to mapping pathways forward inspires me. Knowing that so many are now undertaking community-centered efforts big and small gives me hope that journalists can share power and contribute to more connected and inclusive communities.

# Community-Centered Journalism

INTRODUCTION

The Case for Shared Community Stories

Chicago, Illinois, May 31, 2016

I met Gwen[1] in a leafy green park about fifteen miles south of Chicago's downtown as her friend was giving her a golf lesson. She said she was surprised to look up from practicing her swing to see me. "I don't see people walking through the neighborhood and talking to people," she explained. "Quite honestly, I was like, 'Why are these white people over here?'"[2]

For many, the South Side of Chicago evokes images of "Chiraq" or what Donald Trump cynically labeled "American carnage." Rampant gun violence. Blinding poverty. Gwen, who is Black, acknowledged that the area has real problems. But she took issue with how the media crudely referenced the vast geographic expanse of the majority African American South Side whenever an incident occurred in a single neighborhood. She recalled her brother in California calling her in the middle of the night after he heard a news report about violence on the South Side. "And I'm like, 'That happened [in] so and so, that's not where I'm at.'"

Gwen's brother is not the only one influenced by how Chicago is represented by the considerable number of news outlets covering it. Chicago is the third largest media market in the United States. It is home to subsidiaries of all the major television networks and is one of the few large cities that continues to host two daily newspapers, as well as numerous nonprofit and public media initiatives. But in Gwen's estimation, in the ecology of local news resources she could access, word of mouth often proved to be more reliable than these media sources. She gave the example of a front-page story in one of the dailies. The paper referenced her neighborhood as the site of a "bad story" about gang activity. But when she spoke with her neighbors, they found an inaccuracy in the story's geography: "All the neighbors that I know and people that were talking about it was like, 'That wasn't even our neighborhood.'"

Gwen argued that these kinds of journalistic inaccuracies resulted in negative coverage that did not reflect the reality she experienced in her neighborhood. This was more than irresponsible and sloppy, she argued; it also had harmful consequences. Negative coverage made people fearful. It made some avoid the South Side entirely. And it didn't offer a nuanced understanding of the larger structural reasons behind problems or how to address them. For that to happen, she argued, journalists needed to "learn communities, like really *learn* the communities." After talking with her neighbors, Gwen concluded that if journalists wanted to do a better job, there was a path to do so: "I think the community should play a bigger role in how their community is represented."

Beaver Dam, Kentucky, May 19, 2017

The diner in Beaver Dam was one of only a handful of restaurants in this part of rural Ohio County, Kentucky. I met with Steph at a booth in the back. After perusing a menu with a smiling anthropomorphized catfish on the cover, we ordered drinks. Over coffee, Steph, who is white, expressed a similar frustration with reporters coming to the area and focusing only on the bad.

In this part of Kentucky, the majority is non-Latinx white and voted for Trump—and Steph is part of this majority. In her area, far fewer media sources are available for local news. While there is a weekly newspaper and a hyperlocal online news site, she said she usually got her local news from the town's commercial radio station, which mostly played music but had some talk programming and announcements. Much of her frustration with media came from the regional and national media portrayals of the area that she mostly viewed on Facebook or her Yahoo homepage. She described what she perceived as a distance between her day-to-day experiences and what she saw in media depictions of the region.

"I don't think they get a lot of what I really truly call grassroots opinions and perspectives," she explained. "What happens on the political front affects us differently because if you have a farming community, a coal mining community ... when they start shutting down coal mines, I've got family and friends that are unemployed."[3]

Steph felt frustrated not only with media coverage of economic and political issues but also with media's overall focus on crisis and negativity. "I know that that's what catches everybody's attention," she suggested. But that was not what she was looking for. Steph wanted more positive stories. She wanted local media to highlight characters in her community who reflected what she knew and who challenged people's stereotypical assumptions. She gave the example of a neighbor of her mother's: "The community sees him as just being a loudmouth, beer-drinking redneck." But Steph recounted how he regularly checked on her mother, and when he learned she was ill, "he brought the first potatoes and peas out of his garden. He said, 'Fix these for your mama.'" She offered other examples of community initiatives, including one addressing homelessness, that never got any news coverage. People won't know about these activities and voices if the media doesn't reflect them, she argued.

Like Gwen, Steph saw unfairly negative portrayals of her area as a deliberate act by journalists motivated by what they think will sell: "I get the feeling that they stand back and they wait and they watch and find the person that's got about four teeth, you know. I feel like they look for the person that looks the worst physically and probably is not very articulate and would come across as being uneducated."

So much of the narrative of division in the United States centers on the distance between communities like the mostly Democrat and Black South Side of Chicago and the mostly Republican and white rural Kentucky. But these women's experiences highlight another kind of distance: the one between residents and media, one that leaves a shared distaste and distrust when journalists extract stories that residents feel are distorted and disrespectful. Both Gwen and Steph have bones to pick with how journalists represent their communities. And while they are separated by some four hundred miles and have never met, both have come to some common ground regarding potential alternatives to the status quo. Both want to see media outlets connect with residents like them to share and cocreate stories grounded in local context, representing a fuller spectrum of their communities' experiences.

In this book, I examine local journalism initiatives that are attempting to narrow the distance and connect the links between media, residents, and other community stakeholders. These efforts respond in many ways to concerns raised by both Gwen and Steph about the need for journalists to be embedded in communities, to have relationships with community members, and to offer a fuller representation of community life. Some of these projects have been led by newsrooms, others by third-party organizations, a few in collaboration with researchers, including myself, and others by groups of community members. All of these efforts challenge or at least grapple with the boundaries of dominant journalism norms and practices that often act as barriers to strengthening ties within local storytelling networks. Some, more than others, attempt to decenter journalistic power in order to share power with marginalized communities.

From Los Angeles to Chicago, Beaver Dam to Philadelphia, I focus on these local U.S. journalism interventions because each applies a variation on two practices that will be explored in greater depth later in this chapter and throughout the book: *solutions journalism* and *engaged journalism*. Solutions journalism holds that a journalist's role is not only to report on problems but also to rigorously report on "responses to social problems."[4] Solutions journalism initiatives offer an alternative for residents like Gwen and Steph who are alienated by the constant drumbeat of negative local news. Engaged journalism refers to a range of practices that aim to build relationships between journalists and the public and involve the public in the process of cocreating journalism. The cases in this book employ strategies from both of these practices to varying degrees, and both Gwen and Steph have participated in these projects.

When applied at the local level, solutions journalism and engaged journalism practices intervene in what communication infrastructure theory, or CIT,[5] calls "storytelling networks"—that is, the network of residents, community groups, and local media that are all involved in circulating community stories. In this book I show how these interventions are changing the nature of narratives circulating in local storytelling networks and reveal the extent they are and are not strengthening ties between different parts of the network. I argue that when applied in combination, local solutions journalism and engaged journalism practices can contribute to a communication environment with greater trust between media, community members, and organizations, where residents feel more connected and invested. But, I caution that these practices will neither strengthen storytelling network ties nor build trust with marginalized communities unless they are reflexive about journalistic norms, like objectivity, that reinforce hierarchies of race, class, and geography. By looking at these different initiatives through a CIT lens, I offer a model for *community-centered journalism*—not a prescription for a project but rather for an intervention *process* that responds to communities' needs and assets in its attempt to strengthen storytelling networks and build trust. By engaging residents in the process of reimagining local news and information, these interventions have the potential to offer shared spaces for dialogue and action on community issues. As such, while the book does offer a vision for rethinking journalism norms and practices, it is less concerned with strengthening journalism for journalism's sake than with strengthening the communication health of communities.

A Participant Observer

I came to this project as an outgrowth of my own experiences and experiments as a journalist. In the late 1990s and into the turn of the twenty-first century, I produced a global affairs program for WBEZ public radio, the National Public Radio affiliate in Chicago. While I had a great appreciation for my job, I found two elements frustrating. First, covering global conflicts on a daily basis quickly became depressing and desensitizing. And second, I became more aware of the demographically limited nature of our listenership. While our particular program had a loyal and vocal following of listeners from immigrant and refugee communities, our station's audience, like most public radio outlets in the United States, overall was disproportionately white. Our listenership did not look like the majority Black and Brown city of Chicago, and it had higher than average levels of education and income. Likewise, our listenership seemed to sit within an ideological bubble—certainly my Republican parents across the border in Indiana were never going to tune in to NPR.

Responding to these circumstances and the affordances of the early days of the Internet, my colleagues and I began exploring ways to offer coverage that went beyond stating the facts of war or genocide. We experimented with crowdsourcing, like a weekly series that invited listeners to nominate a person or group with Chicago ties doing work to address a global challenge.[6] From people starting solar oven projects in Angola to health programs in India, these stories were always our most popular, and people turned out in large numbers to public events to learn more about ways to get involved in the issues or programs featured. We also attempted to deepen community involvement by hosting interactive public discussions about issues critical to immigrant and diaspora communities in the region. And I occasionally mentored community members to cocreate radio stories about their personal experiences. This work was not without complications. As a white woman I was often working with communities that do not look or sound like me and with whom there were uneven power dynamics. I had to be mindful not only of the need to invest time to establish trust but also to critically interrogate how I was imposing my own assumptions (tied to cultural and whiteness norms) about what a "good" radio story sounded like. In addition to navigating difference with the communities I worked with, I also at times faced resistance from within our radio station. Some projects were met with concerns about slipping into advocacy journalism. At other times, people questioned the willingness of our audience to listen to a person speaking in accented English.

At the time, the terms "solutions journalism" and "engaged journalism" had yet to surface. Nevertheless, these nascent experiences with similar practices stuck with me. While I ultimately decided public media did not need one more middle-class white woman's voice on the radio, I continued to explore some of the concepts I first encountered there twenty years ago both in research and practice. For this reason, throughout this book I take a normative stance that a more inclusive and connected local communication infrastructure is a goal that can and should be pursued through both academic scholarship and practice. I not only have researched solutions journalism and engaged journalism initiatives but also have gotten my hands messy attempting to help to organize them. As such, I make no claims to be an objective outsider. I am doing this research because I want to understand how I too can help facilitate this work more effectively.

Journalism Interventions in Context

Before I delve into case examples of local journalism interventions, it will be helpful to reflect on the larger context in which these cases emerged and to define what is meant by some relevant terms and theoretical frameworks. Here I focus in particular on concepts such as trust, solutions journalism, engaged journalism, boundary challenges, and communication infrastructure theory.

"Trust" in Local Journalism

Numerous studies have consistently shown a decline in trust in U.S. journalism,[7] as well as in other institutions.[8] To put trust in historical context, scholars of journalism history have noted that the idea of an objective, neutral, and professionalized press—one that deserves to be trusted—is a relatively recent phenomenon.[9] Attempting to explain the rise and fall of trust in journalism, scholars have pointed to a unique set of conditions in the mid-twentieth century that allowed for the growth of trust, at least among a majority of the population. As political scientist Jonathan Ladd argues, this was a time of low political polarization and limited economic competition. These circumstances encouraged higher levels of trust in journalism as they "led to less elite political media criticism and more 'objective' hard news coverage."[10] This era, characterized more by field reporting than by political talking heads, coincided with the economic conditions that media scholar Magda Konieczna argues allowed for the blossoming of public service journalism in the United States, thanks to a trifecta of subsidies: family ownership of papers, the bundling of public service journalism with more profitable content, and the provisions of the Fairness Doctrine.[11]

Of course, subsequent to this era, consolidation, market failure, and a lack of sustainable business models have left many communities with news outlets that have been gutted of resources or have become news deserts.[12] Yet at the same time local news has been hit by financial distress, local news offers a promising area for exploration on the question of trust. In the United States, a number of studies report higher levels of trust in local news than in national outlets,[13] leading some to conclude that local news itself may act as a "building block to rebuild trust" due to its proximity to community concerns.[14]

But exactly what is meant by "trust" in the context of journalism is somewhat muddier. In many efforts to assess how people do or do not trust media, studies have left the concept of trust open to the interpretation of respondents[15] — in terms of what trust means and the object of trust (local, national, and international outlets of all mediums being compressed into "the media"). Often in journalism studies, trust is closely associated with the credibility of news sources, with models accounting for how media outlets select topics and facts and the accuracy of their depictions and journalistic assessments.[16] Other models have focused more on the relationship between the trustor and the trustee. Roger Mayer, James Davis, and F. David Schoorman's model defines trust as the trustor's willingness to assume risk and be vulnerable to the actions of a trustee. In their model, a trustor evaluates trustworthiness based on factors including how he or she perceive the ability, benevolence, and integrity of the trustee. But trustworthiness also varies based on the trustor's propensity to trust and on the context.[17]

The idea that trust is dependent on the relationship between actors is developed further by Sue Robinson in her study of marginalized communities within larger media ecologies. Robinson points out that trust fluctuates based on the dynamics of relationships, place, and power: "Trust must be attained, like capital, and is something that can be gained and lost fluidly."[18] As Robinson shows in her study, "Trust as a relational practice is inevitably caught up in issues of power and privilege."[19]

For the purposes of this book, I also take trust as a relational concept to look at the local level. I focus on how different actors in local storytelling networks, residents, and representatives of different local media and community groups talk about their relationships with each other in terms of trustworthiness factors. I adapt Mayer, Davis, and Schoorman's factors, conceptualizing "trust" as perceived accuracy and credibility, respectful and equitable representations, and benevolence of motives. Engaging with journalists and the communities they are attempting to reach, I ask how both parties can form relationships of mutual trust and what these would look like. Because I focus on case studies of interventions in communities that have been stigmatized or marginalized, I pay special attention to how power dynamics and questions of representation affect the negotiation of trust between community members and journalists. By inviting study participants to share open-ended reflections on their relationship with media rather than imposing a fixed quantitative scale of trust, I focus on how participants talk about their relationships in terms of trustworthiness factors.

"The Whole Story"

At the beginning of a Solutions Journalism Network (SJN) training for journalists in Philadelphia, the trainer invited all the participants to take an online quiz. The "Gapminder Test" posed a series of questions about the magnitude of a range of global social ills, from poverty to education to public health. Participants' scores were generated automatically, and the trainer invited us to raise our hands when she read out our score—starting with the highest possible score and counting down. Almost no hands were to be seen until we got well below what would be a passing score in any context. Almost everyone had overestimated the extent of the problems in question (myself included). This led the trainer to prod reporters and editors to reflect on whether the reporting they and others produced could be part of the reason so many have a grim view of the state of the world and such limited awareness of efforts to address challenges or progress that has been made. Emphasizing only the negative stories leaves the public with distorted perceptions and an incomplete understanding, the SJN trainer pointed out. If journalists are responsible for informing the public, she suggested, surely they should offer "the whole story"—not only spotlighting social ills but also highlighting how they are being addressed.

Since 2013, SJN has been making the case for solutions journalism through outreach to journalists and newsrooms. The concept challenges the traditional norm of emphasizing conflict as a news value,[20] heeding calls by scholars such as Herbert Gans to look at the "newsworthiness" of "solutions for the country's problems—advanced by people outside the mainstream."[21] SJN has been careful to distinguish solutions journalism from what it is not, including "good news" or "advocacy journalism." The goal, it says, is not to advocate for a particular solution but rather to critically explore a response to a problem—looking at what is working or at how it works—including its limitations and insightful failures. Likewise, SJN argues that stories focusing on exceptional individuals or heroes do not meet the criteria. By centering critical and systemic explorations of responses to problems, it avoids the formula that media sociologist Gaye Tuchman warned of: solutions journalism stories do not seek to "soothe the news consumers even as they reify social forces" by ensuring the public that "legitimated experts and authorities are doing everything they can."[22] Rather, SJN draws parallels with investigative reporting standards of rigor and practices such as emphasizing evidence and data.

SJN was founded by two *New York Times* journalists, David Bornstein and Tina Rosenberg. Unsurprisingly, given their professional backgrounds, their conception of solutions journalism walks a careful line, adhering to many journalistic norms—for example, as with their wariness of advocacy. But, critically, it challenges the theory of change of watchdog journalism. One of the slides used in SJN presentations suggests that journalism's theory of change is that "journalists act as whistleblowers and expose wrongdoing" and that "pointing out social problems will spur reform."[23] This logic conforms to Walter Lippmann's idea of "the great healing effect of publicity"—that exposing unseemly interests to sunlight will neutralize them.[24] But SJN argues that "covering the problem without addressing associated responses omits critical information necessary for society to create change."[25]

While challenging watchdog journalism's tendencies to focus on the problem alone, SJN positions solutions journalism as an alternate form of accountability journalism. By highlighting how a problem is being addressed, often in another locale, it argues that solutions journalism removes the excuses used by authorities who claim a problem is intractable. In a presentation, SJN cofounder Bornstein offered the example of solutions journalism reporting done by the *Cleveland Plain Dealer* on lead poisoning. In their series "Toxic Neglect," the reporters broke down the dimensions of the problem, but rather than stopping there, they also reported on how other cities had responded to the challenge of lead through various strategies.[26] Bornstein shared how this coverage was followed by a number of reforms in Cleveland, including personnel changes, new home inspection policies, and postings of warning signs. Bornstein argued that when journalists highlight responses to problems, "a problem that had been seen as unavoidable comes to be seen as unacceptable."[27]

The practice of solutions journalism has been adopted by a growing number of news outlets in the United States and other countries. SJN itself has grown from a small staff led by the pair of veteran *New York Times* journalists to a team of twenty-nine. By mid-2019 it had over two hundred "engaged newsroom partners," which one of SJN's staff members defined as teams that had "broad institutional and editorial support for solutions journalism"—most of whom had received training from SJN.[28] In addition, the network holds an annual summit, collaborates on a workshop for journalism school educators, and has translated its toolkit into eleven languages. Recently it partnered with the organization Report for America to place journalists into newsrooms in the U.S. Mountain West region who committed to report on issues from a solutions journalism frame. SJN tracks and archives solutions journalism stories it learns of, and solutions journalism projects and newsroom collaborations have received a number of high-profile awards.

Peace Journalism and Public Journalism

Solutions journalism is not entirely new. Many journalists have found their way to equivalent practices prior to any awareness of this as a concept or brand.

And the practice has resonance with previous schools of journalism that have attempted to prioritize more constructive news norms. Starting in the 1960s and 1970s, sociologist Johan Galtung put forth the concept of "peace journalism."[29] Galtung advocated that rather than use a conflict-oriented frame, journalists draw from a frame more common in health reporting, where journalists are encouraged to examine causes of disease as well as strategies for their prevention.[30] While peace journalism largely was aligned with traditional journalism norms, it had some points of departure. Notably, its advocates at times took an interventionist line by encouraging stories with an agreement orientation rather than focusing only on points of difference (for example, in cases of coverage of peace negotiations).[31] Critics suggested this approach placed too much responsibility on journalists to forgo objectivity and correct global ills.[32] Its defenders, however, argued that objectivity was actually an impediment to journalism playing a constructive role in public life.[33] Galtung and others have continued to advocate for peace journalism. In recent years, proponents of "constructive journalism" in Europe (a sister practice to solutions journalism that puts more emphasis on the positive psychological effects of solutions-oriented coverage) have highlighted Galtung's concerns around the negative bias of news.[34] However, overall, the practice of peace journalism has not become widely known or adopted among journalists.

The public or civic journalism movement of the 1990s similarly advocated for a more constructive orientation to news, with an emphasis on the active role citizens could play in the process. Jay Rosen, a founding proponent of this school, called for journalists to "1) address people as citizens, potential participants in public affairs, rather than victims or spectators; 2) help the political community to act upon, rather than just learn about, its problems; 3) improve the climate of public discussion, rather than simply watching it deteriorate; 4) make public life go well, so that it earns its claim on our attention."[35] Part of the public journalism push involved an emphasis on setting a "citizens' agenda" that offered a "bottom-up framing" of the news.[36] Throughout the 1990s, researchers documented a blossoming of a number of civic and public journalism initiatives, with at least a fifth of all U.S. newspapers undertaking initiatives. Tracking these initiatives, Lewis Friedland and Sandra Nichols reported that "the goals of news organizations show a strong commitment to the traditional public news values of informing the public and, to a lesser extent, the civic and democratic values of problem-solving and increased deliberation." They noted that 78 percent of the stories they examined from these initiatives included reporting on possible solutions.[37] Other researchers charted cases that managed to increase their use of nonelite sources representing a broader cross-section of the public.[38] Despite these gains, public/civic journalism faced pushback from traditionalists in many outlets, as well as critiques that it did not clearly spell out a practice for how journalism could more effectively support democracy.[39] While it left an imprint on many practitioners, it largely faded from mainstream journalism discourse.

Both civic journalism and peace journalism originated prior to the widespread adoption of mobile and networked online communication. The subsequent emergence of these media infrastructures enabled more multidirectional interactions between makers and users of media, opening doors for some media outlets to consider more participatory bottom-up storytelling.[40] Media tools alone did not determine changes in professional culture or editorial gatekeeping.[41] However, for some, new technologies enabled new ways of thinking about how publics engaged with and shared stories.

Engaging "the People Formerly Known as the Audience"

Solutions-focused collaboration, crowdsourcing, coproduction, crowdfunding, inclusion, interactive media, mobile chat, public convenings, and training—these are some of what the Democracy Fund, a private bipartisan foundation, calls "key categories" in a taxonomy of "engaged journalism."[42] Each category, the foundation explains, grapples in different and at times overlapping ways with the relationship between newsrooms and community members. Beyond this taxonomy there are related terms, including "participatory journalism," "social journalism," "people-powered journalism," and "reciprocal journalism."[43] The terms and practices associated with them can vary considerably—from community events, to soliciting story ideas on a website, to training community storytellers, to interactions on social media. Despite this variation, most initiatives share a genealogical link to a combination of civic and public journalism or community and citizen media.[44] Uniting them is a more active imagining of journalism's relationship with "the former audience"[45] or "the people formerly known as the audience."[46] Rather than a one-to-many model of news, these genres of journalism emphasize participatory and multidirectional flows of media.[47] As Lindsay Green-Barber, a consultant and researcher who has worked with a range of engaged journalism projects, outlines, engaged journalism can be thought of as "an inclusive practice that prioritizes the information needs and wants of the community members it serves, creates collaborative space for the audience in all aspects of the journalistic process, and is dedicated to building and preserving trusting relationships between journalists and the public."[48]

Among practitioners, what it means to "do engagement" has at times been a messy if not murky concept. Confusion over what constitutes engagement can in part be traced to the term's association with social media (where it can mean whether one clicks on a story or shares it or how long one spends on a page) or to comments and discussion on an outlet's website or social media page. In these areas, engagement is often positioned as a technique to increase audience members' financial loyalty,[49] or "trust, connectedness, and social capital."[50] Often, digital engagement has been leveraged with an eye toward how sentiments generated may make the audience better consumers and benefit a bottom line. Engagement here is positioned as a means to an end of more financially sustainable journalism. Other times, some of the same practitioners emphasize engaged journalism as a means to an end of community and civic engagement. This can mean additions to the engagement toolbox such as offline outreach[51] and interactive dialogue, participatory storytelling, or other community-driven tools and tactics that push toward deeper or "thicker"[52] engagement. Andrew DeVigal of the Agora Journalism Center has argued that this range of approaches to engagement can be plotted on a continuum from transactional to relational.[53] Due to these different orientations, with some exceptions,[54] measuring the success of engagement has often been problematic as it lacks an agreed-upon definition or metric.[55] Measuring what makes a core audience spend more time with a media product is quite different from measuring the impact of initiatives that attempt to connect with communities that are not traditionally part of an outlet's "audience" and whose members may feel their concerns have not historically been well represented.

While recognizing the critical nature of questions of economic sustainability, this book primarily focuses on questions of relational or deep engagement as a means to the end of civic participation and strengthening community storytelling networks. As such, it goes beyond the question of what engagement practices can do for a given journalism outlet to focus instead on what engagement practices can do for the health of communities.

The Boundary-Work of Building Relationships and Centering Community

On the more relational side of the engagement spectrum, practitioners undertake community outreach and organizing work that strengthen connections between storytelling network actors, like local media and residents. This work at times pushes the boundaries of journalism norms. Is it the work of journalism to set up a table asking for questions and story ideas at a community event? Or to host a convening where residents and various organizations discuss a local issue and efforts to respond to it? And are there points when journalists should go beyond "engagement" to share power and allow communities to step into the center? Do we need a new kind of journalist to do the work of strengthening ties between local media, residents, and community groups? Can journalists act as relationship builders, building ties and trust between communities and media? What competencies do journalists need to do this work, and how might other fields like community organizing offer guidance?

Many journalism observers and critics have grappled with the questions of what makes journalism "journalism" and who get to call themselves "journalists." These conversations have grown louder as tools for telling and distributing information and stories have become increasingly accessible. Journalism studies scholars have added value to this conversation by adapting sociologist Thomas Gieryn's concept of "boundary-work."[56] Boundary-work looks at how groups compete in ever changing contexts to define what falls inside and outside a social boundary.

Matt Carlson adapts the concept to journalism in a matrix looking at how the boundary-work of expansion, expulsion, and protection of autonomy applies to journalism's participants, practices, and professionalism.[57] Many boundary-work conversations in journalism studies have focused on challenges arising from technological changes, such as the rise of Internet bloggers or social media practices. However, Carlson's matrix has room for more low-tech challenges, such as those coming from engaged journalism. For example, those who see community engagement as a threat to journalism may seek to keep "out non-journalistic informational actors" like citizens. Likewise, those who aim to expand the boundaries of journalism could try to make it acceptable to adopt practices used in community organizing, such as holding one-on-one meetings or tabling at local events.

In her analysis of boundary challenges undertaken by actors in a media ecology, Robinson, who draws from Pierre Bourdieu's field theory,[58] notes the range of boundaries would-be challengers face. In her case, residents and activists had to reckon with physical, virtual, rhetorical, and mediated boundaries as they attempted to participate in public discourse around education. For example, even if a person got access to a meeting room or a Facebook group, he or she had to know the professional lexicon in order to function with authority. An actor's success in challenging this range of boundaries often came down to "field positionality and the ability to network within the dominant doxa."[59] In the boundary-work of engaged journalism, as will be explored in greater depth in chapter 5, practitioners and members of the public similarly have varying success challenging boundaries based on their ability to navigate dominant norms and values in the field of journalism.

It is important to acknowledge that many engaged journalism initiatives (and solutions journalism initiatives) remain centered on the newsroom in ways that can be difficult to access, for marginalized communities in particular. Many newsrooms are composed of journalists who are majority white and of a higher socioeconomic status and who are positioned as reaching out to communities of color that have less socioeconomic status. In such center-periphery relationships, there is some resonance with the critique of postcolonial theorist Gayatri

Chakravorty Spivak. In her essay "Can the Subaltern Speak?," the subaltern can be heard only by adopting the colonizers' ways of knowing and expressing.[60] In cases where communities are kept at the periphery, marginalized residents are legible to "mainstream" journalists and audiences (who are often also white and of higher socioeconomic status) only when they interact on the newsroom's terms, often using the newsroom's tools. Likewise, postcolonial scholar Homi Bhabha argues that framing such efforts as showcasing cultural diversity can be problematic if adherents present their welcoming of diversity in a way that actually *contains* cultural difference—for example, "These other cultures are fine, but we must be able to locate them within our own grid."[61] Critical race scholars have similarly warned against projects to increase diversity without first changing underlying conventions and practices; as Ruth Frankenberg has argued, such projects can result in "valorizing cultural difference but doing so in a way that leaves racial and cultural hierarchies intact."[62] These critical concerns underline the importance of initiatives that share ownership with communities and make room for people to speak and be heard in ways that recognize difference and do not force conformity to journalism practices that are usually tied to norms of whiteness and class. Journalism initiatives can be seen on a continuum in terms of the degree that they adhere to norms that reinforce whiteness and power versus those that center and share power with communities.

Accounting for this continuum, both solutions journalism and engaged journalism constitute potential boundary challenges, particularly to U.S. journalistic norms of objectivity[63] that construct journalists' primary responsibility as introducing strings of facts to an audience that is kept at a distance. They also stray from adversarial watchdog journalism that focuses exclusively on problems. Solutions journalism, then, pushes the boundaries of *what* stories are worthy of coverage, while engaged journalism may help solutions journalism to circulate by challenging norms of *how* journalists connect with audiences. In many ways, both practices are aligned with communication scholar James Carey's ritual view of communication. In Carey's ideal, the press does more than transmit information. The value of the press comes from creating a space for the public to understand information through public discourse and by "encouraging the conversation of its culture."[64] Likewise, news media that is engaged and solutions-oriented requires journalists to expand how they see their role—to be open to facilitating dialogue and a more participatory public.

Solutions-oriented and engaged journalism practices do not inherently go together. One can practice solutions journalism without practicing engaged journalism, and vice versa. Likewise, there is a continuum along which such initiatives may or may not share power with marginalized communities. However, in the sections that follow, I argue that these practices offer optimal value to address the communication challenges many communities grapple with when considered in tandem and designed in ways that are community-centered.

Sharing Stories, Connecting Communities: CIT's Insights for Local Journalism

Employing both engaged and solutions journalism practices allows practitioners to make an intervention into the storytelling network of communication infrastructure theory.[65] CIT was developed by communication scholar Sandra Ball-Rokeach and her Los Angeles–based Metamorphosis Project research team in the early 2000s.[66] The theory grew out of a desire to understand the role communication plays in building and maintaining community cohesion and also the processes of social change at the local level. Because of this, while journalism scholarship often places journalists at the center of the information health of a community, CIT positions them as only one actor in a larger network where other actors also have agency. According to CIT, this "network" refers to the discursive relationships between residents, community organizations, and local media, who are all "storytelling actors" involved in circulating stories about their community (see figure 1). When these actors are linked to each other, they offer the potential to circulate a common story of a shared community, akin to Benedict Anderson's concept of an imagined community.[67]

CIT offers a framework for understanding the communication health of places. Assessing the strength of storytelling network connections makes it

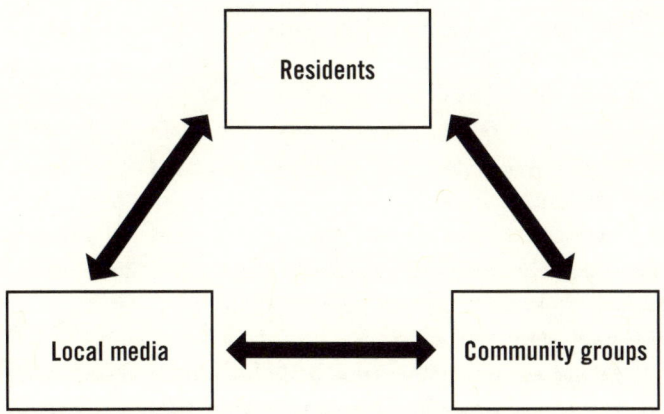

Figure 1. Communication Infrastructure Theory's "Storytelling Network"

possible to diagnose the communication health of a community in a way that goes beyond determining whether an area is a news desert or not. For example, understanding the communication infrastructure involves not only examining the presence of a local newspaper and its circulation but also looking at the content of that paper's coverage (are stories truly place-based and addressing community issues?) and how that content was or was not informed by residents and community groups (who may link residents to each other and let local journalists know about key community issues). In communities where different storytelling actors are more connected to each other, researchers have found higher levels of civic engagement and a greater shared understanding of community issues. But in a number of communities, researchers have documented missing links, particularly between local media and community organizations. When these or other links are weak or fragmented, or when the content of stories circulating in the network are overwhelmingly negative, residents connected to the storytelling network are less likely to report a sense of shared belonging, collective efficacy, or civic participation.[68] Fragmented storytelling networks are less likely to be able to organize to advocate for change or access local policy and power structures.

In addition, communication infrastructure theory is centered on place-based communities rather than on news outlets. This makes CIT compatible with explorations of the importance of place-based identity and power dynamics. Like Christopher Ali's work exploring "media localism"[69] and Lewis Friedland's concept of "communicatively integrated communities,"[70] the local is privileged as critical to a healthy public sphere. Ali's contention that the "local is contextual and contingent upon mobility, class, and life cycle"[71] complements CIT's concept of "communication action contexts" that can either facilitate or constrain connecting to the storytelling networks. The context in which a news narrative is processed in Boston will vary when read in Baltimore, let alone in Bristol, Indiana. Indeed, the context of place and power will exert meaningful differences depending on whether a story is heard by residents of North Philadelphia or when it is heard three miles away by those who live in Philadelphia's Center City. While scholars focused on local news and place, such as Ali, have examined primarily critical questions of access and policy, the cases in this book will focus in a complementary way on more granular questions of how residents make sense of the content of stories circulating about their community; on the points of connection between journalists, residents, and key community stakeholders; and on the possibility of journalistic practices and outreach to alter these relationships. I use CIT as a framework to analyze these case studies rooted in place that to varying extents attempt to tackle different links in community storytelling networks.

These case studies build on CIT's tradition of focusing on communities that historically have been either neglected by news outlets or affected by stigmatization—a layering of a reputation for crime and disorder onto a place and people.[72] For example, in some neighborhoods of Los Angeles, researchers have identified communities where the only news circulating was perceived to be negative, and residents connecting to these storytelling networks tended to lack a sense of collective efficacy and to express negative sentiments toward groups of people who were portrayed in an exclusively negative light.[73] Similarly, the case studies in this book largely explore communities that have been the focus of negative media coverage, highlighting the subjective experiences of residents. Like Ruth Palmer's exploration of how residents use folk theories to make sense of the work of journalism and the power of journalists,[74] the case studies here explore the narratives residents construct about how journalists represent their community, journalists' motives, and the daylight between the perspectives of residents and journalists. These narratives illustrate how residents think about trustworthiness factors (accuracy, perceived motives, representation) and how such factors affect storytelling network links. Working with these communities, I do not ask, "How do we restore trust in media?" This is at base a problematic question when trust has never been earned in many marginalized communities. Rather, I ask how we can make more trustful communities by strengthening storytelling networks.

In cases where weaknesses in the storytelling network have corresponded with low levels of civic engagement or a lack of community cohesion—for example, when local government elections go uncontested or cultural and linguistic divisions stymie organizing efforts—researchers have at times collaborated with practitioners to design communication interventions. These have included a range of approaches, from health communication campaigns[75] to coalitions connecting residents with organizers and policy makers to plan for sustainable development.[76] Several projects have also used CIT to inform the design[77] and evaluation[78] of media and journalism interventions.

One of the most ambitious examples has been the case of the hyperlocal news site Alhambra Source. Researchers at the University of Southern California[79] collaborated with journalists to launch a trilingual (English, Mandarin Chinese, and Spanish) website in response to studies that revealed ethnically and linguistically fragmented storytelling networks in a suburb of Los Angeles whose population had shifted from majority non-Hispanic white to majority Asian and Latinx. The city of Alhambra had no independent local media outlets, and so unsurprisingly residents lacked a shared resource to learn about community issues or civic life. Alhambra Source initially sourced its content primarily from community contributors[80] and included a number of community outreach events. While Alhambra Source has struggled to secure ongoing funding, preliminary research suggests it has had a substantial impact, especially through its accountability journalism. Over the course of several years, Alhambra Source coverage was influencing local officials, helping to mobilize the formation of community organizations,[81] and producing investigative coverage of city government expenditures.[82] In addition to accountability coverage, Alhambra Source attempted its own version of deep engagement by training youth and adult contributors and hosting events.[83] In planning its activities, it took care to be mindful of the racial coding and power dynamics of places,[84] attempting to create spaces that were welcoming across linguistic and cultural divides. Alhambra Source's efforts demonstrate how a CIT framework can be used to assess community information needs and inform journalistic interventions.

Bearing these contexts in mind, this book demonstrates how solutions journalism and engaged journalism offer promise for potential interventions to strengthen local storytelling networks. I argue that solutions journalism provides an alternative to exclusively negative content circulating in storytelling networks, a critical intervention particularly for residents who perceive their geographic, cultural, or political communities to be stigmatized by news media. At the same time, engaged journalism practices are needed to connect residents to solutions journalism content. Beyond this, engaged journalism practices, particularly when they share power and ownership with communities, present boundary challenges to dominant journalism norms like objectivity that act as impediments to leveling power imbalances and building trust. Challenging those norms is a prerequisite to strengthening storytelling network ties between journalists, residents, and community groups. When engaged journalism and solutions journalism, then, are taken together, both practices can more effectively build relationships of mutual trust. Through more solutions-oriented stories, residents may shift community narratives from "Who's to blame?" to "What can we do?" At the same time, engagement practices that are community-centered can connect residents to media, organizations, and fellow residents to mobilize—to better understand and address shared community issues. By strengthening local communication infrastructures, these journalism reform movements offer the potential to contribute to communities where residents are more likely to feel a sense of belonging and participate in civic life.

Overview

This book tackles the question of how to build trust between communities and media, particular in areas that have historically been marginalized or divided.

It follows interventions that attempted to strengthen local communication infrastructure undertaken by various combinations of newsrooms, community stakeholders, organizations, and researchers. Starting in Los Angeles and Chicago, I chart how they did and did not affect relationships between local media, residents, and community groups. I then outline how I worked with local journalists and community stakeholders in Kentucky and Philadelphia to develop and test a model for designing and evaluating interventions that aimed to strengthen ties between communities and media. In addition to these cases, I survey the landscape of engaged and solutions journalism initiatives taking place elsewhere in North America and the challenges of supporting and funding this work. I argue that while there is no one-size-fits-all intervention project, there is value in following a process model that is participatory and focuses on building relationships that share power between journalists and community stakeholders.

To analyze this series of qualitative empirical case studies, I used a communication infrastructure theory framework. While I offer a more extensive discussion of methods in the appendix, I generally followed a process of conducting a research study (often employing a combination of focus groups, diaries, and interviews), convening a discussion about findings with key community stakeholders and journalists, developing a pilot intervention in consultation with these stakeholders, and then implementing the pilot and monitoring its progress. The methods used in each chapter varied slightly due to the nature of the cases (some focused on a particular link in the storytelling network, others followed interventions undertaken by a third party, and so on). In each case, I include perspectives from both communities and journalists. I also include reflections from practitioners connected with these and other projects who occupy roles that straddle the worlds of journalism, engagement, and community organizing.

In chapter 1, I focus on the storytelling network link between local media and community organizations. I do this by analyzing a solutions journalism intervention in South Los Angeles, a majority African American and Latinx area that has historically been stigmatized. I detail the media intervention that colleagues from the University of Southern California's Metamorphosis research group and I organized to connect and build trust between local media and community organizations. This led to the collaborative production of a series of solutions journalism stories, which we then discussed with community members who expressed enthusiasm for the solutions journalism approach but shared lingering concerns about power imbalances in news production and a lack of input into the production process. I reflect on how solutions journalism initiatives, particularly those that involve community groups, have the potential to build trust within storytelling networks. But I underline that these interventions can be effective only when paired with engagement.

In chapter 2, I look more closely at the storytelling network link between residents and local media, centering on a case where a media outlet has attempted to involve community members in the process of producing journalism. The chapter follows *Curious City*, a Chicago public media initiative that uses the digital engagement platform Hearken to invite listeners to nominate questions about Chicago that they want reporters to explore. I focus on their yearlong outreach project that aimed to expand participation in the series, primarily by conducting outreach to African American and Latinx neighborhoods. I follow their attempt to determine the efficacy of various outreach methods: face-to-face outreach, outreach via community partners, social media marketing. Through this I show how their outreach did and did not strengthen storytelling network links between Chicago public media, residents, community organizations, and hyperlocal and ethnic media. The case highlights the limits of engagement that is not community-centered. It reveals how engagement practices can close the gap between "community" and "audience," but only when engagement tools are paired with outreach that meets communities where they are.

After looking at the link between local media and community groups in chapter 1 and between local media and residents in chapter 2, in chapter 3 I look at the entire storytelling network, synthesizing lessons learned about solutions journalism and online and offline engagement. In this chapter I introduce a model for designing research-based local journalism interventions. The case explores a majority Republican area in Western Kentucky where distrust of media is intertwined with political and place identity. The chapter examines how political polarization has affected local storytelling networks. I then recount how we organized a workshop with residents, local media partners, community organization representatives, and journalism organizations to discuss findings and brainstorm possible projects to strengthen networks and address gaps in trust. Several of these projects have subsequently been implemented as pilots, including a rural hyperlocal's efforts to conduct listening sessions and to develop a community contributors program. I review preliminary findings that suggest the local outlet's engagement efforts have increased trust and a sense of shared investment among participants, though it is premature to say it has strengthened overall network ties between local media and the broader community.

In chapter 4, I make the argument that while community-centered journalism projects may not be scalable due to the necessity to respond to place-specific needs, research-based participatory processes to develop these projects may be portable. I apply a process similar to the one I used in Kentucky to two sites within the Philadelphia metro area: a historically African American neighborhood that has experienced various challenges, including disinvestment and the threat of displacement due to gentrification, and a majority white suburb where nearly half of presidential votes cast in 2016 went for Donald Trump. After examining how participants navigate issues of trust with fellow residents and media, I highlight some of the project ideas generated from a series of participatory workshops. I then explore one of the projects currently being piloted that is led by community members and researchers rather than by a media outlet. By putting these in conversation with the Kentucky initiative, I emphasize the influence of place and power dynamics and the context of regional media landscapes. The pilots that emerged from this process illustrate how community assets, even more than community needs, determine the shape and form of interventions that come from a participatory design process.

In chapter 5, I put these cases into the context of their larger fields, reviewing the spectrum of practices under the engaged journalism and solutions journalism umbrellas. I argue that for engaged journalism and solutions journalism initiatives to strengthen ties between local storytelling networks, new roles and competencies are needed. Drawing from interviews with representatives of projects including City Bureau, Free Press News Voices, Outlier Media, Resolve Philadelphia, and more, I share perspectives from practitioners on how they navigate and challenge boundaries of journalism and how they measure the impact of their work. I also look at opportunities and limitations within philanthropy for supporting this work, including the possibility of making philanthropic funding itself more participatory. I examine how initiatives address different links in local storytelling networks and how some projects practice a sort of engaged journalism 2.0, going beyond traditional norms to center and share power with communities—often drawing from community organizing practices.

Finally, in the conclusion, I circle back to examine how lessons learned from these cases may help in the design and evaluation of future interventions, not only to strengthen local news but to strengthen communities.

Through insights from both community members and journalists, the book translates communication infrastructure theory into a guide for assessing and designing place-based interventions to build relationships grounded in trust. It explores what is required from various actors—journalists, community members, researchers, third-party organizations, funders—to implement these interventions, how engaged and solutions-oriented practices may require reimaging traditional roles, and some of the barriers and challenges these efforts face. Looking at each of these cases in combination allows us to focus on different elements of intervention in the storytelling network, from connecting community organizations to local journalists, to connecting local journalists to residents. Examining not only where these interventions offer promise but also where they fall short allows the book to offer insights on building trust grounded within the context of local places. By focusing not on a project but rather on a process model for community-centered journalism, this book most of all offers strategies that may be adapted by practitioners to meet the needs of their communities—whether they be on the South Side of Chicago or in rural Kentucky.

CHAPTER 1

Shifting Stories with Solutions Journalism

For six days in August 1965, the streets of South Los Angeles's Watts neighborhood became sites of conflict between residents and law enforcement following the traffic stop and arrest of an African American motorist. By August 16, thirty-four people were dead (twenty-eight of whom were Black), most shot by police or National Guard troops. Just under four thousand people were arrested, and some $40 million of property had been damaged.

This incident would become known as the Watts Riots to some and as the Watts Uprising or Watts Rebellion to others. While the term "riots" implies senseless destruction, "rebellion," the term I will use in this chapter, implies a reaction to injustice or an alternative to protest for people who lack the power to protest.[1] Following the Watts Rebellion, the governor of California appointed a commission to investigate the causes of unrest. More than two years before the Kerner Commission[2] would come to similar conclusions about civil unrest across the United States, the McCone Commission outlined discriminatory practices and the toll they took in areas such as community-police relations, employment, housing, transportation, and health. The report also issued a plea to news media: "The press, television, and radio can play their part. Good reporting of constructive efforts in the field of race relations will be a major service to the community. We urge all media to report equally the good and the bad."[3] While the report's call to media seemed more focused on discouraging coverage of "inflammatory incidents," it also critiqued the tendency of journalists to "report the dramatic and ignore the constructive."[4]

Nearly fifty years later, in 2015, leaders of community organizations gathered for a workshop at the University of Southern California to reflect on media coverage of South LA. Some familiar sentiments emerged.

"It's balance that I'm looking for," explained Sarah, who worked with an organization providing social services. "Yes, we do have gangs; we all know that. So we're not saying that that's not happening in our community, but let's talk about what are some of the positive aspects of the community." Sarah herself was in South LA during the Watts Rebellion. She remembered the grocery stores and markets that were burned down and not rebuilt. But she wanted the media's gaze to go beyond what was missing in the community: "I'm tired of hearing about the deficits, you know; I want to look at the strengths of the young people that we're working with and the families that we're working with. And how can we help them to build on those strengths."[5]

Social scientists have long argued that media coverage can contribute to the stigmatization of communities, particularly communities of color. A reputation for crime and disorder can be layered onto a place and its residents—and this can have material consequences.[6]

As the community members (who represented a mix of community development groups, churches, and service providers) sat around the table thinking about how they wanted their area to be represented fifty years after the unrest in Watts, they did so in the shadow of more contemporary unrest in a different part of the country. For the past six months, protests had been simmering in Ferguson, Missouri, after a police officer shot Michael Brown, an unarmed Black man, and left his body on the pavement for four hours.

It was with an eye to this context that I worked with a group of researchers and journalists affiliated with the Metamorphosis Project and USC to think about the impending anniversary coverage of the Watts Rebellion. We wanted to know what kinds of South LA stories would be valuable for community stakeholders. And we wanted to explore whether we could help to strengthen the local "storytelling network"[7] in South LA, the network that connected local media, organizations, and residents who were all in their own way circulating stories about the community.

In this chapter, I offer an overview of our efforts as a way to understand how communication infrastructure theory[8] can be used to diagnose the state of local storytelling networks and to organize a place-based intervention that includes a solutions journalism approach. This particular case illustrates the importance of place and of looking at links between all the major nodes in the storytelling network—media, community organizations, and residents. It highlights not only the value of an intervention that focused particularly on the relationship between community organizations and local media but also on the shortcomings that can result from lingering weaknesses in links between local media and residents.

To begin this case, we reviewed research that identified points of tension in particular between community organizations and news media in South LA. After meeting with each group separately, my colleagues and I reached out to community organizations and local journalists to bring these groups together for a joint workshop. We wanted to see if doing this would allow them to produce a different kind of local news coverage.

It did.

The journalists who participated developed a series of solutions journalism stories about South LA. We then circled back to residents of South LA to see what they thought of this coverage. In a series of focus group discussions, we talked about what it was like to read solutions-oriented narratives, particularly in a community with a long history of being portrayed in a negative light. Residents shared what they saw as opportunities in this approach but also where they anticipated limitations.

Tracing this process shows how the concept of the storytelling network and interventions that try to make it stronger have value not just for journalists but also for the community more broadly. We began this intervention by focusing on the link between news media and community organizations. We invited both of these parties to question their assumptions about each other—particularly given that both defined themselves as serving the public. But we found when we got started that there were quite a few assumptions to untangle about what constituted a "story." As will be discussed below, there was a sizable gap between the norms journalists held about the elements of a "quality" story and the perspective of community stakeholders. And this was made more complicated by the kinds of stories community organizers noticed being told about their neighborhoods.

The South LA Storytelling Network

When asked what the media is looking for when covering South LA, representatives of community organizations in attendance at our USC workshop quickly offered a list of unpleasant incidents.

> **ANTOINE**: South LA is accidents, if you're talking about . . .
> **CLAUDIA**: Shootings, drive-bys . . .
> **SARAH**: Shootings.
> **ARTURO**: Anything wrong with police.
> **ANTOINE**: Police raids.
> **SARAH**: Right.

WILL: All the drama, people dying, folks beating each other's ass, excuse my language, anything having to do with violence.

Everyone agreed that press coverage was almost always negative. As Arturo complained, this kind of coverage "paints a very particular picture of a community." As a result, when he organizes an event in South LA, many outsiders don't come because they think it is dangerous.

In South LA, this stigmatized storytelling must be interpreted through a lens of history, race, power, and demographic change. Like much of Los Angeles, cultural claims to place in South LA are contested and layered. Before World War II, the majority of residents were non-Hispanic white, with pockets of African American and Japanese American residents. The combination of the internment of Japanese Americans during the war and the Second Great Migration of African Americans led to a concentration of Black residents in the few South LA neighborhoods they were allowed to live in due to racist housing covenants. When these covenants eased starting in the 1950s, African Americans became a majority in more neighborhoods throughout South LA, with many white residents leaving.[9] The demographic balance would change again, starting in the 1990s, when many African Americans left the area and the population of Latinx residents grew, resulting in the current estimate of 76 percent Latinx and 21 percent non-Hispanic Black residents.[10]

Changing demographics have also led to changing media narratives. In South LA in recent years, this has meant a considerable amount of coverage of stories of both physical violence and economic conflict between Black and Brown communities. As Manuel Pastor has suggested, overreporting Black-Latinx conflict shifts the focus from racist structures to racist attitudes: "an attempt to portray all groups, and not just whites, as having to overcome prejudice." While there are real differences between the Black and Latinx communities and their needs, he says, "competition is overstated"—and this narrative presents an obstacle for building real and needed coalitions between these groups that "not only share fences in areas like South L.A." but also "share critical social needs: healthy neighborhoods, good schools, decent public transportation, well-paying work, and neighborhood safety."[11]

Journalists may not see it as their role to facilitate coalition between Black and Brown communities. But those who argue that their role is strictly to objectively cover these communities should be mindful that scholars have found a relationship between practices associated with objectivity, such as maintaining a distance from communities, and the reinforcement of white supremacy.[12] Practices associated with journalistic "objectivity" can pose a barrier to establishing trust between local journalists and community stakeholders. For example, when journalists insist on using only named sources, they may exclude vulnerable groups with less power and are more at risk,[13] or when they seek out perspectives from authorities, they may contribute to the "over-accessing" of (often white) elites in privileged institutional roles.[14] Journalists, like all people, grapple with implicit bias and, in addition, are influenced by journalistic norms that position conflict as a news value.[15] Studies of media coverage of communities of color have repeatedly shown that Black and Latinx people are disproportionately depicted in a negative and criminal light.[16]

Previous research in the communication infrastructure theory tradition has highlighted the toll that these negative media narratives can take. In their "fear and comfort" mapping exercises, Sorin Adam Matei and Sandra Ball-Rokeach found that residents from around Los Angeles were more likely to note a "spatial fear" of South LA, a majority Black and Latinx area, than of other majority white areas of the city with similar crime rates. This was even more the case for participants who indicated they got most of their local news from television, suggesting stigmatized coverage of crime could have a lasting effect on how spaces are coded and perceived.[17]

Negative narratives have also affected local storytelling networks within South LA. Researchers with USC's Metamorphosis research group previously found that Black and Latinx residents connected to distinct ethnically bounded storytelling networks, largely accessing different media, organizations, and interpersonal networks. Because negative stories circulated within these networks, residents who were more connected to them tended to have more negative perceptions of Black-Brown relations in South LA.[18] For many residents, negative media narratives were hard to avoid due to their presence in dominant media outlets. Community organizers like Arturo, and others, were particularly frustrated with these narratives. The negative media narratives resulted in storytelling networks where the links between community groups and local media were often strained at best. The weakening of the network mattered because when community groups were not connected to local media, the stories and issues these organizations had access to were not shared with the wider community or city. Instead, the narratives shared about communities like South LA tended to be told by "parachuting" outsiders reporting on moments of crisis, if at all. Such disconnects reinforced inequitable power structures by continuing to circulate stigmatizing narratives that contributed to the marginalization of communities.

It was in this context of fragmented and fragile storytelling networks that the Metamorphosis Project set out to design an intervention. We wanted to address both the content and valence of stories circulating, as well as the strength of network ties between local media and community organizations. But before we dared try to connect journalists and community organizers to each other, we first needed to establish a shared language to begin our discussion.

An Intervention: Connecting Local Media and Community Groups

Perils of the "Pitch" Process

Before we could start building connections between journalists and community organizations, we first had to address a source of bad blood and misunderstanding between the two parties. One of the biggest complaints organization representatives had about news media was the difficulty they had in trying to get coverage of their work and community events. While both community organizers and journalists talked about wanting to cover community stories, they seemed to have very different understandings of the story development process.

To prepare for our intervention and workshop, I sought the perspective of journalists about the experiences of getting "pitched" story ideas by community groups. "I think the main challenge is that people just want to say, 'We do good work'—which is important but doesn't necessarily make for a story," a reporter for the *Los Angeles Times* explained. She said that there often seemed to be a lack of awareness of what journalists were looking for and how they defined "a good story." For example, she received a lot of pitches about upcoming anniversaries or a group's partnerships. She said she imagined that things like partnerships were "really important to funders," but she had doubts that they were "important to an average person" reading her newspaper.[19]

The reporter offered some advice for the organizations participating in our workshop:

> What makes for a kind of better pitch would be something that talks about something that's changing, some kind of conflict, something that's new in some way. For instance, if your organization is trying something different that's been really effective. If there's a particular person who is really interesting and maybe unexpected to be involved in that kind of work. . . . You know, a story needs to have some clear kind of progression or change. And so that could be, like, a change in how your organization does things; that's interesting. Or maybe a change external to the organization that affects it. Think in terms of what's current about it. What's different, what's new. And not just kind of what's good about it.

In her advice to community organizations, which we shared in our workshop, the reporter emphasized key ingredients to a "good story"—qualities such as novelty, conflict, story arc, and compelling or unexpected characters. No matter how good the work done by the organization was, its value as a "story" came largely from the form in which it was told. This advice illustrates how journalistic norms about what makes a quality story can limit what information gets circulated in local media and can pose a barrier to strengthening connections between journalists and community stakeholders.

Prior to our workshop connecting local media and community groups, we first held discussions with groups of media and community organizations separately. Many of their experiences resonated with the reflections of the *Los Angeles Times* reporter.

In conversations with local journalists, most participants spoke about story pitches as "PR," and they did so with a sense of wariness (due to the heavy volume of pitches) and a dose of skepticism. Hector, an editor of a Spanish-language newspaper, acknowledged he also got a lot of PR pitches. But he explained how at times he was able to find value in these, if not in the way the groups had originally intended: "Sometimes they have good ideas. Sometimes you get the idea and you go and you're not necessarily gonna report what they are asking you. From there, you can have a different approach."[20]

In their separate discussion, community organization representatives shared the flip side of Hector's observation—frustrations with their lack of influence on the editorial direction of stories. The story they pitched, they noted, often did not match the story that was later published. Will shared his experience with a local news outlet he had tried to get to cover an issue:

WILL: It was not good.
MODERATOR: Why?
WILL: Because the piece they came out with, the angle of the piece . . . didn't allow for our perspective on it and was . . . really biased from our perspective.
MODERATOR: What do you think it is about that that didn't work?
WILL: Well . . . the piece was very heavy on the other side, the other opinion. . . . They were definitely weighing more on the opposition, [the] other project, versus, like, giving that balance, perspective, and neighborhood voice to it.[21]

Will and others shared frustrations with how coverage was often determined by the subjectivities of individual reporters and the reporters' backgrounds, views, and relationships. Often the organization representatives noted that journalists were coming from outside their community. When they spoke of the positionality of reporters, they often did so in reference to trustworthiness factors, such as how they viewed the reporting's accuracy, fairness of representation, and motives. Reporters they saw as outsiders were generally connected with more negative assessments of these trustworthiness factors.

From the reporters' vantage point, however, sourcing stories from an organization's pitches was seen as a less desirable and more passive way to find stories. Steve talked about the value of finding story ideas by driving around a community, equating that with being "part of the community." He contrasted that tactic with the passive process of receiving pitches, as other journalists nodded their heads in assent: "PR people out there, . . . they're pushing their agenda because they want their thing. And the PR person actually gets paid to get their play out there or their act or this and that. And you're bombarded everyday with emails from, 'Come see my thing,' 'Come and cover it,' 'Give me press.' Because it's free advertisement for their thing."

This idea that pitches come from paid professionals did not always square with the realities of small community organizations with limited resources. Most of the groups in our discussion could not afford to have permanent communication staff. Brenda acknowledged that paying a professional did make a difference: "The only times really where I would say we've had any coverage is if we pay money and we hire a media consultant, which can be very, very, expensive. And then they know somebody and they can maybe get someone like ABC, NBC to come out." But this was a luxury these groups could rarely afford. More commonly, press outreach was referenced as one more obligation on top of what was seen as the more core work of organizing, service provision, or grant writing.

Community organizers said it was important to showcase their work because it offered a more nuanced narrative of South LA. But they believed one of the reasons they had difficulty getting coverage was because media outlets favored stories about conflict and negativity. Steve, an editor for a hyperlocal paper, acknowledged coverage of South LA was often negative: "A lot of protests, a lot of shootings, a lot of parents, kids that they've lost or violence. There's a lot of violence in South LA, so there's no getting around that. A lot more than [in] other communities." Steve said that while his paper did also cover positive community initiatives, "there is more of a focus on the bad just because people find that disturbing and [it] gets their attention, and if it does happen to the house next to you, you are really shaken up and it means, you know, something to you. You need to do something about it." Steve saw his paper's coverage of violence as responding to what he believed audiences wanted. While this journalistic practice frustrated community organizers, journalists like Steve saw it as a way to connect with residents, albeit based on assumptions about their preferences.

This idea that the public is inherently attracted to negative news has a long history in journalism folk wisdom, as well as among some researchers. Some political science studies have suggested that audiences give negative stories greater weight and are more influenced by negative assessments about issues such as candidate preference.[22] Similarly, a number of psychology studies have found that people devote more attention to processing negative information[23] and are more likely to think it is true[24] or to remember it.[25] At the same time, other studies have countered these findings, suggesting that negative framing can have mixed results in political or humanitarian campaigns[26] and can tend to reduce people's likelihood to seek preventive care in health communication.[27] Furthermore, a number of studies report that some people are more likely to avoid news and disengage from it due to feelings of negativity.[28]

Despite challenges to the concept of a negativity bias, the prioritization of problem- and conflict-centered narratives continues to influence how journalists construct and vet their news coverage. News norms have little room for stories of positive stability,[29] and positive stories continue to be viewed with skepticism if seen to be an outcome of public relations efforts.[30] Nevertheless, some of the local journalists in our discussion shared an interest in going beyond norms of negative coverage. Mercedes explained, "For a long time . . . media and also TV have focused a lot on the bad issues from South LA. So I think it's important that we start to do stories not only about the accidents, the big number of accidents, or pedestrian killings, and gangs, and all this stuff. Because there [is] a lot of richness in this community that we need to pay more attention [to]." Mercedes's perspective highlighted that local news media, particularly hyperlocal and non-English-language media outlets, cannot be viewed as a monolith. Particularly when journalists came from the same community they were covering, the kinds of stories they prioritized for coverage tended to bear a closer resemblance to what community organizers wanted to see.

Representing Black and Brown

As previous research has demonstrated,[31] South LA residents have largely gravitated to different storytelling networks depending on whether they identified as African American or Latinx. The community organizations and local media participants we consulted expressed awareness of divides between Black and Brown communities and had varied perspectives on questions of bridging.

Among the local journalists participating in this project, many were either affiliated with Spanish-language outlets or with outlets historically serving African American communities. Among these, most acknowledged that not only their audience but also their content was associated with either one community or the other. Speaking of his Spanish-language newspaper, Hector expressed regret that it did not do more "integration stories." He suggested there may be more his newspaper could do to address relations between Latinx and African American communities:

> We as a media . . . we are part of the problem. . . . A lot of times, the communities—particularly young people—they don't seem to really get along, or they start some problems. They're social issues; it is not one group against another, but there are social issues. . . . I think we are missing a lot not covering more issues,

like in the case of the African American community, because [we] are growing together [in] some areas.

Hector explained that he at times encountered pushback when he tried to cover other communities: "The main chief says, 'Oh well, they want a Latino face there, no matter what; it has to be Latino.'" For Hector, this was a missed opportunity.

Journalists from outlets associated with the Black community said they faced similar resistance when they tried to do stories about other ethnic groups. Imani shared her experience of doing a story about a Korean R&B singer: "I wanted to talk to some community members and they're like, 'No.' It's like, 'Why?,' [and] they're like, 'Well, if you want to cover that kind of story then you should do that for, like, *Korean Times*." South LA has a history of tensions between African American and Korean communities in the area. One of the contributing factors in the 1992 LA Uprising was the killing of fifteen-year-old Latasha Harlins by a Korean American store owner the previous year.[32] With these tensions in the background, Imani's attempt to profile a Korean American who talked about his admiration for African American R&B did not go over well: "A lot of them [the readers] were offended. Like, I even got emails, phone calls saying, 'You guys should not print a story that is dealing with another community in an African American paper.' You know, like, I was getting resistance from my editor. He was, like, 'No, this is an African American paper.'" Imani said she found it frustrating that she couldn't "cover another minority inside of a minority paper." Another reporter at another historically Black paper agreed: "There's such a struggle; I have to put a Black face on everything. It has to be a Black face. For me, I'm just a reporter, I want to share everyone's story, but it's the editorial decision, and that's the paper I work for."

Of course, this prioritization of representing specific communities of color must be viewed within the larger context of a "mainstream" media landscape dominated by whiteness. Prioritizing representation of a community that is largely under- or misrepresented in citywide or national outlets is an understandable goal. Though, among outlets serving communities of color in South LA, this also has the effect of reifying divisions between the storytelling networks of different communities of color.

For organizations, interactions with media, including "mainstream" media, often left them feeling like they were being forced into an identity box—even if they saw their work as serving multiple communities. Sarah explained her frustration with being treated as a "monolithic people" and expected to have the same values and opinions as every other African American: "If I don't believe what you believe and we're both African American, one of us is wrong."

Discussing this among the group, and at times veering into sarcasm, community organization leaders agreed that the work they did deserved more nuance:

> **SARAH:** There are various opinions across the spectrum. And so we have to be able to have all those opinions reflected because that's who we are. And if you only put it in a box of "Ok, this is the way [Arturo] thinks, therefore the Latino community thinks this way"—
> **ARTURO:** Right, we represent Latinos.
> **SARAH:** —he represents all the Latinos in the world.
> **ARTURO:** I'm just the Salvadoran.
> **WILL:** So you guys speak for all Black people right now?
> **SARAH:** Yeah, all the time, when I'm in the room by myself.

Between coverage that relied on essentialized and simplistic representations of communities and coverage that focused almost exclusively on one community, all community organization representatives we spoke with agreed that there was work to be done if coverage was to reflect the multiplicity of South LA communities. Otherwise the storytelling network was likely to remain fragmented. With no shared networks, residents would be less likely to make common cause to address community issues.

Demystifying the Production Process and "Speed Pitching"

Once participants from community organizations and local media outlets had an opportunity to voice the frustrations they felt about the media production process and each other, our workshops at USC attempted to establish some shared understandings, as a sort of first step to creating stronger communication infrastructure links. Meeting with media and organizations separately first, we attempted to share issues raised by the "other" side.

For community organizations, this meant we walked through a module on the journalistic process, from story pitch to production. This included a discussion of how a reporter would vet multiple pitches—looking for story elements such as novelty, strong characters, compelling "action," surprise, and visual or audio elements depending on the medium. We reviewed how a reporter would often then need to pitch a story idea to his or her editor and how he or she needed to be prepared to respond to the editor's questions. We also discussed the time and resource issues many of these journalists faced and how that shaped the production process. Based on these factors, we invited organizations to brainstorm possible story pitches and discussed the elements they would include. For journalists, we likewise reviewed some of the time and resource issues organizations faced, as well as some of their concerns and frustrations around negative coverage and "parachute journalism."

These separate sessions were then followed by a combined workshop, where we connected local journalists and representatives of community organizations. This workshop included eight representatives from community organizations and eight local journalists (two from Spanish-language outlets, three from newspapers historically associated with the African American community, and three from the regional public radio station), as well as six reporters from a hyperlocal student media outlet.

During the joint workshop, in response to concerns about negative coverage in the storytelling network, participants were introduced to the concept of solutions journalism. As discussed in the introduction, solutions journalism is a practice defined by the Solutions Journalism Network as "rigorous and compelling reporting on responses to social problems." Workshop participants discussed what distinguished solutions journalism stories from "good news," advocacy, or "hero" stories. Drawing from SJN's "toolkit," an online solutions journalism training guide, we reviewed how their understanding of the practice necessitated critical reporting on what is working but also on limitations and additionally examined the importance of integrating evidence into reporting. SJN's interpretation of solutions journalism largely followed dominant journalism norms, apart from centering not just on problems but on responses to them. The workshop participants also discussed resources for sourcing story ideas, including using databases to look for cases of positive deviance.

Workshop participants then explored how the approach of solutions journalism could be used to offer alternative narratives around the fiftieth anniversary of the Watts Rebellion. They discussed the areas identified in the original McCone Commission report, such as community-police relations, employment, housing, transportation, and health, and how contemporary initiatives were and were not addressing some of the challenges that persisted in these areas. In small groups, community leaders and journalists then brainstormed ideas for possible solutions-oriented stories about South LA.

Perhaps the most valuable portion of the workshop was the most simple: we adapted the concept of "speed dating" to "speed pitching." Community organization representatives and journalists rotated around the room talking to each other in groups of two or three. This offered a chance for journalists to learn about the work that organizations were doing, as well as to hear some of the story pitches they had been developing following the first workshop they had participated in separately. At the same time, community leaders learned about what the various media outlets were looking for—for example, community trend stories as opposed to an organization's new project—and the best ways to work together.

The goal of these interactions was to begin to build a bridge between local media outlets and community organizations in South LA, starting by strengthening network ties between participating journalists and organizers. Participants, of course, did not resolve all their differences and doubts in the course of a one-day workshop. Addressing concerns raised would require both journalists and community organizations to make changes in their day-to-day interactions around pitching and developing stories. This was not a small ask of two groups with historical reasons for skepticism. But the workshop was a first step. The main takeaway was a plan to follow up to develop a series of solutions-oriented stories about South LA to be presented in a series called "Watts Revisited" in the lead-up to the fiftieth anniversary of the uprising.

For the series, stories were produced for each media partner's outlets, with many running on the front pages of the print outlets. They were also posted on a shared project website. Journalists followed up with community organizations as they developed stories on issues such as redevelopment, public space, and job training. This process resulted in stories that had a greater solutions orientation than would have been likely otherwise. For example, one reporter shared how he had planned to do a story on new numbers showing disproportionately high jobless rates in South LA. However, after talking with a community organization representative about local job training initiatives, he was able to do the story in a way that featured the experiences of community members participating in some of these initiatives. There were also collaborations between journalists. The public radio station, a historically African American hyperlocal, and the student hyperlocal all did stories exploring the redevelopment of abandoned lots, including a story about converting lots to playgrounds that received 2,885 shares ten days after airing (a high number of shares for the outlet). The collaboration also included Spanish- and English-language media outlets, contributing to one of the project's objectives of building connections between often ethnically bounded storytelling networks.

Several of the series' stories were featured as part of a public forum held at USC, which included a panel of journalists and community leaders and invited area community members to participate in interactive small group discussions. Beyond the Watts Revisited project, some journalists and community groups reported developing other stories not related to the series from relationships formed at the workshop. Many participants expressed a desire for the workshop to be followed up with other opportunities for informal networking in order to continue to develop these and similar relationships.

This intervention was modest and time-bound, connecting a group of local journalists and community organizations in a region that had historically been stigmatized by negative news coverage. The effort grew from several years of research diagnosing weaknesses in the storytelling network—namely the fragmentation of Black and Brown storytelling networks and the lack of trust and connection between organizations and journalists. Overall, this intervention made modest gains. These gains were limited by the fact that the intervention centered on a one-off project rather than on a longer-term collaboration between institutions. Nevertheless, connections were made between journalists from regional, Spanish-language, and historically African American media outlets. Critically, ties were developed and strengthened between journalists and community organizations working in South LA, two key actors in local storytelling networks that had a history of mutual mistrust.

Reading Solutions Journalism in Stigmatized Neighborhoods

Following the Watts Revisited series, our Metamorphosis research group wanted to understand how community members from South LA felt about solutions journalism stories about their community.[33] The university-media-community organization partnership was meant to be an intervention in the local storytelling network. We could see how it was addressing the connection between journalists and community groups in this network, at least in a small way. But we wanted to understand what it meant to circulate solutions-oriented stories in a network that usually was dominated by negative narratives. How would it affect the local storytelling network if the valence of stories shifted? And would this intervention affect the connection between local media and residents?

Working with community organizations and service providers (different from the ones who participated in our workshops to develop the stories), we planned a series of six focus group discussions at a community center in South Los Angeles. We wanted a better understanding of how residents of South LA interpreted media coverage of their own communities and how they responded to solutions-oriented stories, particularly ones that had been informed by the perspectives of community organizations. Our six groups included twenty-nine African American and nineteen Latinx residents (twenty-three women, twenty-five men; ages twenty-one to fifty-nine). All had lived in South LA for at least two years, and all reported reading news articles at least occasionally. Participants noted using a range of local news sources, including ethnic print and broadcast media (Spanish- and English-language) and local and regional radio, television, and print. These included the news outlets that participated in our Watts Revisited project as well as others. Because previous research on South LA communities suggested Black and Latinx residents were often using different media and connecting to different community groups, we segmented our focus groups by ethnicity and language.

When discussion participants arrived, they were invited to first read an article adapted from the Watts Revisited project. We created two versions of a story about vacant lots and the lack of outdoor park spaces for children in South LA.[34] In the first (A) version, we followed the original solutions-oriented story that examined initiatives to transform vacant lots into parks. The other (B) version was more like a traditional news story. It was not solutions-oriented, and we only looked at the problem and issues raised. Apart from the solutions or problem-focus, we attempted to ensure that stories met a similar standard. We then gave four of the six groups the solutions version of the story first, while the other two read the non-solutions version first. This allowed us to have a point of comparison to see how participants would react to a more traditional story format.

Once our discussions started, we invited participants to talk about their own news habits and their perspective on how outlets covered South LA. The residents referenced the coverage of various outlets, what they liked or disliked, and how they adapted their habits in response. As part of this, they talked about what they thought was a "typical" South LA media story. They then talked about the story they had read from the Watts Revisited series and how it compared with the "typical" story. Participants reflected on how the story made them feel and had suggestions for doing the story differently. After this, we gave them the alternate version of the story to similarly read and discuss. Finally, we directly introduced the concept of solutions journalism and invited their feedback and thoughts. Participants were also invited to share advice they had for journalists covering South LA.

Bad News

In July 2015, social media lit up with rumors that area gangs were seeking to kill 100 people over the course of 100 days. Some sources suggested the killings were in retaliation for a murder; others that it was part of a competition with a rival gang.

Raven heard these rumors. She said the killings were transpiring in areas she often went, so when she heard, she stayed home. She said in this instance she was grateful for reporting on bad news (even if from less-than-official sources): "I appreciate that you're informing me about that situation, so I know. . . . It stopped me from walking into an ambush."[35]

It turned out that these rumors were unfounded. As the police chief responsible for South LA told the *Los Angeles Times*, "We did have a bad week that week, but really we only had one homicide."[36]

Raven wasn't alone in expressing an appreciation for the utility of news about crime in making day-to-day decisions about safety. For some, access to local news was not just a way to find out about community events or local politics; particularly in marginalized communities of color, local news was about safety and survival. But Raven's experience also illustrates the muddiness of South LA communication ecologies. Raven's preferred place to get news was YouTube because it gave her some control over what she was seeing and how negative it was. Instead of using legacy media outlets, she said a great deal of her local knowledge came from interpersonal sources: "We learn from each other what's going on in the street." Raven's case highlights how the dominance of negativity in storytelling networks can weaken ties between residents and local media due to news avoidance.[37] In Raven's case, avoiding conventional news media removed a potential check that could have helped her to verify information from interpersonal networks. This preference by some for interpersonal or social sources over traditional media, combined with a larger context in which crime is overreported in media, offers a ripe situation for the spreading of rumors. Raven's particular incident also serves as a reminder that the stakes of avoiding local news are not the same for everyone. Not needing to pay attention to local news is a privilege that is not distributed equally. For residents of communities with higher risks of violence, staying informed about local developments can literally be a matter of basic survival.

While many admitted that negative news could have its time and place, most discussion focused on the gap between what was seen as ubiquitous negative news and observed experience.

Marisol, a lifelong Angelino in the Spanish-speaking group, explained that she generally preferred a variety of Internet news sources over television. Television overall received some of the harshest critiques. "In local news the only thing they report on are bad things, only negative things," she said. "They are not showing us how to change the community."[38] Marisol complained that the news was more likely to focus on entertainment than on the community information she wanted. Her desire for information that could help lead to change hints at a disconnect between her ideal of journalism and journalistic norms of simply reporting "objective" information. In addition to complaints about an overreliance on entertainment, participants decried a lack of investigative and accountability coverage, as well as a lack of follow-up coverage on stories. Many contrasted their observed experiences with the news that was reported about their neighborhoods. Others shared examples of events they had witnessed that never made the news—particularly positive activities like community festivals.

Many attributed a lack of what they saw as accurate coverage to what they perceived to be commercial priorities, which did not highly value embedding in and serving the community. A few mentioned turning to ethnic and community media as alternatives, but these were often brought up in the context of limited resources—such as a community newspaper that had become difficult to find. Some associated media outlets with more sinister and deliberate motives. Jamal equated the media to bread and circuses: "They give you a little bread, they give you a little Jerry Springer. Throw in some Judge Judy with that. And they keep you out of focus on what's really going on."[39] For these participants, local news media failed to meet the trustworthiness factor of benevolence or integrity,[40] weakening the storytelling network link between local media and residents.

For some, not only was local news dissatisfying, but the negativity was cumulatively harmful:

> DUANE: Because it's a lot of weight coming from negative exposure to media. Like, somebody was attacked; somebody was injured. Some accident happened.
> JAMAL: Right.
> DUANE: But you never really see any background on who's responsible. Who's going to look out for more of this kind of stuff in the community, or things like that.
> MODERATOR: Like, who's going to do something about it?
> DUANE: Yeah. It can have a heavy negative mental or psychological effect on you. Because it's a lot of . . . meteorite crashes. [*Laughs.*] You know. It's like, you have stuff going on in your own life, but then you hear about something bad that's happening and it's not even related to you. It can make it feel even worse.[41]

In addition to a feeling that negativity could be internalized, others added concerns about how excessively negative coverage could stigmatize residents to outsiders:

> RAUL: You hear about rape, drugs, gang-related shootings, and, you know, a lot of negative things that . . . South LA is portrayed as. And it just kind of, like, lowers . . . the perspective in which people view South LA.
> ANDRES: Like a bad impression . . .
> GUILLERMO: They only give negative stuff.
> ANDRES: Yeah. . . . It makes us look like mostly criminals live around South LA
> RAUL: Street scum.[42]

Participants' concerns that negative coverage may give outsiders a negative impression of them and their community may not be unfounded. Previous studies focusing on the Los Angeles metro area have found that coverage of crime, particularly on television, disproportionately represents African American and Latinx people as "lawbreakers."[43] Subsequent research found that people who were more exposed to local news coverage were more likely to view African Americans as violent.[44]

As residents processed this coverage and how they believed it stigmatized their community, they did so within the larger context of race and representation within the United States. Tyler explained that he often would sit with his eighty-six-year-old grandmother watching TV. While he scrolled through Facebook checking news, she would get her news from the television: "I'll hear her say things like, 'Lord have mercy,' or, 'God just move with us.' . . . or stuff like that. . . . I start feeling kind of strongly about it because I see the pain that she feels for people she doesn't even know." Tyler, an African American man, found it disturbing to see what he saw as racialized representations in TV news:

> As I sit and I watch the TV with her, I get filled with a bunch of emotions when I see the biased opinion of the media—when, say, a white guy goes out and starts shooting up places, they probably wouldn't even show his picture. But if it was an African American male, he would be blasted all over the media as an infamous person. So I guess that even though I can't do anything about it now, I guess I watch to observe exactly what is going on and what changes need to be made.[45]

Tyler and several other participants pointed to how the negative coverage of South LA was part of a larger pattern of negative coverage of communities of color in the country. Indeed, researchers in the United States have traced a long history of people of color being represented more negatively, particularly around issues of crime. A number of case studies[46] have shown Black and Latinx people overrepresented as perpetrators of crime—for example, a study in New York City found that local news represented three of four criminals as Black, when the New York Police Department's actual Black arrest rate was only two of four.[47] As Robert Entman and Andrew Rojecki point out, "Blacks in the news tend to look different from and more dangerous than whites even when they commit similar crimes."[48]

As part of these issues of representation, participants also pointed to how the selection of sources by reporters could stigmatize the community. Jamal, a fifty-six-year-old African American man, recounted an encounter he had with a reporter in a park. The reporter was looking for someone in the park to react to an incident that had just happened: "He picked out the cats that's been sleeping on the bench all day to describe what just happened. And I'm standing right there. I'm fresh, I'm pressed . . . I'm literate." Jamal complained that the reporter was essentially "picking the worst grape" of the bunch.[49] By not including articulate community voices, the coverage was perpetuating negative stereotypes. Many pointed out that these kinds of choices and habits were likely happening because reporters covering South LA were not of and from the community. As outsiders, they had less of a stake in the stories and were not always mindful of issues of representation and history. This fed a sense that representations of the community were not respectful or fair, a key trustworthiness factor.

Some participants suggested that reporters could at times make local tensions worse by appearing to favor one group over another. For example, Duane, an African American participant, shared the example of a television news report about violence between Black and Latinx gangs. Closing the story, the reporter, who was Latinx, "made a comment that was, like, really offensive . . . something about leaving a 'black eye on the community.'" To him, because of the reporter's ethnic background, the comment was perceived to be a racial slur. He said that these sorts of insensitive word choices by journalists could "create barriers."[50] Duane's experience was a reminder that media content might be interpreted through a lens of microaggression,[51] coded speech,[52] or what John Jackson has called "racial paranoia"—or "distrustful conjecture about purposeful race-based maliciousness."[53] For Duane, while the intentions of the reporter are not known, the reporter's remarks nevertheless resulted in a felt harm.

Faced with coverage perceived as overly negative or disrespectful, participants adapted their news habits in a number of ways. Some spoke of avoiding news or limiting their use in order to minimize what they saw as the "stress" of negative coverage, illustrating how at least in historically stigmatized communities, the concept of news avoidance has been around long before post-2016 concerns. Others shared how they found alternative sources to get community information, such as alternative weeklies or ethnic newspapers. Many spoke of using the Internet to verify information, often in combination with interpersonal sources. For example, a participant said instead of television, she checked particular Internet sites her brother had recommended. A number of participants expressed greater faith in the reliability of interpersonal sources, be they face-to-face or through social media. Some spoke of using legacy media but with an oppositional reading, then contacting trusted friends or family members to verify what was "really" going on.[54] Overall, participants described how they were accounting for the negative nature of stories and a lack of confidence or trust in news outlets by adapting how they engaged within their storytelling network. For many, this meant a weakening of links between residents and local media.

In this discussion of what they saw as the status quo of local news coverage of South LA, a number of participants made recommendations for local news that was less negative. Duane, who had found the negativity of coverage to be stressful and frustrating, suggested that news outlets should cover stories where "somebody is trying to start something to change something." He even proposed creating a story feed "focused on who's actually looking for solutions."[55] He shared these thoughts before we introduced the concept of solutions journalism, suggesting there may be at least some appetite for the practice.

Solutions Storytelling

After reading the news story about efforts to transform abandoned lots into parks and playground for children in South LA, most focus group participants expressed appreciation for the solutions orientation of the story. Many connected the story to their own lives:

> **MARIA:** It is motivating. I felt like, "Oh, there is an organization that does this. Perhaps in the future I can call and ask how can I get involved?"
>
> **GABRIELLE:** How to participate, right?! What came to my mind is how I could volunteer.
>
> **MARISOL:** This motivated me more to take my kid out more, to the park. She doesn't really go out, for the same reasons of safety. But she could benefit from going to the park.[56]

This solutions-oriented story was the first time these residents learned about particular organizations working to improve their community. We aren't able to know whether they followed up on their intentions to volunteer, but this example illustrates how there is at least the possibility that exposure to stories that have a constructive orientation may generate new connections between residents and community groups in local storytelling networks. Some participants, like Duane, even looked beyond the particular case of parks to think about other possibilities for community action and collective efficacy: "You can look forward to changing something yourself if you have the same goal in mind."[57]

When groups read the non-solutions version of the story first (exploring the challenges of vacant lots but not outlining how they were being addressed), participants often suggested without prompting that the story would be strengthened by ideas for how to develop the lots to serve community needs. However, some said that even though this story was problem-centered, it was still more valuable than what they had characterized as the "typical" South LA story (which they associated with such words as "violence," "death," "robbery," "crime," "poverty," "unemployment," "drugs," "gangs," "prostitution," "homelessness," "police brutality," and "gentrification"). The problem-centered story about vacant lots was negative, but several noted that at least the story was in-depth and included articulate voices from community members—a key ingredient many saw as lacking in "typical" stories. This illustrates that for many residents, what was troubling about "typical" news was not only that their neighborhood was depicted in a negative light but also that its residents were shown in ways that were disrespectful and that reinforced stereotypes. Because of this, solutions journalism was framed as a valuable intervention, but so was more problem-centered but community-engaged reporting.

Participants also shared some reservations with solutions journalism stories. Perhaps unsurprisingly, given the longer arc of media systems and histories of coverage of South LA, there was a skepticism that this approach would bring meaningful change: "That's just like one story.... Where we come from, that's like a drop in the bucket."[58] Participants also cautioned that it was important to continue to investigate and cover problems. Javier was concerned that an emphasis on solutions could inaccurately suggest that there is no need to continue to press for action on the problem: "If all of it is positive it kind of glossed over the problem," the fifty-nine-year-old Latinx participant said. "It kind of also gives you a feeling of, 'Oh, no problem.... It's taking care of itself.'"[59] Javier suggested stories should offer analysis of problems in addition to solutions, as not everything can be "sunshine and lollipops in life." Here, Javier seems to reference Gaye Tuchman's warning against false promises that "reify social forces" by suggesting everything is in hand.[60] Of course, advocates of solutions journalism like the Solutions Journalism Network would suggest that good solutions journalism looks critically at both problems and solutions.

When sharing advice for journalists covering South LA, participants' preferences revealed a range of at times contradictory perspectives on the role of journalists. For example, one group came to a sort of consensus that the media was simply supposed to "tell the truth." But minutes later, many of the same participants suggested that media had a responsibility to "make us aware and give us a solution."[61] Many participants pushed beyond dominant norms of journalistic objectivity, suggesting that news should facilitate positive community change: "News needs to be an actual participant in what's happening rather than just reporting on it."[62] Overall, the problem-solving orientation of solutions journalism resonated with what many saw as a more active understanding of journalism's ideal purpose. In some ways, participants' ideas were aligned with the concept of "active objectivity"[63] that recognizes the interpretive nature of journalism and "privileges citizens as the recipient of media loyalty and emphasizes community trust building as an essential part of news gathering."[64]

While making recommendations, participants also suggested that solutions journalism could do more to critically challenge assumptions about South LA. Several believed this could be done via more follow-up coverage of stories, tracking the extent to which a problem was or was not resolved. Others thought the stories would be more meaningful if there were more opportunities for community input throughout the storytelling process. In terms of the storytelling network, they expressed a desire for a discursive link that travels in both directions between local media and residents—unlike the situation in South LA, where stories at best traveled one way, from local media outlet to resident. Critically, several participants expressed a desire to see media outlets hire reporters from their community so they could report on their community with an insider's perspective and knowledge. Overall, there was a sense that journalists had a responsibility to think about the community throughout a cycle of storytelling—from idea generation to after the story was published or broadcast.

Despite these reservations and calls for improvement, most indicated that they would be more likely to read or watch solutions journalism stories than traditional problem-oriented coverage. Many were also enthusiastic about sharing these kinds of stories with friends and family because they had an action orientation: "It offers more of a platform not to just discuss it, but . . . to tell them how we can get involved to try to change it or try to make something different."[65] In this way, participants' sentiments offered context to the findings of quantitative national studies, which suggest readers of solutions-oriented stories spend more time on the stories and report a greater sense of self-efficacy and optimism than readers of non-solutions stories.[66] But beyond this, connecting to the idea that community members could be involved in giving their input on solutions and possible stories, Jamal even suggested that such a process could help to strengthen communities that had been fragmented: "It would actually bring the community . . . back together."[67] For these participants, circulating solutions-oriented stories and involving community members in the storytelling process presented an opportunity to mobilize around community issues.

Strengthening the South LA Storytelling Network?

The effort to connect community organizations and local media covering South LA was a pilot intervention. As explored in this chapter, the initiative undertaken by USC's Metamorphosis Project did succeed in bringing together representatives of community groups and local and ethnic media. Given the layers of distrust between local media and community groups, this was no small accomplishment. Even getting these stakeholders into the same room with a recognition that they shared some common interests was a substantial step toward building trust in these relationships in local storytelling networks (see figure 2). Participating organizations and local media established a common understanding of their goals and ways of working. This allowed both parties to question assumptions about the other—for example, helping a community organizer realize why a journalist didn't respond to her press release, or allowing a journalist to understand that many grassroots organizations did not have public relations professionals and rather were simply trying to share community stories on top of their normal duties. Through this process of talking about their orientation toward the larger community, they were able to recognize in each

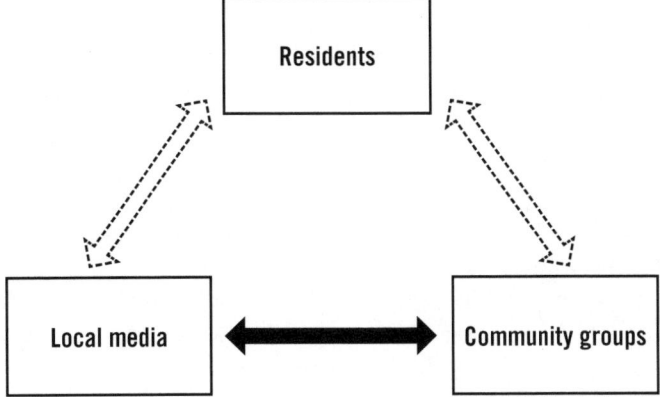

Figure 2. Communication Infrastructure Theory's "Storytelling Network": South LA Case

other trustworthiness factors such as benevolence and integrity.[68] By collaborating, they learned how a news outlet defined a "story" and how an organization could more effectively communicate their work.

By producing a series of solutions journalism stories, the Watts Revisited series also contributed to circulating shared stories about South LA—stories that were not exclusively negative and stigmatizing and stories that included respectful representations of community members. Here again this was significant, given the context of place. In the storytelling networks in South LA, links between residents and local media had been weakened. Participants recounted a combination of news avoidance, due to the overwhelming negativity of stories circulating in the network, and a violation of trustworthiness factors. Their accounts illustrated how factors like the perceived motives of journalists and how they saw their community represented led to distrust, damaging links in the storytelling network.

Reflections from residents who participated in our focus groups suggested that those who came into contact with these solutions-oriented stories were likely to react with a sense of efficacy, believing they could engage with the community issues raised. At the end of our discussion sessions, participants asked us how they could learn more or get involved in the issues raised. At the same time, there were lingering concerns about structural inequalities—like the larger history of negative coverage and the lack of journalists of color reporting on their own communities. Changing the valence of stories alone was not enough to repair damage and bridge gaps in trust between residents and media. Some residents suggested greater participation in the storytelling process would offer a pathway to building trust. More work was needed to focus on this storytelling network link between residents and local journalism.

This communication infrastructure theory–informed pilot intervention was not continued as an ongoing project.[69] Thus, it is difficult to make claims about its long-term impact on the South LA storytelling network. Relationships between journalists and community organization representatives did continue to an extent. However, the lack of a supported project makes it difficult to assess the impact on relations between media and organizations in the storytelling network over time. Likewise, additional support for solutions journalism storytelling and research would be needed to follow how solutions-oriented content affects residents over time in communities that have been stigmatized. The fact that this project did not grow from a pilot stage to an ongoing project foreshadows a challenge that many local journalism projects grapple with and will be discussed more in later chapters. Maintaining these types of interventions requires a sustained investment over time—and for many projects working in marginalized communities with limited resources, this requires additional philanthropic support. Building relationships of trust between stakeholders with a history of mutual skepticism is not a quick fix.

Nevertheless, the incrementally improved relations between local media and organizations and the promise expressed by residents in reaction to solutions journalism stories suggest there are points of value in this intervention to be considered further. This intervention offered promise for the storytelling network link between media and organizations and illustrated the necessity of simultaneously addressing the link between media and residents. In the following chapter, I explore a program in Chicago that attempted to tackle this latter storytelling network link and with it one of the concerns raised by South LA residents—to involve community members more in the process of storytelling from story generation to publication and beyond. In it we dig into the role engaged journalism can play in local storytelling networks.

CHAPTER 2

Connecting Journalists and Community Members

It all started with the recycling. In Chicago, the city encourages residents to deposit their paper, plastic, and aluminum into blue plastic bins or "blue carts." But as the staff of the radio program *Curious City* learned, these bins were a source of considerable public skepticism. Lots of people wanted to know where the content of their blue bins was ending up.

Curious City is an initiative, what its website calls "an ongoing news experiment,"[1] at WBEZ, Chicago's public radio station. Since 2012, the series has invited listeners to ask questions about "Chicago, the region or its people" using an online form. The submissions received by the program's staff have been wide ranging—from historical curiosity to accountability questions to city planning trivia. What's at the bottom of the Chicago River? Do lottery dollars really fund education? Why does Chicago have so many wooden fire escapes?

Once they got these questions, the *Curious City* team went through a process for choosing questions to answer. Answering them meant a WBEZ reporter would follow up with the question asker and do the reporting needed to satisfy his or her curiosity—usually making a radio story in the process.

The series has been popular, and stories that grew out of this process have often been some of the best performing content the station has produced, particularly when it comes to social media analytics. But fairly early on in the series, editor Shawn Allee began noticing some patterns that gave him pause. "I figured that we were probably going to be running into a problem where we're kind of captured by our own audience in some way," he explained.[2]

Allee said it was actually the recycling questions that crystallized his concern. He explained the program got numerous questions about the blue bins (which the team did eventually answer),[3] almost all from areas of the city that were considered to be strongholds for public radio. This made Allee wonder what audiences the show was *not* serving. *Curious City*'s mission, he noted, was to get questions about and from the entire region of Chicagoland, but he and his team seemed to be missing many suburbs and areas of the city. "I just had a sinking suspicion that this was a problem," Allee noted.

Responding to his hunch, Allee set out to map the origins of question askers from the summer of 2012 to February 2016 using the zip codes entered on their online form. As he feared, the resulting map revealed question hotspots that largely corresponded to areas of Chicago associated with WBEZ listeners, primarily on the North Side of the city. Few questions were coming from the city's majority Black and Latinx South and West Sides, or from a number of predominantly white suburbs. While this was not exactly surprising, it was disappointing.

Allee said this map underlined the gap between the radio program's mission to cover the whole region and the reality where coverage super-served existing audiences. He wanted to take action to address this gap between the audience and the community, to get residents from around the region participating in the program, but he wasn't sure how. "I needed to run an experiment where we could really try different approaches to gathering questions from people who are not familiar with the station at all," he concluded.

In this chapter, I follow *Curious City*'s experiment in trying to strengthen connections between itself, as a local media outlet, and community members in areas of the region the program had not been reaching. By focusing primarily on the relationship between local media and residents, this case offers an example of an intervention in the local storytelling network, which builds on what was missing in chapter 1's South Los Angeles case. In it, I look at the strategies *Curious City*'s staffers attempted as they intervened in the local storytelling network, at what we can learn from the efforts that worked effectively, and at the areas where they came up against dominant journalistic practices and the limitations of their own structure. By looking at this link between community members and local journalists, this example also offers insights into principles of engaged journalism.

A More Participatory Story Cycle?

I learned about *Curious City*'s intended experiment just after wrapping up work with the Metamorphosis Project's initiative in South LA that connected local media with community organizations to produce a solutions journalism series. Residents participating in that study had been vocal about wanting there to be more opportunities for community members throughout the process of story production. Because of this, *Curious City*'s efforts to include residents in the process of gathering ideas for stories and reporting them caught my attention.

I was also interested because of where *Curious City* had been conceived. WBEZ was considered by many in the public media system to be one of the most innovative U.S. public radio stations. It had birthed renowned national initiatives including *This American Life*, *Wait Wait... Don't Tell Me!*, and the Third Coast International Audio Festival. It also had a history of award-winning local news coverage, including investigative news coverage, highly produced documentaries and features, and collaborative series such as *Chicago Matters*.

When I worked at WBEZ as a radio producer from 1999 to 2008, the conversation about how to involve communities in the process of storytelling was already underway. This was a time of transition, where we were grappling with the possibilities and realities of the Internet. While a number of our programs had a history of hosting face-to-face community discussions or inviting listeners to call in, with the Internet we could ask listeners to email us and later to fill out basic web forms. In addition to crowdsourcing ideas for existing programs, WBEZ took the bold step of starting a sister radio station called Vocalo, which was originally intended to showcase user-generated content.[4] These creative efforts to engage community members in the process of making radio were due in no small part to the station's CEO at the time, Torey Malatia.[5] From 1995 to 2013, Malatia ran WBEZ. He was a considered a visionary if at times eccentric leader in public radio, as apt to quote communication scholar James Carey[6] in a staff meeting as to talk about market shares. Reflecting back on the public media climate in the days before *Curious City*, Malatia explained the dominant mindset toward the public at the time:

> Everybody was concentrating on what's the formula, what's the best practice. And it was all sort of inside this radio bubble that was about ratings and audience flow and consistent appeal and churn—and, you know, all this kind of stuff that was being talked about. And what was missed in all of that was, "What is the institution supposed to be doing, and how does that go beyond what happens to be on the air at a given time?"

These industry "best practices" focused on the audience but not on the larger community. Malatia took umbrage with this. The airwaves were a public asset, he said. "Your responsibility goes beyond the people who use the service."[7]

When Malatia encouraged initiatives at WBEZ that moved in the direction of public engagement, there was pushback. "It was horrible," he recalled. "It was a huge kind of culture problem. It was at just about every level—members of the audience, members of the board, members of staff." At one point prior to the development of *Curious City*, he proposed an outreach project to find out about community priorities to help inform coverage. It did not go over well:

> I remember having a conversation with someone in the newsroom who said, "Well, why would you do that? I know what to cover." [*Laughs.*] Well, that's the problem! You think you do know that. And you know some of it. There's no question. I mean, you work hard at this. But you've gotta be open to this notion that they [community members] know better than you do. Because they're living it every day.

Before *Curious City*, these initiatives mostly hovered on the outskirts of the station's core operations. Literally. The physical layout of the station was such that the newsroom sat in the center of an open office plan, but many of the engagement efforts bubbled up from other corners of the office—from special projects or partnership initiatives from the marketing department. Key editors in the newsroom at times expressed skepticism of these projects and concerns that they posed the risk of tainting the station's brand with the dreaded "advocacy journalism" label. Even when projects were not particularly controversial, they were often dependent on enterprising individuals working on them on top of their primary duties or via unstable funding streams. When a staff member left or a grant ended, the associated engagement initiative often fizzled. But unlike many of WBEZ's previous engagement initiatives, *Curious City* was positioned *in* the newsroom. What would this mean for its relationship with journalism norms, like objectivity, that governed the newsroom? Would the fate of *Curious City* be different from other outreach efforts?

Curious City first started at WBEZ in 2012 with funding from the Localore Project. Localore was an initiative of the Association of Independents in Radio, which paired independent producers with radio stations to produce projects— many of which had a community engagement component. *Curious City*'s founder, Jennifer Brandel, had been working as a contractor reporting and producing at WBEZ when she got the idea to ask the audience what questions they had that they wanted reporters to follow up on. Brandel explained she didn't have a traditional journalism background and often wondered why it was that she and others sitting inside the station got to play the role of gatekeepers, setting the agenda and deciding what made a good story idea. She wanted to create a new editorial pathway powered by questions from members of the public. The Association of Independents in Radio article describing her Localore project quoted her as saying that the *Curious City* platform "shares the power of the press with the everyman."[8]

After launching *Curious City* at WBEZ, Brandel went on to create the company Hearken. Hearken includes a digital engagement platform for gathering and managing questions from the public as well as a consulting service to help news outlets engage the public throughout the "story cycle" of journalism. *Curious City* has continued on as a client of Hearken and has since been joined by more than 150 newsrooms in eighteen countries.[9]

At the core of Hearken is the philosophy of "public-powered journalism." This means a shift in how the public is involved in the story cycle of newsrooms. Whereas in what Hearken calls the "traditional story cycle" the public gets involved only when the story is published and they share comments, in the "public-powered story cycle" the public is involved throughout the process, from the pitch (asking questions), to assignment (voting on their favorite questions), to reporting (accompanying the reporter), and finally to feedback.[10]

Of course, this story cycle is the ideal. A study by Thomas Schmidt and Regina Lawrence found that while newsrooms using Hearken often share the philosophy of public participation, few are able to involve audience members throughout the story cycle.[11] While the fifteen newsrooms they studied involved the public early in the cycle to gather questions, few involved the public in the reporting phase. In such cases, members of the public were influencing the basic agenda of what stories circulate in their community but not the shape or valence of the content.

For Brandel, just harvesting questions and not following up with the question asker puts the model at risk of being extractive. "You're actually losing out on a lot of relationship building," she explained. In terms of communication infrastructure theory's storytelling network, simply taking questions meant the link between local media and residents was flowing in only one direction, benefiting local journalism but not sharing power. Brandel acknowledges that how newsrooms use Hearken's technology can vary widely, but through the company's consulting it encourages best practices: "The pinnacle of the Hearken model applied would be—it's almost extractive to the newsroom. The public is able to say, 'I need something from you. You're experts at getting that information. Will you give it to me? And in return, I may give you my attention. I may give you my donation or my membership or subscription. I may tell my friends; I may not.'"[12]

This statement has a whiff of what journalism scholars Seth Lewis, Avery Holton, and Mark Coddington call "direct reciprocity," where "individuals give without expecting anything in return but nonetheless are likely to receive something of value in return."[13] Indeed, looking at case studies of how Hearken has been used in public media, researchers Valerie Belair-Gagnon, Jacob Nelson, and Lewis argue that journalists using the platform saw it as part of their efforts to pursue engaged or reciprocal relationships.[14] Brandel has claimed that Hearken also can offer "measurable value for partner newsrooms," converting users into paying subscribers or helping newsrooms to win awards. But beyond this, Brandel has contended that Hearken can change journalism. She suggested that the model brings "the public closer to the newsroom and to one another to exchange information" and that Hearken offers the public the opportunity "to contribute to shaping the narrative that comprises their realities."[15]

The ambition of Hearken's story cycle, then, is a potential intervention in the local communication infrastructure. If the practice of using Hearken connects the public to newsrooms, this could have an effect on CIT's concept of the storytelling network—strengthening the link between residents and local media. This matters because researchers have found that in networks where local media, community groups, and residents are more connected, people tend to feel a greater sense of belonging and to share an understanding of key community issues.[16] Such a goal of connecting the public and media also would take a step toward what James Carey argued had originally been the role of the press, to reflect and animate public conversation—where "the value of the press was predicated on the existence of the public and not the reverse."[17] But of course there is also the question of whether this model, being centered on newsrooms, will do enough to share power with marginalized communities, or whether such a structure is inherently tethered to journalism norms that reinforce hierarchies of race, class, and power. To understand whether any of Hearken's and *Curious City*'s aspirational changes might be happening, I return to *Curious City*'s experiment to try to engage the public in a more inclusive way.

An Intervention: *Curious City*'s Question Experiment

On the map of Chicagoland used by the producers of *Curious City*,[18] the areas that the program did not get questions from—mostly majority Black and Brown communities on the South and West Sides and some majority white suburbs—were colored in a pale beige. For editor Shawn Allee, how to begin to turn these beige regions to the darker colors that indicated more participation posed a dilemma. What was the best strategy to expand the program's question base? "I literally didn't know," Allee admitted.

Rather than guess, *Curious City* put together an experiment. With support from the McCormick Foundation,[19] producers outlined a plan to test three main strategies for increasing questions, focusing on Chicago's South and West Sides and a few suburbs where participation had been dismal. The first strategy involved hiring an outreach producer to go out to communities and invite people to ask questions face-to-face. The second strategy was to partner with community organizations, institutions, and businesses for their help in gathering questions. This included leaving question boxes at cafés and libraries, setting up tables to collect questions in person, and collaborating with hyperlocal and ethnic media outlets. The third and final strategy they undertook was a Facebook advertising campaign.

As they went about this process, I shadowed the outreach producer and observed team discussions. I also conducted interviews with *Curious City* journalists and participants, various institutions they partnered with, and community members they reached out to as part of their experiment. I wanted to trace how *Curious City* was involving the public through the stages of the story cycle. And because *Curious City* was attempting not only to connect with residents but also to involve community groups, libraries, and hyperlocal media, I wanted to understand whether the team's efforts were affecting the local storytelling network.

Face-to-Face

A considerable portion of *Curious City*'s outreach project was spent in cars. Getting to one of the beige areas targeted for outreach from the radio station or outreach producer Tom's home sometimes meant driving for more than an hour. Herein lay one of the biggest challenges of the project's mission to encourage participation throughout the region. To state the obvious, Chicago is big. It is one of the largest cities in the world by land area.[20]

Of course, the way its nearly 10 million people are spread across the nearly 11,000 square miles of metro Chicago, with more than seventy-seven official "community areas"[21] and two hundred unofficial neighborhoods,[22] is uneven and mired in a history of racist practices.[23] As sociologist Robert Sampson points out, the "neighborhood facts" or "spatially inscribed social differences" of Chicago vary greatly from one part of the city to another.[24] A Chicago resident's likeliness to experience crime, poverty, or child health issues, for example, correlates strongly with the neighborhood he or she calls home. Chicago continues to bear scars from its legacy of government-regulated housing segregation,[25] which was followed by lingering customary practices.[26] These drew and then hardened racial lines in an attempt to confine African American residents to what became the Black Belt on the South and, later, West Sides of Chicago. Chicago's now large Latinx community was initially viewed as a buffer population between white and Black neighborhoods,[27] though as Latinx communities have grown there are now sizable populations in suburban areas as well. At the city level, according to the 2017 American Community Survey, Chicago residents were divided fairly evenly among residents who identified as Black (30.5 percent), non-Hispanic white (32.7 percent), and Hispanic (29 percent).[28] Diversity on paper at the city level belies the fact that at the level of neighborhoods, Chicago usually scores at or near the top of the list of most segregated cities.[29] Today, the average white resident lives in a neighborhood that is 71.5 percent white,[30] mostly in North and Central areas of the city. Meanwhile majority Black neighborhoods, even middle-class ones, continue to feel the effects of disinvestment and have been largely untouched by gentrification.[31]

At the time of the *Curious City* outreach experiment in 2016, Chicago was also garnering national and international media headlines due to record-breaking levels of gun violence (even before Donald Trump labeled it the home of "American carnage") and police brutality—but also for dynamic protests and grassroots activism. The moment led many to reflect on the very different lives led by residents of different parts of Chicago. For example, a *New York Times* survey found that expectations about safety, schooling, and job discrimination varied dramatically based on where a resident lived, largely coinciding with race.[32] These different Chicagos rarely connected, in part due to the stigma placed on South and West Side communities due to their reputation for gun violence.[33] Such differences in experience extended to perceptions of media as well. The city has had a historically vibrant Black and Latinx press. However, when it comes to perceptions of "Chicago news media" overall, studies of South and West Side communities have found that residents of these neighborhoods are more likely to feel misrepresented by media than their peers on the city's majority white North Side.[34] Because of this context, as with South Los Angeles, place had a significant influence on how local storytelling networks functioned, particularly in how residents interpreted trustworthiness factors within these networks.

Lived experiences of segregation shaped how residents perceived the simple act of showing up in many of the communities in which *Curious City* sought to conduct outreach—particularly when media outlets sent white reporters to cover communities of color. Tom, the outreach producer, and I, who are both white, at times would not see any other white people as we walked around talking to residents. That was the case when we met Gwen, from the introduction of this book, who expressed surprise to see us come to talk about a media project in her majority Black South Side neighborhood.

While Gwen was getting a golf lesson, Dorothy, an eighty-two-year-old African American woman, was walking laps around the park. I talked with her after the outreach producer had asked her if she had questions she would like to share for *Curious City*. The experience had been unexpected for her. "I don't know journalists or newspaper people who come to the South Side to find stories. I just don't see that," she said. Despite this, Dorothy explained that she liked the idea of *Curious City*, because it departed from how she usually saw the South Side treated:

> **DOROTHY**: We're on the South Side. They don't care about people on the South Side. In my opinion.
>
> **ANDREA**: Who doesn't care? The media?
>
> **DOROTHY**: Not necessarily the media. The politicians. And, of course, the media follows the politicians. You know they follow whatever they do or say. They're with them and what they're doing. But I don't know if it's the media or not. I think they're part of the whole picture. The big picture.[35]

For Dorothy, media was part of a larger inequitable structure. Journalists' habits of how they went about contacting people for quotes, or sourcing, led to what Stuart Hall and his colleagues would call the "over-accessing" of people in power at the expense of communities, especially communities like Dorothy's. Those who had positions of institutional authority were allowed to be "primary definers" of local issues in the news media.[36] This may contribute to a layering of distrust as studies have found a correlation between a lack of trust in political institutions and a lack of trust in news media.[37] As actors in the local storytelling network, members of the local media, in Dorothy's assessment, had not demonstrated the "trustworthiness factor" of benevolence.[38] They had not prioritized the needs and perspectives of residents in her community.

I encountered similar sentiments from other residents when shadowing Tom, the outreach producer. In the same park, I also met two women who complained that media outlets usually portrayed their neighborhood as "the scum of the earth" and the "second thing to hell." They attributed negative coverage to a financial motive of journalists to sensationalize their community: "It's like we're reality shows. The more crazy people act, the more they watch." One of the women said she wanted *Curious City* and other media outlets to look at the positive elements of the community: "My kids are not gang-bangers. They do good in school. What about us?"[39]

Over and over again, like the South LA residents in chapter 1, Chicago residents told me they were frustrated with overly negative depictions of their communities and eager for more positive and solutions-oriented stories to circulate.

Kyle, a twenty-one-year-old man I met sitting on a bench in the same park, also complained that his neighborhood was "misunderstood" by negative media representations that showed his community "from the outside looking in." Beyond that, he referenced one of the only times it was common to encounter journalists in his community—when reporters came in to cover crime or violence. In these instances, he saw what he interpreted as aggressive behavior from reporters and found them frustrating and insensitive. He called out television reporters in particular for "coming up, 'Oh what happened? What happened?'" He offered advice for journalists: "Put your microphone down."[40]

This didn't mean Kyle didn't want to talk to reporters. He said he actually found the *Curious City* experience fun because the process felt more like a relaxed conversation and "people love to be heard." He suggested other reporters try a similar approach: "Instead of me talking to you like a reporter, talk to you like a person. Talk to me as a friend. You know. Not getting to know me—but so I don't feel like it's your job that you want. Make me feel more comfortable." Kyle wanted more of a relationship than a transactional exchange. For him, members of the media had to do more to listen and show that they were "out there keeping with the community" before community members would reciprocate with their trust. A lot of this had to do with timing—showing up when there wasn't breaking news and listening even when they weren't just trying to get a quote. Kyle's experience highlights the role that relational exchanges can play in strengthening links in the storytelling network. When journalists build relationships with community members, they demonstrate trustworthiness factors—particularly by showing they have benevolent motives and are interested in offering a more complete representation of communities. Building this trust through relational work is a critical prerequisite to strengthening local storytelling networks and developing a healthy communication infrastructure.

The reflections of these residents also illustrate an important reality for any journalist attempting to do outreach and engagement work. When journalists enter community spaces, they are not entering with a blank slate. Beyond their own preconceived assumptions, residents will make sense of journalists' presence, efforts, and motives in the context of the layers of experiences they have had with those who came before—even if they were coming for very different reasons or from different kinds of media. Journalists who want to acknowledge and grapple with this reality may have to adjust some of their routine practices and find ways to spend more time in communities when they are not reporting particular stories.

While Tom garnered goodwill from residents by showing up on an ordinary day to listen, this didn't always translate into getting the questions he needed. Part of the issue was that many of the people he talked to had never heard of WBEZ, or if they had, they were not familiar with the *Curious City*. Why did he want them to ask a question? What kind of question was a good question?

Part of the goal, of course, was to reach beyond listeners already familiar with the program. But explaining everything quickly enough to clarify the purpose before someone's patience ran out or the bus they were waiting for arrived could be challenging.

Tom would select a location based on where he thought there would be a lot of foot traffic. While he tried to go to a variety of places, from city parks to suburban shopping malls, he acknowledged there was nothing scientific about his process of selecting where to gather questions: "Partially I just go to places that look interesting to me too, like, selfishly. This would be a fun place to spend an hour."[41]

Approaching strangers and asking them if they had a question they'd like to ask, of course, did not always yield a result. At the South Side park, he said his response rate was pretty good: "Today, probably 60 percent yes, 40 percent no. Usually it's more like 20 percent yes, 80 percent no. It just depends on the day. Maybe [on] how I'm looking that day. If I'm approachable." Tom did not have any sort of orientation or training on best practices for this kind of outreach before going into the field. There was no set playbook, and he and his team saw themselves largely as experimenting to see what worked best. As a result, he explained that he tried varying how he presented the request—his wording, the examples he gave. Sometimes he asked, "Do you have a minute to be on the radio?" Other times he'd explain, "We're from a news organization and we're collecting questions from the public." Sometimes he tried to talk people into it if their first answer was no. If they agreed, he tried to help them with how they framed their questions.

"I don't think I'm looking for any particular question," Tom explained. "I'm looking for a level of depth to the question." More specific questions lent themselves better to the reporting that would follow. Whereas members of the public who already listened to *Curious City* may have had an idea of what made a "good" question based on the stories that they had heard, this was not so for residents lacking a reference point. "I think a lot of people start with statements," another producer who helped gather questions observed. "Like, 'I've seen blah blah blah and then . . . what's up with that?'"[42] Tom said he typically took the questions people asked verbatim, but at times he would try to clarify things and make them more specific. On a few occasions I observed him coaching residents through the question-asking process. Often this happened when residents started more with a topic, story idea, or hypothesis than with a question. This process took time and was certainly swayed by Tom's own understanding of what kinds of question had the most value for reporting. But it allowed Tom to bring more community members into the process. Still, the challenges of this process also illustrated how the structural setup of the project unintentionally made it complicated for marginalized voices to express themselves on their own terms. The project was centered at the WBEZ newsroom, and it required reaching out to a periphery of people unfamiliar with that center. For community members to participate, they needed to adhere to the project's format of asking a question, a request that could be confusing and did not always match with a resident's priorities.

The *Curious City* and Hearken models are rooted in the philosophy that genuine wonder expressed in the form of a question can lead to a different kind of storytelling. But, when it came to questions of accountability in particular, the program's editor, Shawn Allee, acknowledged that having a hypothesis could actually be valuable. He referenced one of the stories that came from Gwen, who posed a question to Tom in the South Side park. Gwen suggested a story on unequal resource distribution between the city's North and South Sides. After some discussion, she settled on the question, "Why can't viaducts on the South Side have beautiful murals like the North Side?"

"I think we needed to be really clear with the listeners that she's not coming from a vantage point that she doesn't think she had an answer already," Allee said. Having witnessed Gwen's exchange with Tom, I saw that this was true. She was convinced the explanation behind this resource gap was structural racism and inequality. Her story was assigned to a reporter to investigate, who then followed up with her, checking in with her several times.

That was a standard part of the *Curious City* process. As one reporter explained, she liked to start the process by making sure she was interpreting the questions as the question askers intended: "What I try to understand from them is if I'm understanding their question properly.... And then I say, 'Ok, now I'm going to do a little reporting, then I'll get back to you. We're going to look for opportunities for you to come out with me to do some of this reporting.'"[43]

Some interactions did not go any further—especially when the source wanted to be anonymous or did not have time to join in the reporting. But in cases like Gwen's, the question asker would be asked to join the reporter in the field. And that is how Gwen ended up offering the *Curious City* reporter a tour of the dismal mural-less viaducts in her neighborhood.

In the finished story that was broadcast, the reporter tells Gwen about information that complicated her hypothesis about the disparity in murals. He explained how in some North Side cases murals were the result of participatory budgeting and how other South Side neighborhoods with participatory budgeting had not voted for murals. He suggested this meant perhaps residents of those neighborhoods didn't want murals. But Gwen pushed back, challenging the reporter's interpretation. She was African American and from the South Side, while the reporter was white and not from the South Side. Gwen argued that larger historical realities of structural racism led to South Side residents needing to make different choices—not because they didn't want murals but because their basic infrastructure was crumbling.

Allee explained why they included that exchange between the reporter and the question asker in the final story: "It was useful, because she was able to critique some of the things that we found. In a meaningful way, but not in a mean way.... That gave us the space to deliver things that maybe she should rethink, or at least consider in her analysis." In this particular case, *Curious City* not only centered a concern from a member of the public, but they also provided transparency in the storytelling process.

Transparency was one of the aims for involving question askers in the reporting more generally. For example, a producer explained that if the question asker joined for an interview and asked a source a question, he included that: "I want people to hear that and be like, 'Look, she just asked him a really interesting question. Normally you'd expect the reporter to do that, but that was just someone like me.'"[44] He hoped that this behind-the-scenes glimpse would encourage other residents to participate.

Despite these forms of participation, *Curious City* retained editorial control—deciding how the piece on the murals was scripted and what tape it did and did not use. But by including the question asker at several points in the story, listeners were able to draw their own conclusions. They could choose to walk away with the idea the reporter presented, which in some ways complicated the narrative assumed by the question asker. Or, they might feel the reporter didn't fully comprehend the question asker's point and that even his complicating evidence was intertwined within racist structures.

Having played this story as part of discussions in a number of classes, I have anecdotally heard multiple interpretations from listeners to the story. While most all expressed appreciation that the story involved the question asker, some focused on the contrast between the reporter, a white outsider, and Gwen, the resident. Some suggested the reporter seemed out of touch or naive by relaying advice given by officials that the resident could simply call her alderman to solve a problem, when Gwen pointed out that the alderman never answered her phone. While transparency has been touted as a key strategy to increase audience trust in journalism,[45] this case illustrates the need for additional research to understand how transparency is perceived based on the positionality of the reporter, sources, and audience members. Audience members assess the authenticity and credibility of information based not only on the process of reporting but also on their perceptions of the reporter and that person's relationship to power structures. Additional research on how transparency practices are perceived may offer a fuller understanding by looking more granularly at the identities of both the audience members and reporters involved.

While getting usable questions for *Curious City* was sometimes difficult in many of the communities, Tom, the outreach producer, explained that there were secondary benefits that came from the exchanges he had. In one instance I observed as he spent a considerable amount of time speaking with a young African American man waiting for a bus in a suburb. The man did not share a question but expressed a number of concerns. As part of that, he explained how his family wanted to leave the Chicago area. Tom was taken aback by what the young man said: "I've never heard people say, 'My family's been struggling for generations. There's no future here for African Americans.'"[46] But the man's aspirations to leave the region fit within larger demographic trends. Cook County, the county home to Chicago, has the largest non-Hispanic Black population in the country. But from 2010 to 2018, the Black community lost over 61,000 people, while the county's overall population grew by over 16,000.[47] Given this context, this young man's perspective likely represented a considerable portion of the population, just not one the journalist had encountered.

By spending time talking to residents in communities where most reporters did not live or frequent, *Curious City*'s outreach also functioned as listening sessions,[48] opportunities to gather perspectives from members of the public. Tom explained that while he did not get a question to use from that young man, he did walk away with ideas for possible stories. While these would fall outside the domain of *Curious City*, they could end up elsewhere on WBEZ's airwaves. In this way, the outreach sometimes indirectly increased the range of perspectives circulated in the local storytelling network by WBEZ.

By the end of the yearlong outreach project, Tom had gathered 137 questions by driving around to various neighborhoods and suburbs to solicit questions face-to-face. Through these interactions, *Curious City* was able to establish connections with members of the public who largely had not previously been listeners, let alone participants in the process of creating stories.

How did these cases match up to the Hearken and *Curious City* story cycle models that aspired to involve residents from the beginning (pitching and assigning), to reporting, and to feedback following publication or broadcast? By conducting face-to-face outreach in communities, *Curious City* did involve the public in pitching story ideas. Those whose stories were selected were also involved in the reporting process. However, there was a gap at the point of assignment and follow-up. When Tom spoke with residents, he often gave them his card, but he didn't have any sort of flyer or other way to let them know how to find the *Curious City* website or FM station. Because of this, it was highly unlikely that they would participate in story selection.

Ordinarily when questions came in, they were entered into a question "pool" and then vetted by the producers and the editor, who would discuss their appropriateness and viability in meetings. From there some questions were selected for a "voting round," where anyone visiting the website could vote on what question they wanted answered next (usually choosing from a list of three options). Occasionally, the editor would select questions for production without first putting them through a voting round.

Reporters said the *Curious City* process altered the standard practices of gatekeeping and agenda setting—and in some ways gave reporters more freedom. One reporter pointed out that she liked how getting questions allowed the team to consider ideas that might be outside the view of typical "types of newsroom people." She said while these processes alone were not enough to address the limited diversity in the public radio newsrooms, they did allow reporters to consider story ideas beyond the cliché of "what your editors saw while driving into work."[49] Another reporter explained that he appreciated how the process helped him to justify stories that lacked a traditional "hook or news peg" but had audience interest: "Sometimes I think [when] the focus [is] on what's important to what's happening in the news right now, you lose sight of the fact that there are things just sitting there that are worth writing about, reporting about."[50] At the same time, while there may have been some loosening of the boundaries of what was considered newsworthy, the editorial team still decided what stories made it into the voting rounds. As former WBEZ CEO Torey Malatia explained how radio stations used Hearken—*Curious City* in particular—"We're not turning over anything." Professionals were still the keeper of an editorial process that "we and we alone can do."[51] *Curious City* was not sharing power when it came to what made it on the air.

Residents whom *Curious City* journalists met as part of their outreach not only were unlikely to connect with voting rounds but also were unlikely to hear finished *Curious City* stories when they broadcast—unless the story was about their question and they had shared their contact information. While *Curious City* stories aired in multiple time slots on the radio, online, via podcasts, and on social media, none of these channels were likely to reach residents not already connected with WBEZ or *Curious City*. A lack of outreach or marketing made it improbable that residents in the communities targeted for outreach would stumble across *Curious City* on the radio dial or in online spaces. This presented a significant limitation for the project's ability to build relationships of trust with communities. In conversations in outreach areas, a number of residents expressed frustration with media outlets for their lack of follow-up on community issues—and for the sense that they "parachute in" to take stories and then are not to be seen. One resident cautioned that members of the public may be reluctant to participate in engagement efforts because of a lack of a track record of follow-up or change: "We never see results, so it's like, why get involved if anything's not going to happen? And I get that. So that's basically what it is; it's not going to change, so why get involved?"[52] For these residents, if they were not included in the broadcast or follow-up discussion of stories, even if the stories circulating about their neighborhood were changing, they had no way to know about it.

Curious City did take some measures to engage the public beyond the point of broadcast, including hosting public events. Team members invited listeners to auditoriums for several events where they presented stories through a variety of creative means, including a puppet cinema. They also hosted interactive Twitter chats where reporters and experts were on hand to respond to questions about stories from the public. However, these engagement efforts largely served WBEZ listeners who would find out about them through on-air announcements, visits to the website, or emails to electronic mailing lists. While *Curious City* staffers conducted outreach in communities to gather questions, they did not return to let these communities know how to listen to the answers. There was no marketing campaign. This was largely a question of resources—there was no budget line in the foundation grant for such marketing. Team members acknowledged that even basic materials like a flyer or bookmark would have been valuable—simply having something to hand out to community members with basic information about how to find out more about *Curious City* and how to participate in the future.

Not involving residents in the distribution and feedback portion of the story cycle matters. In communication infrastructure theory's storytelling network, it means the network tie between media and residents flows in only one direction, from resident to media (see figure 3). Not only does this limit the degree the local storytelling network is strengthened, but it reinforces problematic flows of information. Such a situation risks creating extractive relationships—for example, when a white reporter goes into a community of color on the South Side and works with a community member to tell a story, but then that story

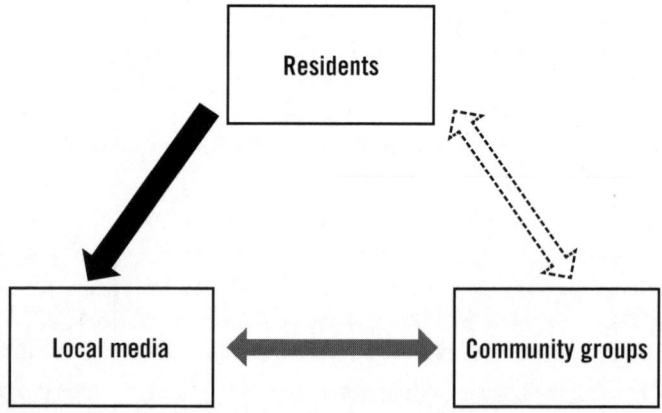

Figure 3. Communication Infrastructure Theory's "Storytelling Network": *Curious City* Case

is heard only by a majority white, majority North Side public radio audience. While, in this case, outreach may expand the perspectives circulating in the storytelling network, residents in affected communities are not given access to participate in public discourse around community issues.

Curious City's example also illustrates how the concept Lewis, Holton, and Coddington called "sustained reciprocity"[53] offers the potential to strengthen CIT's storytelling network—and how its absence can pose a barrier to developing relationships of trust. *Curious City*'s face-to-face outreach did allow residents to participate more actively in shaping the agenda of what stories were considered in the editorial process. But the degree this intervention strengthened ties between residents and local media in the storytelling network was limited by the lack of basic marketing and follow-up to maintain relationships with residents over time—what would have been sustained reciprocity or engagement. While program staffers positioned their efforts as an experiment, their emphasis remained fixed on connecting with residents for the purpose of enhancing the programming rather than on circling back to engage with the communities themselves.

Community Partnerships

In addition to face-to-face outreach, such as going up to residents in public spaces to ask if they had questions to contribute, *Curious City* team members also tried partnering with various community institutions as part of their experiment. This step was significant because it raised the possibility of connecting two key actors in CIT's storytelling network. Media outlets' conducting outreach to the general public offered the potential to build relationships with individual residents. Connecting to organizations offered the possibility of amplifying their efforts by extending out to community networks, particularly when working with partners with a deep history of organizing with communities and a trusted reputation. *Curious City* tried working with a range of partners—from community organizations to brewpubs to libraries. Each partner had a different set of constituents that *Curious City* hoped to connect with. But building and maintaining shared expectations with partners proved challenging, and the results of the experience varied widely from partner to partner.

One of the first approaches *Curious City* staffers tried was to set up question boxes inviting patrons of the various locations to submit a question idea on a slip of paper. The boxes included a little sign and some sample questions. They set these up in a suburban microbrewery café and several libraries. Tom explained that when he went around with the boxes, they were well received by the library branches. At one branch, he described how he had shown the librarian the *Curious City* question box and then stepped away to use the restroom.

"They were like 'Curious City'? OK.' And they, like, got a Curious George doll and a Curious George book and they tied it to the thing. And by the time I came out of the bathroom I was like, 'Wow, you really personalized this box.'"[54]

At another library branch, the librarian helped make signage for the box in Spanish to appeal to the area's large population of Spanish speakers. But this initial enthusiasm did not translate into productive interaction with the question boxes. Because these libraries and cafés were spread across a considerable geographic expanse, Tom did not regularly check in with them. When he returned later to see about the boxes, several had been moved. He noted that most were not located near someone who could explain them or draw people's attention to them. Perhaps unsurprisingly, the boxes yielded a dismal number of questions. They were mostly empty—generating a paltry three questions.

Another way *Curious City* tried to partner with community groups was by inviting them to appeal to their constituents to gather questions. On the city's West Side, the program's staffers worked with the head of a youth organization who appreciated the project's effort to solicit community input: "This is what we need. Seldom do we have an opportunity to say what we want covered. Very seldom." He contrasted *Curious City*'s effort with the way he usually saw his neighborhood covered by journalists reporting breaking news, where "once the lights and camera go off that reporter is gone."[55]

But the relationships *Curious City* sought to form with community groups were not immune from the sorts of tensions that arose between media and organizations in South LA in chapter 1. Shawn Allee, the show's editor, explained that he appreciated the value that community organizations provided in helping the team connect with residents: "Their mediation is helpful, in that it exposes us to new people." However, the show's producers were also guarded, recognizing that these organizations may be pushing an "agenda" that conflicted with *Curious City*'s self-image as a neutral journalistic actor. The outreach producer explained that when he edited stories, he generally removed information about organizations that felt "like free advertising for them." He didn't want to do promotional work for an organization: "I don't see the need to carry water for any particular group."[56] There was a point at which the journalists expressed a need to reinforce boundaries of editorial control and norms of independence within their practice.

In some cases, partnerships with community groups didn't work out because of this tension. Allee offered the example of an organization that had been gathering questions from its community. Most of the questions its leaders shared with *Curious City* were related to the issues that the organization focused on. The editor had told them that the program wanted questions on any topic the residents were interested in. But the leaders of the organization saw that this was a rare opportunity to share important community concerns with influential segments of the city that listened to WBEZ. They did not want to squander this chance by asking frivolous questions on random topics. Allee explained that the program was limited in its number of stories on any one topic or tone. He wanted the outreach to get participants who would return to *Curious City* multiple times with different types of questions.

Allee said these gaps in expectations led the team to move away from more advocacy-oriented community groups to partners they saw as more neutral. He suggested that libraries in particular had a mission that was aligned with the program.

"Our mission is to provide a path to empower and support learning and discovery," Emily, a staffer at a suburban branch library, explained. To her, collaborating with *Curious City* seemed like a natural fit. Getting patrons to ask questions supported the library's goal of discovery: "If our reference staff engages a patron with something they're interested in—'What's your question for WBEZ?' Maybe it's the Superfund site. . . . What resources can they then connect them to here in the library so they can learn more?" Emily said she saw potential for library staff to encourage participation in *Curious City* in various ways—from the reference desk to English as a second language courses. And she pointed out that libraries could help to connect journalists to residents who may otherwise have reservations speaking with reporters. She offered to assist in this area by making flyers in both English and Spanish that indicated the library's partnership: "That would go a long way. People trust the library. We worked really hard to build a reputation. People come here and they feel safe. For a community that has a significant population of undocumented immigrants, that is really important. So having our name be on there helps with respect to that population."[57]

Curious City producers saw libraries as different from other community organizations because they did not perceive them to have an agenda. However, one library staffer acknowledged that she hoped the partnership with *Curious City* would help to build goodwill with WBEZ more broadly. Her library occasionally sought press coverage of its activities, some of which were grant-funded. As with community groups, libraries also worked to develop relationships that they hoped would lead to positive press coverage. Nevertheless, the *Curious City* team did not see such complications as problematic within the scope of this outreach project.

The partnership between *Curious City* and libraries was seen as mutually beneficial. It was also the most productive element of the program's outreach experiment. While leaving question boxes did not prove fruitful, team members attempted a hybrid of their face-to-face outreach in collaboration with several branch libraries. They would set up a table in the lobby of a branch or just outside it when the weather was good. *Curious City* staffers were stationed at the tables, displaying WBEZ banners and tablecloths, ready to talk with residents when they approached. They explained the premise of the project, invited people to ask questions, and showed a display of other sample questions. This method offered the best of both the face-to-face and partnership strategies. It provided the flexibility of face-to-face interaction, allowing journalists to tailor their explanation to community members. At the same time, people could choose to approach the table on their own terms, which was different from being approached on the street in a context that made many defensive. The program also benefited from the added credibility of association with the library. Through this process, *Curious City* gathered 159 questions over the outreach period.

Overall, *Curious City*'s attempt to use partnerships to gather questions had mixed results. Team members' efforts illustrate the challenges of connecting media outlets with community groups, a key step to creating stronger storytelling networks. Building these relationships took an investment of time—something the single outreach producer had in short supply. Further, with *Curious City*'s particular model of gathering questions, the journalists involved were not comfortable working with groups seen to be advancing an agenda beyond that of curiosity or accessing information. This illustrates how journalism norms around objectivity and neutrality can present barriers to building trust between local news outlets and community groups. At the same time, the process did uncover a major finding of their experiment. *Curious City*'s producers settled upon a sense of what their ideal outreach method was—working with a partner seen as sharing a complementary mission and employing face-to-face outreach in collaboration with the partner. Through their efforts, while they didn't significantly strengthen storytelling network links between themselves as members of local media and all community organizations, they did build ties with libraries, an important community institution.

Hyperlocal and Ethnic Media Partnerships

Another avenue *Curious City* explored as part of its outreach experiment was the idea of connecting with area hyperlocal and ethnic media outlets. Chicago is home to numerous community newspapers serving particular neighborhoods, as well as outlets associated with the African American community and multilingual outlets serving the city's many immigrant and refugee communities.

Tom, the outreach producer, began sending queries to a few outlets to see if they would be interested in adapting *Curious City* content for print and including a solicitation for readers to share their questions. One of the outlets Tom tried was a Polish newspaper, Chicago being home to one of the largest Polish communities outside of Poland. At first he was having difficulty reaching its office. He worried he may have offended the publishers: "It might be kind of insulting in some ways ... [like,] 'We're fabulous, take our great content.'" But in the end, they did connect and the newspaper was happy to take the free content. The newspaper ran translations of *Curious City* stories that focused on Chicago's Polish community. Yet despite this success in sharing content to a different audience, *Curious City* was not able to measure whether any of the questions the program got ended up coming from the readers of this newspaper.

Producers tried only a few of the region's numerous outlets, even though they saw partnerships with hyperlocal and ethnic media as a way to reach previously unreached publics. Here again *Curious City*'s relationships were mostly going in one direction—in this case, going from *Curious City* to the smaller outlets. The team did not explore the potential to go in the other direction, to adapt content from these outlets or to coproduce content. This is understandable given the limited scope of the program's experimental project. Nevertheless, two-way exchanges of content or collaborative productions offer a potentially valuable way to strengthen the local storytelling network and, in this case, an opportunity to benefit WBEZ more broadly. Such partnerships are loaded with complexity—establishing and managing expectations and differences in resources and power. However, collaborative journalism initiatives have been undertaken by a growing number of outlets in the United States and internationally in recent years. This has included regional efforts such as the Center for Cooperative Media[58] in New Jersey, citywide projects like the Resolve Philadelphia's solutions journalism series,[59] and the Charlotte Journalism Collaborative,[60] and in Chicago the organization City Bureau[61] has collaborated with a range of outlets on engagement activities.[62]

Going forward, deepening some of the relationships *Curious City* began to explore and developing others may offer one avenue to grapple with WBEZ's limited reach within communities of color, as well as within more conservative suburban areas. Building such partnerships would require a substantial investment of time and careful navigations of power relationships. But beyond the potential benefits for the public radio station or the hyperlocal partner outlets, creating such relationships would enable the circulation of shared community stories across local storytelling networks, strengthening the region's communication infrastructure.

Social Media Marketing

The final strategy *Curious City*'s producers attempted in their outreach experiment was a social media marketing campaign. The online campaign presented a challenge to the program's impulse to openness in terms of types of questions and the profiles of question askers. To run a campaign on Facebook, they had to deliberately choose whom they would target to see the Facebook ad. Working with WBEZ's marketing director, they first selected the zip code of the areas their outreach campaign was focusing on. This was the easy part. But beyond that, they had to build a profile of whom they were targeting based on Facebook users' demographics and groups and issues they had "liked."

Staffers decided they would target demographic "look-alikes"—people who shared characteristics with WBEZ listeners but who were residents of the target geographic areas. They varied the profiles slightly, including people with "some high school" and people who had expressed interest in local history. But the list of interests they selected largely overlapped with their core audience: WBEZ, *This American Life*, NPR, *NPR Morning Edition*, *Wait Wait ... Don't Tell Me!*, urban design, architecture and design, environmentally friendly, urbanism, the *New York Times*, urbanization, smart growth, sustainable living, *The Atlantic*, public broadcasting, history, sustainable development, urban planning, environmentalism, architecture.

In their face-to-face outreach, team members had found that it was helpful to localize their request to participate. For this reason, they decided to split their pool of several hundred thousand residents into three geographic zones: underrepresented areas of Chicago (largely on the South and West Sides), suburban areas, and Northwest Indiana (which is also part of the metro region and WBEZ's coverage area). For each of these areas they varied the questions and the ad design. For example, Facebook users in Northwest Indiana would be asked, "Curious about something in the Northwest Indiana or Chicago region?" Accompanying this question would be a banner with a graphic that included houses and trees instead of the design of Chicago's skyline that Chicago residents would see. Users who clicked on the ads would be sent to geographically specific landing pages for the campaign. Each of these included the question form.

By the end of their three-week campaign, the *Curious City* team had spent $4,500 on ads that reached just under 200,000 people. Of these people, 1,920 clicked the ad to get to the landing page. But after all of the effort and expense, only 14 people asked questions. In their own reflections, the *Curious City* team agreed this was a poor result. For a campaign this size, they expected at least 10 percent of those who visited the site to ask a question, but they received closer to 1 percent. This social media strategy did not seem to offer potential for strengthening the local storytelling network.

Curious City's Conclusions on Outreach

At the end of *Curious City*'s yearlong outreach project, team members stepped back to evaluate the results of their engagement experiment. While they were certain the Facebook ads and question boxes had been a bust, what about the other strategies they had attempted? Over the course of the year, *Curious City* gathered 313 questions through outreach to targeted geographic areas. This was a third of all the questions they had received over the year (976 questions in total). They looked not only at the number of questions gathered but at the resources required for each strategy: face-to-face outreach, outreach with partners, and online marketing. Far and away the most productive approach was a hybrid of the face-to-face outreach and collaboration with partners, specifically collaborating with libraries. They gained 137 questions by having outreach producers approach strangers to solicit questions. However, this was the most time- and resource-intensive strategy, requiring numerous trips and staff hours. In comparison, just three Saturdays at branch libraries netted 159 questions.

Editor Shawn Allee also reflected on what kinds of questions came from their outreach. He had been deliberately cautious at the start of the project not to assume he knew what residents from underrepresented communities were interested in: "What I can predict is that if we ask more people from these communities, we'll get more questions. We'll get more voices. And since part of our job is to be genuine and listening to them, then, I can sleep better at night at least knowing that I listened—and that it informed my editorial decision-making."[63]

Allee wanted to leave the door open for the range of questions *Curious City* tried to include—from historical trivia to more serious reporting. By the end of the team's outreach project, Allee noted that a number of questions from the geographies they focused on were questions of accountability. Many residents asked about issues within local governance or issues around city resources and equity. Part of this may be explained by the participants' lack of familiarity with *Curious City* and its track record for including quirky stories. But many participants came from areas with histories of deep inequality, so accountability questions were not surprising.

Reflecting on *Curious City*'s overall outreach efforts, the team also looked at how they represented the region as a result of their project. They concluded that the outreach project did "move the needle closer to geographic parity."[64] The percentage of questions coming from targeted geographic zones grew at a faster rate (78 percent for Chicago's West Side and 53 percent for the South Side) than WBEZ's core audience areas (20 percent). Participation from targeted suburbs and exurbs also grew faster than the core areas, with the exception of Northwest Indiana, where questions remained flat. Allee said he hoped going forward they would be able to shift from a model of experimenting to one of deploying the most effective strategies in a way that could be sustainable.

Offline Engagement and the Storytelling Network

Curious City's outreach intervention did not hit every mark as far as strengthening the connection between local media and residents in the storytelling network. Through offline outreach, staffers were able to connect to residents who were not familiar with public radio and who rarely had the opportunity to tell their own stories or shape the local news agenda. This was not a small accomplishment, particularly given that many of the communities they connected with had a history of being stigmatized by negative media coverage. At the same time, the outreach experiment failed to create a feedback loop. By gathering questions without letting residents know how to participate in the future, they were not adhering to the ideals of Hearken's story cycle model.

Following their experiment, *Curious City* staffers did attempt to address some of these gaps and to deepen the involvement of residents in later stages of the production cycle. The team has focused on working with libraries. But now when they go out and set up tables, they make sure to bring flyers telling people how they can listen to the stories that are produced and keep participating. They have tried to make this a more sustainable practice by including budget lines for this outreach in their underwriting sales (so, for example, when a museum purchased underwriting for its podcast, it included funds to be used to buy a branded tablecloth and to print flyers). They have also worked to build outreach and engagement into the institutional culture. This effort at times has been challenging, as staff who are used to public radio events intended to recruit members have different expectations from what is needed for outreach to encourage participation in programming. But Allee has tried to work with staff to develop shared goals. For example, he made it part of the goals for a reporter's annual review to organize presentations to share *Curious City* stories at some of the outreach libraries. These presentations aim to close the feedback loop—letting residents hear and discuss stories that their fellow neighbors proposed and having the opportunity on the spot to suggest more questions. The team also has tried other tactics like involving members of the public in group edits of stories when possible, allowing them to have more input on the editorial process, at least in these cases.

Implementing these changes takes time and an investment in building relationships. *Curious City*'s experience illustrates how engagement platforms like Hearken on their own are dependent on sustained engagement or reciprocity and on an investment in both building and maintaining relationships. A media outlet can at a given moment have the public participating in generating story ideas, selecting them, reporting, and feedback. But then in other circumstances it may involve residents only in gathering story ideas. *Curious City*'s experience also illustrates the importance of storytelling network links flowing in both directions to prevent the media outlet from going into a community and extracting a story rather than engaging residents in dialogue about the community issue.

Curious City's outreach effort also highlights the value of building storytelling network ties between local media and community institutions. For the program, working with libraries was the most efficient pathway to connect with residents in communities where it lacked broad listenership. In recent years, a number of projects have explored the potential synergies between news media and libraries.[65] Many have pointed to libraries' comparatively high levels of trust among the public. For example, a Pew Research Center study suggested 78 percent of adults believe libraries help them find trustworthy and reliable information.[66] Following their outreach experiment, *Curious City* producers have continued to develop relationships with libraries, especially on the South Side and in the suburbs. They may work on more regular visits to particular regional libraries to deepen their connection.

At the same time, there may be value in looking back at some of *Curious City*'s less successful partnerships, with community groups or hyperlocal media, to explore whether with more investment the radio team may have yielded valuable results. Had community organizations and media outlets undertaken a process of learning to understand each other, as groups did in South Los Angeles, it may have been possible to find mutually beneficial ways to collaborate. *Curious City*'s interactions with community organizations perceived to be advocating for particular issues illustrate how difficult it can be to navigate journalistic norms of objectivity and neutrality that tend to come up when media outlets and organizations connect.

In Rhode Island, where former WBEZ CEO Torey Malatia now runs "The Public's Radio," the station is looking to use Hearken to strengthen its connections to community organizations. Malatia shared the example of how the station may let an organization committed to water preservation post a Hearken widget to ask for community questions to help inform its own planning process. "We'd be able to learn from it," he explained. Sharing access to the platform (which would indicate it is normally connected to the public radio station) would introduce Hearken to potential new audiences. At the same time, it would indirectly benefit reporters by exposing them to "whatever the conversation is that the institution needs to have, so that we just know more about our community."[67] Here, Malatia's conception of Hearken's value connects with the idea of direct reciprocity[68] and also holds promise to strengthen links between community groups and media in the local storytelling network. While a number of public media projects pursue mutual benefit, the direct benefit often goes to the media outlet (for example, in the form of content gained), with community stakeholders benefiting in a more nebulous, indirect way. Malatia's proposed arrangement flips the balance of direct benefit to the community organization. It shows other outlets interested in building reciprocal or engaged relationships with communities that there may be paths to working more directly with community organizations.

The outreach efforts *Curious City* has used in combination with Hearken, while mixed, highlight the critical value that offline engagement can offer media organizations that seek to meet residents where they are. This emphasis on the value of offline engagement has been found in studies of other public media outlets. For example, Belair-Gagnon, Nelson, and Lewis examined how two public media outlets that also used the Hearken platform emphasized the value of face-to-face engagement.[69] Likewise, *Curious City*'s attempt at offline engagement outside traditional public radio audience strongholds illustrated the difficulties of attempting to build relationships of reciprocity with broader communities. The outlets in Belair-Gagnon, Nelson, and Lewis's study were similarly trying to balance these dual relationships. To understand the nature of these relationships deeply would require more extensive research from the perspective of community members. What value do they see in these relationships and exchanges? Do they feel their voice can be heard through this process, and is that enough? Do the expectations of residents match that of the journalists who see themselves as providing something of benefit to "the community"?

These efforts can force outlets to confront the gap between their existing audience and whom they imagine as their community. Of course, this gap has always been there. Before online engagement platforms existed, there were countless efforts in public media to connect with communities through town hall discussions and citizen media initiatives. Subsequently there have long been tensions in public media between desiring to serve an elite member base versus appealing to parts of the community who are largely reported *about* and not *for*. However, the advent of online engagement initiatives has led new generations of producers and reporters to grapple with questions of participatory journalism and the gap between audience and community.

Beyond the People Formerly Known as the Audience

Curious City's efforts to create links with communities that fall outside its existing public media audience illustrate both the promise and the structural challenges such initiatives face. The program's editor identified a need and an opportunity to fill *Curious City*'s mission of serving the curiosity of all of Chicagoland. But the steps the team took to address the gap between mission and practice were embedded in a system that reinforced journalistic norms of detached objectivity and public media norms that prioritized serving potential members.

For example, while Shawn Allee's team sought to collaborate with community groups to gather questions, these relationships were constrained by a sense that they didn't want to get too close to groups with perceptible agendas. Here they came up against journalistic norms of objectivity. An allegiance to these prevented them from pursuing stronger links with community organizations.

Meanwhile, while the *Curious City* team fully intended to try to strengthen connections with residents, they initially approached this work with blind spots likely influenced by their position within the public media structure. At WBEZ, marketing activities sit in a separate part of the station. Simple acts of establishing feedback loops and channels of two-way communication were associated with the work of marketing. Reporters did not see it as part of their job to hand out a flyer to let people know how to follow up on, listen to, or give feedback on programs. At the same time, public media marketing departments are designed to build and serve the work of membership, often conceptualizing a target audience likely to contribute financially to support the station. Setting up tables or handing out flyers in marginalized communities with limited socioeconomic resources has not historically been part of public media marketing.

This case also illustrates the potential power of philanthropic foundations to support work that strengthens local storytelling networks. While foundations traditionally fund projects with fixed deliverables, *Curious City* received funding for a process—an experiment to see what method of engagement would be most effective. This represents a forward-thinking approach to philanthropic support of engaged journalism. At the same time, if funders had adapted concepts like CIT's storytelling network, they may have been able to prod *Curious City* to make room in their budget for simple things like flyers or other ways to create two-way feedback loops with communities.

Going forward, if Allee and his *Curious City* team are going to push ahead with strengthening local storytelling networks and creating two-way feedback loops, they will have to find ways to chip away at structural barriers and blind spots. Good intentions alone will not enable WBEZ or any public media outlet to build relationships with communities that historically fall outside familiar tote-bag-carrying and NPR-mug-sipping audiences. Their current plans suggest they may work to build on alliances developed with public libraries and continue using a combination of digital and face-to-face outreach, which ultimately draw from community organizing strategies.[70]

Public media outlets committed to building engaged or reciprocal relationships with community members may also need to question their assumptions about what "mutual benefit" means. When outlets host opportunities for residents to share their experiences and "be heard," on- or off-air, many assume that such offerings are a service to residents. While this may be true, there is a danger of slipping into "giving voice to the voiceless" narratives. Doing so presumes that a voice is bestowed value only when it is heard by (often privileged, often white) public media audiences. Residents of communities already have voices, even if, as Gayatri Chakravorty Spivak argued, they do not speak in the language that is heard by those with power.[71] When public media journalists use their platform to share voices from marginalized communities with their audiences, they may benefit the communities at times by placing issues on the agenda of people with power to make changes. But often the benefit to those communities is murkier, particularly when there are no feedback loops for them to participate in follow-up conversations and exercise agency in the process. Often the lion's share of benefit goes to the media outlet and its audience, who are able to gain a greater understanding of these "other" communities.

Building relationships that go beyond audiences and stretch into the fabric of communities requires deliberate strategy and the sharing of power. While *Curious City*'s intervention was not designed with a CIT framework in mind, it nevertheless illustrates how a CIT framework can be used to analyze how engagement efforts do and do not strengthen local storytelling networks. In many ways the program's outreach efforts demonstrated valuable strategies—such as face-to-face tabling, partnering with public library branches, and showing up in communities that have historically been stigmatized. This said, the lingering areas of weakness in the storytelling network were at least as insightful. To build connections between media, residents, and community groups and to strengthen the local storytelling network, this case suggested that feedback loops must be created and nurtured over time and that projects must be responsive to the local needs and realities that communities face. In the next chapter, I'll examine a process where residents and journalists worked together to design an intervention that aimed to strengthen relationships between local media and the public amid a background of heightened partisan divisions and mistrust of media.

CHAPTER 3

Developing an Intervention

Building a Public Sphere in Polarized Places

Growing up in rural Ohio County, Kentucky, Heather had no intention of sticking around. But then, just as she was finishing law school, the financial crisis hit. Heather found herself moving back to her small town, whose slogan read, "Home of 2,000 happy people and a few soreheads."

When I met Heather, she wore a bright pink T-shirt with "SOREHEAD" emblazoned in white letters, next to her town's name and an image of Kentucky. The shirt seemed to embrace the term as a point of pride, appropriating the idea of the disgruntled "sorehead" townsperson into a marker of town identity.

Heather was now firmly entrenched in local civic life, actively attending meetings and participating in community organizations. And on paper, as a white Republican, Heather conformed to the area's dominant demographic profile. But when she looked outward to news media, she did not see herself: "I didn't vote for Trump. But I live in Kentucky, so from a national standpoint I'm clumped in with a bunch of hillbillies. Right?"[1]

Heather expressed frustration that news media painted only in strokes of Republican red or Democratic blue, but this did not reflect the complexity of her identity. Indeed, I met numerous area residents who confounded traditional assumptions about party and politics: residents who identified as Democrat but voted for Trump, and vice versa. For Heather this lack of nuance was a symptom of a larger problem with how her area was represented: "The national media now makes a decision on how naturally it is to view a rural area like this as dumb and backwards and very conservative—which is frustrating to me, because sometimes that means that we're the last ones to see any kind of growth or see any sort of investment."

Like residents on Chicago's South Side,[2] Heather had identified material consequences to what she saw as stigmatizing media depictions of her area. She expressed concern that beyond offering a distorted view to outsiders and potentially deterring would-be tourists or investors, these limited portrayals affected how residents saw and interacted with each other locally. People internalized negative depictions of the area as a place where "nothing ever happens," she said. "When good things try to happen here, they just keep tearing it down."

A considerable amount of discourse has been devoted to the perils of political polarization, including its link to perceptions of media bias and mistrust.[3] Without trusted institutions, Ethan Zuckerman has argued, citizens find themselves in "polarized media spaces that have so little overlap that shared consensus on basic civic facts is difficult to achieve."[4] But how does polarization and mistrust play out in lived experiences that are inevitably more "purple" than they may appear on an aggregated map? And how does it affect local storytelling networks that connect residents to community groups, local media, and each other?

By zooming in on the lived experiences of Western Kentucky residents, this chapter shifts to a very different demographic context to explore how trust is negotiated, how it is mediated by place, and the toll that partisan divides and mistrust can take on local communication infrastructures. While previous chapters have focused largely on Democrat-leaning urban neighborhoods and communities of color, the Western Kentucky case is situated in Republican-leaning rural areas and small towns that are majority white. At the same time, all of these areas see themselves as marginalized in various ways, and all are more complex and layered than demographic summaries may suggest. By grappling with experiences in these different contexts and places, this chapter aims to work toward interventions that seek to strengthen and repair local storytelling networks by building trust and contributing to communication environments where people feel informed, invested, and respected.

Polarization in Purple Places

From April 2017 to February 2018, I worked with colleagues, local journalists, and community members to research local communication infrastructures in Western Kentucky, particularly in the college town of Bowling Green and the more rural area of Ohio County.[5] The case study first explored how partisan divisions played out at the local level. We then undertook an intervention by bringing local stakeholders together to brainstorm projects and subsequently followed several of the pilot engagement initiatives that emerged from the process.

Kentucky overall is a Republican state. It was one of the first states called for Trump in the 2016 U.S. elections.[6] The only blotches of Democratic blue on the state's map were in the large metro areas of Lexington and Louisville. Nevertheless, even the regions of Western Kentucky where our research was located had minorities of Clinton voters (20 percent in Ohio County, 35 percent in Warren County). Given patterns of polarization at the national level[7] and attitudes toward political "others,"[8] what was it like for political "others" to live in proximity? How did people interact if they went to the same high school sports games or worshipped at the same churches? And how did this affect how people made sense of their community?

For at least a decade, analysts have pointed to a phenomenon of U.S. residents migrating to areas where their political and lifestyle preferences are widely shared. Author Bill Bishop called this the "big sort" in 2008,[9] and more recent studies have suggested that spatial polarization has increased in most states since the 1990s.[10] However, as highlighted by the experience of Heather and other participants in this case study, this kind of ideological self-segregation is possible only with a degree of privilege and resources. For many, moving for political or lifestyle reasons is not an option. As a result, places that may appear as a uniform red or blue on a map may obscure complex histories of class, race, and power that do not always neatly adhere to partisan identities.

Mapping politics onto places can be complicated. In her exploration of "rural consciousness," political scientist Katherine Cramer has outlined the relationship between place identity and a sense of resentment held by rural residents toward city dwellers perceived to be benefiting from unfair allocations of resources. While place identity and party identity often overlap, Cramer argues that place identity is at times more meaningful than partisanship.[11] Likewise, scholars focused on local media have emphasized the importance of recognizing places without reducing or romanticizing them[12] while centering the critical role of local place-based media in healthy public spheres.[13]

Place identity, then, can be seen as influencing what communication infrastructure theory[14] calls the communication action context.[15] As detailed in the introduction, CIT offers a framework to assess the communicative health and cohesion of place-based communities. In communities with strong storytelling networks, residents, community organizations, and local media are connected to each other and share information about community issues. The communication action context is the environment that either facilitates or constrains connection to these networks. In rural Kentucky, this might mean something as simple as a lack of broadband Internet connections constraining people from accessing websites. Or, interpersonal connections could be facilitated through community institutions like churches or establishments like a local diner, but how these spaces are coded in terms of politics, class, or race may shape whether or not these spaces feel accessible and welcoming.

Beyond assessing the state of local communication environments, CIT can also be used to design intervention projects that aim to improve them. As discussed in the introduction and chapter 1, CIT has been used to design journalistic projects. These have included projects that try to connect different parts of local storytelling networks—for example, ethnically Chinese, Latinx, and white residents of a suburb,[16] or community organizations and local journalists.[17] Beyond journalistic interventions, CIT also has a tradition of participatory and engaged projects that work with residents and organizations to imagine, design,[18] and evaluate[19] interventions.

In this chapter, I draw on CIT first as a framework to investigate local storytelling networks in Western Kentucky. After assessing the strengths and weaknesses of the local communication environment, I then use CIT as a map, guiding work with local stakeholders in a participatory intervention design process.

The Places: Bowling Green and Ohio County

On February 3, 2017, Vanessa, like many residents of Bowling Green, Kentucky, awoke to a shock.

"I remember waking up that morning, the morning after. Because I always check Twitter, and that was the thing that was trending. I'm like, Bowling Green Massacre, oh shit, what'd I miss overnight?"[20]

What Vanessa had missed was one of the most infamous cases of "alternative facts" taking over the news cycle. Trump ally Kellyanne Conway had fabricated a story of a terrorist attack in Bowling Green as a justification for Trump's controversial travel ban.[21] Vanessa recalled talking to reporters from the Associated Press and CNN and her amusement when her friends marked themselves as "safe" on Facebook.

For many in Bowling Green, the "massacre," and the lack of understanding about the area exhibited in subsequent news coverage, underlined the disconnect between national media and their lived experience. As a college town, the home of Western Kentucky University, and a refugee resettlement area, Bowling Green is significantly diverse compared with the surrounding region. More than 10,000 refugees from thirty countries have been resettled since 1981. The city has a foreign-born population of approximately 14 percent, and nearly 10 percent of the population speaks English less than "very well." While 71 percent of residents identify as white, this includes a sizable Bosnian Muslim community. Bowling Green is also home to 14 percent of residents who identify as African American, 7 percent as Hispanic or Latinx, 5 percent as Asian, and 4 percent as another race.[22] Politically, it sits as a pocket of purple within a sea of Republican red.

Bowling Green has a spoke-and-hub economic relationship with other more rural areas surrounding it. This includes Ohio County, the birthplace of the father of bluegrass music, Bill Monroe. Ohio County is home to 24,000 residents who are spread across six hundred square miles. While the area has a history of agriculture, manufacturing, and coal mining, 21 percent of residents are categorized as living in poverty, with the per capita income just under $20,000.[23] Ohio County residents, who are 94 percent non-Latinx white and majority Republican, often go to Bowling Green for shopping or dining. In recent years, a number of immigrant and refugee residents of Bowling Green also moved to or commute to work in Ohio County, including a considerable number who work in a chicken processing plant.

The two areas are also home to a range of local media outlets. In Bowling Green, this includes a daily legacy paper and a public media broadcaster, among others. Ohio County has a weekly legacy paper, a hyperlocal news website, and commercial talk radio. A number of community organizations in both areas offer service provision and address a range of local issues. These sites, then, were home to the kinds of storytelling actors (local media, community groups, residents from different backgrounds) that would be needed for a potential intervention to strengthen communication infrastructure.

Following the Bowling Green "massacre," residents clapped back at the national distortion of their local reality, making memorials with candles and flowers and signs reading "Never Forget" and, tellingly, "RIP Truth."[24] Bowling Green may symbolically be associated with misinformation. But my colleagues and I also selected it and nearby Ohio County as research sites because they have valuable communication assets. Understanding the complexity of these places and how residents navigate information needs within them allows us to imagine how communities can strengthen local storytelling networks by amplifying the kinds of local stories that leave residents feeling represented and respected.

Assessing the Storytelling Network

By the time this study began, many words had already been spent warning of increasingly yawning partisan divides at the national level.[25] I opted to focus on the local level. It was at the local level that residents from different political backgrounds were most likely to come into physical contact. Social psychologist Gordon Allport's contact theory[26] suggested this face-to-face interaction could lead to a reduction in prejudice toward the "other," though only under optimal conditions. Concentrating on this local level, I used a qualitative[27] and "audience-centered"[28] exploration to chart how local storytelling networks were or were not affected by challenges of polarization and mistrust and what might be done to address them.

To undertake this work, I collaborated with Sam Ford, a media consultant with lifelong roots in Western Kentucky. Working with Sam offered the advantage of bringing a constructive insider-outsider perspective to the study. Sam was able to contribute his deep understanding of local issue and contexts to ensure we recruited a pool of participants who would offer a range of views and experiences, and he helped with the analysis of our findings. Meanwhile, I was clearly an outsider, having grown up a state away in Indiana but now associated with a university on the East Coast. This offered an advantage in conducting focus groups and interviews, as I was free of associations with local personalities or politics, and I was able to delve into taken-for-granted, assumed knowledge.

Through snowball sampling, we compiled a convenience sample of twenty-one residents from Bowling Green and Ohio County who roughly reflected the demographics and politics of the surrounding area.[29] Participants were first invited to take part in a series of three focus group discussions. Following the focus groups and applying the model of methodological triangulation,[30] I invited participants to complete "story diaries." To keep story diaries, participants tracked for a week up to five stories a day that resonated with them and whether they shared the story or attempted to find out more about it. These were then used as jumping-off points for one-on-one follow-up interviews, where participants discussed in greater detail how they did and did not interact with a local storytelling network (local media, organizations, fellow residents, and so on). Finally, I conducted interviews with editors, publishers, and reporters from six local media outlets[31] to get a better understanding of the challenges and opportunities in the local media environment.

By analyzing this combination of discussions, diaries, and interviews, a picture emerged of the state of local storytelling networks (not only local media but also other communication resources and relationships) and how these were affected by the polarized political climate. In the sections that follow, I share how the larger communication action context of participants has been shaped by partisan divisions and how this in turn has influenced ties between residents and interpersonal networks, community groups and spaces, and local media.

National Media Mistrust

According to communication infrastructure theory, national media is rarely part of the local storytelling network as it is generally not involved in circulating community stories. That said, national media informs the larger communication action context in that the narratives it circulates have the potential to influence how residents connect with and interpret local stories and other storytellers. As will be discussed in the sections that follow, participants often referenced how national narratives made their way into interpersonal conversations and social media exchanges and at times were reflected in interpretations of local issues and media stories. For this reason, I began by asking how residents navigated and adapted their national news media diet.

Some of what participants reported was unsurprising, such as a tendency to gravitate toward media outlets associated with their political affiliations. For example, all but four on the right mentioned Fox News and/or the Drudge Report, whereas all but two on the left referenced CNN. A majority of participants mentioned consulting at least one source that was referenced by both those on the left and the right, though some mentioned watching sources to get "the other side."[32] Using a source did not necessarily indicate that participants trusted said source. Most participants expressed mistrust not only about outlets they did not use or that they associated with political others but also about outlets they felt politically aligned with and used regularly. A number communicated some variation of, "I don't really believe anybody."

These feelings of mistrust and dissatisfaction with national media led many to describe a cycle of shifting from verification efforts to stepping back and disengaging.[33] Faced with doubt about the validity of a story or source, participants described assembling a range of communication resources. Sarah explained how she would "go to the source" to see whom the publisher was. If she was still not certain, she would cross-check the information by looking at the *Today Show*'s website. She said she would also note who shared a story and touch base with personal contacts whom she considered knowledgeable. For others, verification was less about checking facts than about comparing and searching for narratives or keeping tabs on the "other side." For some, this meant seeking out hyperpartisan content. William described how he struggled to find what he considered to be uncensored coverage of issues such as terrorist attacks in Europe. He explained that the only place he could find reporting on such stories was on 4Chan. He conceded that 4Chan had unsavory racist and sexist content, but he saw it as his only option for unfiltered news.[34]

Many of the same participants who shared their verification practices, however, said they had also taken at least intermittent breaks from the news—both from legacy sources and from social media. Many referenced a combination of mistrust and a sense of overwhelming negativity. As Christy explained, "It's so depressing because there's not a lot of happy things in the news. It's always sad."[35] She said she now heard about stories via word of mouth and incidental exposure but avoided news when possible. Vanessa said that she tried to seek out celebrity entertainment stories and avoid all news related to Trump: "Things are so weird in the world that I don't want to wake up in the morning and look at bad news."[36] This sentiment was echoed across the political spectrum, as Tricia, a Trump supporter, expressed a similar pull to disengage: "There's a correlation between the amount of news I'm taking in, and a sense of well-being."[37] These sentiments offer context to Reuters Institute findings regarding patterns of rising news avoidance, which many respondents explained as their way of coping with the negative toll news was taking on their mood.[38]

Another concern mentioned frequently among both left- and right-leaning participants was what many saw as an overabundance of opinion and punditry in news media. Many expressed a sense of loss and a belief that things were better in the era of Walter Cronkite, or even in the early days of CNN when the emphasis was more on field reporting. As Martha lamented, for her it was no longer clear who was a pundit and who was a news reporter: "I don't think the reporters are neutral anymore, are they? They've become stars. It's Hollywood."[39]

Responding to this concern, most participants voiced a desire to double down on what they saw as an ideal of objectivity—to go "back to basics, back to old-school reporting," where opinion and fact were clearly separated. Steph underlined this ideal by paraphrasing Detective Joe Friday in *Dragnet*: "Just the facts, ma'am; just the facts."[40] Critical analysis of how journalists interpret or select which facts to include or what stories to cover was largely absent from these discussions. An alternate approach, suggested by a minority of participants, was for media outlets to be more transparent and own up to their views. As William argued, "When you have the news outlets both on the left and the right pretending like they don't have an ideological bent, that is insulting the intelligence of the American leaders and people, in my opinion."[41]

Interestingly, the process of maintaining a story diary seemed in itself to be an intervention for a number of participants. A majority on the left and right expressed concern about polarized media habits and the concept of filter bubbles and echo chambers—and many stated in the focus groups that they maintained relatively balanced news diets. However, a number of these same participants were alarmed to look back at their story diaries and realize that the stories they noted day to day largely came from one or two sources. As Jason, a participant who self-characterized all his sources (which included CNN, MSNBC, and the *New York Times*) as liberal, stated, "There were no differing views at all."[42] Similarly, Steve expressed surprise that almost all the news stories he had logged came from Fox. The process made him grapple with the idea that "maybe I wasn't as open-minded as I thought."[43] The process also highlighted the value of triangulation, as participants were able to capture a fuller picture of their media habits and to note the gap between what they may have articulated in group discussions and what they documented through the process of keeping a diary.

Overall, participants shared experiences of navigating national news outlets, reportedly with a grain of salt, but often returning to outlets that corresponded to their partisan identities. How, then, did participants' national news diets and the partisan narratives circulating in them influence how they interacted with fellow residents, community groups, and media? Were these national narratives reshaping local storytelling networks?

Local Storytelling: Interpersonal Networks

Steph and her nephew were close. "I mean, we used to get up in the mornings and go away in a dew-covered field just to get pictures of the sunrise and things like that, you know," she shared. But the 2016 election changed everything. Now, "he won't even talk to me." She lamented how she got wind of the impending rift on Facebook: "The day after the election he starts talking about how he shakes at the thought of seeing his Republican step-family." Steph pointed out that she was actually a registered Democrat, though she did vote for Trump. She said they had never talked about politics before, but months later, when they ran into each other at a local restaurant, "he turned his head and walked away."[44]

Like Steph, numerous participants shared experiences of national politics taking a very personal toll on how they related to and communicated with other residents and relatives. In this area where red was dominant but blue was in proximity, participants shared stories of lost friendships and family arguments. One participant even admitted he and his girlfriend had broken up due to disagreement over Trump. For most, even if their immediate family and close friends shared their views, interaction across partisan lines was difficult to avoid. Participants' encounters generally fell into one of three categories: deliberate and mostly face-to-face engagement about an issue or news story; incidental encounters in public or commercial spaces or institutional or family gatherings; or views posted on social media.

Intentional encounters, which were frequently noted in participants' story diaries, almost always involved conversations with people whose views were known to the participant—often a spouse, trusted colleague, or close friend. In most of these cases, the conversation was between people who held similar views on the story or issue in question. Participants were more likely to be brought into confrontation with partisan difference through unplanned encounters in public or institutional spaces or online.

For many, social media was noted as a key factor in upsetting the balance of social ties. Where residents had previously maintained ties across lines of ideological difference, a lack of politeness norms online complicated this, as Mark explained: "The old rule of thumb about not talking about religion and politics in person... people feel completely free to do so on Facebook, and very vocally. And it does kind of make you look at people that you've known for a long time that were your friends. You're like, 'Oh, gosh, I didn't know that's the way they felt.'" Mark and others suggested that these online revelations led to offline adaptations: "Given the strength of what they post on Facebook sometimes, I wouldn't even begin to be presumptuous enough to try to change their minds or even engage in conversation."[45]

Adapting to these new realities, participants shared a range of strategies, from muting status updates of objectionable Facebook posts to self-censoring or avoiding social media platforms to avoid conflict. Living in rural and small-town environments meant that preserving relationships was a priority, as William explained: "It's better to censor yourself and have friends from the limited pool of people around you than to not do that, to have no friends."[46]

In cases where the participants identified with a party that was in the minority in their storytelling network, self-censorship was a tactic to preserve not only social ties. I met closet progressives, for instance, who took great care to conceal their voting choices, something they felt they had to do in order to do business in a majority Republican community. Likewise, a participant who identified as Republican explained how she felt obligated to self-censor around her colleagues associated with the university, as she perceived the bulk of them to lean left.

Everyone I met expressed some sense of regret that encounters across lines of difference had become more fraught and perilous. Arun was nostalgic for an earlier time when he could argue about the news with someone at a bar, then "shake hands and go home—and, next day, you're back to work and friends like ... nothing [ever] happened."[47] Lynn said she worried that the climate was now so toxic that it had the potential to lead to violence: "I think our media and our government [have] put such a great divide between people, and it's very worrisome when you think, like I said, you're either on this side, or you're on this side. Both people think they're right. That's when you start having to fight for what you feel like you believe in, and that's very scary."[48]

For Lynn and many of the participants I spoke with, partisan divisions at the national level had cast a cloud over interpersonal interactions. Most participants still had some interactions with political "others," but these links were often damaged by what some have called "affective polarization."[49] Many referenced incivility on social media as amplifying emotionally charged gaps separating them from others in their interpersonal networks.

While a number of studies have questioned the prevalence of online filter bubbles,[50] participants' experiences illustrate how national political stories may be discussed, processed, and often reinforced in conversation with others with shared viewpoints. For many, the desire to avoid conflict over partisan news meant making adjustments to whom one socialized with and how. The processing of national-level partisan narratives both informed and was informed by interpersonal networks on- and offline. As a result, national divides often had the effect of interrupting the flow of discussion of stories and issues in local storytelling networks.

Local Storytelling: Community Groups and Spaces

Bowling Green and Ohio County have a finite number of choices when it comes to organizations, sports clubs, cafés, and stores. It was not surprising, then, that partisan conflicts that cropped up on social media or through interpersonal networks also affected how residents connected with community groups and spaces.

In Helen's experience, not even Walmart was safe. She shared the example of posting an article about the national health care debate on Facebook. When she saw she was getting a lot of comments on her feed she turned off her notifications. But then she ran into one of the commenters while grocery shopping, "And they were like, 'I can't believe you put that post on Facebook.' I'm like, 'Oh my goodness.' . . . I'm like, 'Where's the salad?'"[51]

Helen said this experience reinforced her belief that self-censorship was the best path for her as a moderate Democrat in a heavily Republican area. Partisanship had already affected her relationship with her predominantly conservative church: "It's so terrible, the week before the election, I didn't go to church because I was tired of hearing it. I was just . . . I go to church to worship, not to listen to the . . . it's my one hour to not listen to all this other. They're trying to tell us who to vote for." Helen was not alone in encountering politics at church, which most participants mentioned attending. Dave recalled when his pastor gave a sermon that criticized Trump's travel ban: "The guy behind me during it was so enraged, and he was saying, 'I'm going to have to find another church. Now I have to find another church.' And I never saw him again."[52]

Apart from churches, participants from all political stripes who were parents talked about attending their children's sports and other activities. But being copresent on the sidelines of a soccer game with other parents did not necessarily amount to meaningful interaction. Ehsan recalled getting into arguments with another father during the 2016 election campaign: "It would get out of hand and my wife said, 'Can you just not talk about politics or the news with these people?'"[53] After that, he switched to talking with other parents with whom he agreed—through the help of linguistic dexterity. While Ehsan himself came from a Middle Eastern background, his Spanish was strong enough to discuss politics with two Latinx mothers. So there, on the same sideline, storytelling networks splintered along political and linguistic lines. Similarly, other parents who reported feeling politically marginal shared stories of avoiding or self-censoring at play dates and birthday parties.

In rare instances, participants mentioned spaces and organizations that had made it possible to maintain relationships across boundaries of politics and demographic difference. These mostly included educational and professional settings but also some community organizations. Even in these spaces, though, political conversations were usually avoided, with some exceptions.

At least one dimension of the storytelling network was actually facilitated by the politically charged environment. In some cases, participants sought out organizations that they saw as offering solidarity, like a letter-writing group that met at the public library. This pull seemed strongest for participants who saw themselves as part of a vulnerable minority in terms of politics, race, gender, or sexual identity. In Bowling Green, in particular, partisan tensions had the effect of exacerbating divisions between a university-centered network and a more conservative storytelling network that included the larger town.

Overall, national divisions did color how residents coded, navigated, or avoided community groups and spaces. As with their connections to interpersonal networks, residents' ties to community groups in their storytelling network were affected as many residents adjusted their habits in order to avoid partisan conflict.

Local Storytelling: Local Media

Within these communication environments that were in some ways strained by national politics, what role did local media play? When participants discussed how their ties with fellow residents or with various community groups were affected by politics, they were usually referencing national media. But, of course, the link between residents and local media was not immune from politics.

Traces of national partisan narratives at times left their mark on local news noted in participants' story diaries. For example, a number of residents mentioned a story about a WKU student government effort to secure reparations for African American students. Residents who identified as both on the left and on the right noted the story, but how the story was interpreted and whom they shared it with varied along political and demographic lines. The local-ness of the story became consumed by politically charged national-level narratives—and, at some point, was even covered by the national media.

But polarized reaction to local stories was more the exception than the rule. Apart from one local newspaper whose owner had a reputation for conservatism, and some concerns about a reluctance by outlets to write anything critical about the major local employer, Western Kentucky University, most criticism of local news had less to do with perceived bias than with a lack of resources and capacity.

"You know, people will ask if I can send someone from the paper, and that's always me," noted the editor-cum-reporter of a rural paper. With his total editorial staff of one, he attested that concerns about limited resources were not unfounded. "I'm the court reporter, the commission reporter, the—you name it, I report it."[54] Participants did notice the multiplicity of bylines in one day and expressed their belief that this could take a toll on quality. Several also speculated about the inexperience of many local reporters at a number of outlets and the challenges of retaining talent. Often participants' reflections on local media were born of first-hand experience, seeing, or not seeing, reporters cover local events. While national press was perceived by residents of all political backgrounds as distant, privileged, and dismissive of local culture, it was not uncommon for residents to have first- or secondhand interactions with local reporters. So while participants could identify shortcomings, there was a base-level familiarity and trust.

Overall, participants selected their local news outlets based on where they lived rather than on their political affiliation. This meant participants from the left and the right were often reading or listening to the same outlets, and a number said they thought local news outlets did "a pretty fair job" and were "a lot better" than national outlets. Several pointed to what they saw as a greater separation in local news between fact and opinion. Some said they trusted the content that came in the local outlets more than they did the national outlets, even if it was about a national issue. So in terms of local storytelling network ties, the connection between residents and local news offered some promise. Unlike relationships with national media or interpersonal networks, this link was not substantially damaged by partisan mistrust. As a result, local news was one of the few communication resources shared across political lines.

At the same time, while participants voiced less concern about negativity in local news than they did in national news, several critiqued what they saw as excessively negative coverage—particularly around crime. It was still a tradition for rural papers to report details of arrests, which were a fairly regular occurrence in a region struggling with the opioid epidemic. Indeed, the editors of one local news site joked that they may as well rename their site "Death and Mayhem, Death and Destruction."[55] One of the editors lamented that the most intensive traffic to their site came from obituaries and crime stories, even though he had determined that only 20 percent of their stories were devoted to crime over the course of two months. However, in his view, the reach of these stories was amplified because they were shared and commented on more frequently on social media: "Facebook is set up to have people see what they want to see instead of what they need to see. They see the garbage and not what they need to see."[56]

Not everyone wanted to see these crime stories, though. Or at least they didn't want to see *only* them. Participants shared frustrations about what they viewed as information needs that neither national nor local nor social media was filling. In particular, several spoke of trying to get local coverage for constructive community initiatives, like a volunteer project to help a homeless resident. Others suggested that local news outlets could do more to engage with residents and let them know about community events taking place in the county's different small towns. As Heather said, "I'd like to see more community involvement."[57]

Overall, while there was a definite sense of room for improvement, the links connecting residents with local media did not seem to be as frayed by mistrust or partisanship as they were with national U.S. media outlets.

Storytelling Networks, Place, and Community Issues

Using communication infrastructure theory to analyze the local communication environment in Bowling Green and Ohio County revealed a picture of a region with at least three distinct storytelling networks of residents, community organizations, and media.[58] These included a network centered on Ohio County, where conservative perspectives were dominant. Here, polarization had taken a toll on how residents interacted with each other and community spaces, but residents of all political stripes generally accessed the same local media. In Bowling Green, residents described connecting to two largely distinct networks: a purple network of city residents and a comparatively blue network attached to Western Kentucky University. Residents connected with the WKU network often expressed a lack of connection to the community beyond the university, including interpersonal networks, organizations, or city media.

According to CIT's communication action context, place mediated how residents were accessing local storytelling networks. The communication action context—referring to all the elements of a community that would make it easier or more difficult for different actors in the storytelling network to connect—either facilitated or constrained residents from connecting to local storytelling networks. The mediating role of place included the presence or absence of shared public spaces where people might come into contact and exchange information—be it a local school, a café, or a clinic. The communication action context also accounted for whether such local communication assets were accessible and welcoming. Were people able to easily get to the local library? Were churches one of the only places people gathered on a regular basis? Did people have access to broadband Internet to find out about local issues online?

Accounting for this context, place was a more salient variable than politics in many ways. Residents mostly connected with local media outlets based on place, regardless of politics. Likewise, there was a correlation between what residents noted as pressing issues and place. For example, in Ohio County, residents were more likely to mention jobs as a key issue, regardless of political affiliation (reflecting the area's comparatively higher unemployment).[59] Holding shared concerns indicates that residents were sharing a storytelling network, at least to an extent, according to communication infrastructure theory.

Residents from both Bowling Green and Ohio County had similar opinions in two areas of interest. First, residents expressed a dissatisfaction with how their region or others like it were depicted in national media coverage. While this sentiment was even more adamant among residents from more rural and right-leaning backgrounds, it was expressed by residents with all political beliefs. There was a resentment toward reporters whom they saw as "parachuting in" and depicting their communities in stereotypical and overly negative frames. Second, residents of all backgrounds expressed an interest in less negative, less partisan, and more constructive coverage of local issues, including coverage of issues such as addiction and unemployment.

At the same time, partisan narratives circulating in the national news did influence the local storytelling network (see figure 4), particularly links between

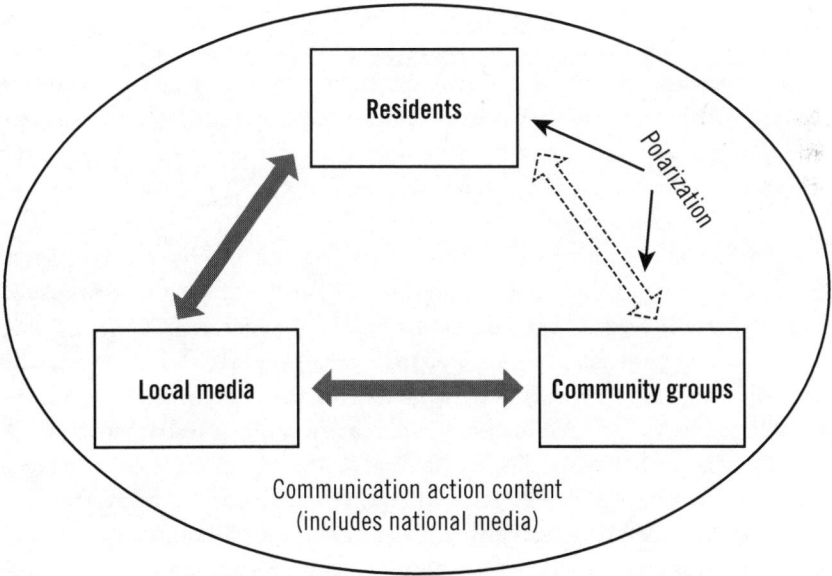

Figure 4. Communication Infrastructure Theory's "Storytelling Network": Western Kentucky

residents and community groups. Partisan national media narratives were also part of the larger communication action context. These shaped how some residents moved through their community—avoiding certain groups or gravitating toward others to minimize partisan conflict. For the most part, relationships between community members and local news media were minimally affected by partisanship, though it contributed to how some local stories were interpreted and to a general attitude of skepticism toward journalists. However, weaknesses in the local news landscape made it hard for narratives about local issues to be heard above the din of louder partisan narratives from national news.

Storytelling Network Interventions

Now that a CIT-based assessment had revealed the state of local storytelling networks, my colleagues and I wanted to explore our findings and brainstorm potential interventions with those who had a stake in strengthening storytelling networks in Bowling Green and Ohio County. In August 2017, we brought together representatives of local and regional media outlets, rural journalism initiatives, and community organizations and several of the study participants for a workshop. We also invited representatives of groups working on engaged journalism and solutions journalism initiatives (including Hearken, Listening Post Collective, Solutions Journalism Network, and Spaceship Media) to share experiences from their work around the United States.

Along the way, we invited workshop participants, particularly editors and other journalists, to raise questions and doubts. For example, several editors initially balked at the finding that residents were overwhelmed by negative news and were interested in more solutions-oriented stories. They pointed to the high metrics they regularly received for stories about crime and other negative issues. However, through the discussion with community members, a consensus emerged that wanting solutions-oriented coverage did not mean residents would not continue to take in inherently negative news. Rather, residents wanted to have more choices, to get a fuller picture of their communities. In the end, most of the journalists were interested in exploring these concepts further, particularly given that they saw them as aligned with their efforts to make stronger connections with their audiences as potential subscribers and supporters.

After sharing and discussing our findings and hearing examples of engaged journalism initiatives, participants worked in small teams to brainstorm ideas for projects to strengthen ties between residents, community groups, and media and to address some of the concerns and issues raised in the study. They then shared these with the larger group and additional community members, revising and further developing ideas for possible projects.

Two of the project ideas to emerge sought to build communication ties between residents across demographic and ideological divides through initiatives that included dialogue groups. One idea was for a project to address "town and gown" divides (which often coincided with political and cultural divides) by bridging the university and city storytelling networks of Bowling Green. Participants proposed a Town and Gown Club, which would include a diverse mix of participants—half associated with the university, half from other communities in Bowling Green. In some ways, this club reimagined a more inclusive version of the local tradition of "literary clubs," invitation-only social groups where members take turns hosting salon-style discussions. The Town and Gown Club would identify an important issue that the city faces, such as homelessness, and focus on potential solutions and ways the city might work to tackle it. In addition to their own activities, the group would collaborate with local university and city media to produce complementary solutions-oriented reporting for a wider audience.

Another project idea sought to connect residents from refugee and immigrant backgrounds with multigenerational residents of the region, who are primarily white and conservative. While Bowling Green is a refugee resettlement area, the areas in rural Ohio County where many refugees work have little infrastructure to manage cultural and linguistic difference. Participants suggested connecting these two populations by starting with a point of common ground—for example, recruiting mothers for a dialogue on culturally informed healthy eating choices (a need identified by a participant who had done work with the area chicken plant where nineteen languages are spoken). In conjunction with community groups and local media partners, the mothers would collaborate with each other to document personal stories and recipes, with local media partners publishing the results and hosting community discussions over shared meals.

These two proposals have yet to be initiated at the time of writing, though local stakeholders continue to express interest if and when resources materialize. However, several other projects were undertaken, including efforts to combine digital engagement tools with in-person outreach.

Two of the organizations participating in the workshop teamed up to produce the Bowling Green Civic Assembly. The *Bowling Green Daily News* and the American Assembly, a think tank based at Columbia University, collaboratively organized an interactive digital town hall where residents shared and voted on comments about local issues using the Polis engagement tool. Following an online discussion in which more than 2,000 people participated, they organized a face-to-face town hall where they connected more than 250 residents and local officials to discuss the issues raised in the online forum. This was followed by a community workshop to explore possible continued civic engagement and dialogue. The organizers argued that the online discussion illustrated that there are actually more local issues that are consensus issues than divisive issues—and that the project highlights the value of connecting residents and local media.[60] The groups continue to explore follow-up activities, and several organizations in other states have expressed interest in undertaking a similar process.

Reimagining Community Traditions in Ohio County

The workshop also generated project ideas that centered on the more rural area of Ohio County, and one of its media participants in particular.[61] The hyperlocal online news site the *Ohio County Monitor* is run by brothers Dustin and Lee Bratcher. Following the workshop, the Bratchers developed a series of engagement experiments that sought to understand how a combination of digital and offline outreach would affect their relationship with residents. Given that they shifted from an advertising-based model to a subscription model in mid-2017, they also wanted to see whether these initiatives would have any impact on their subscription rates.

Consultant Sam Ford and I worked with the Bratchers, drawing on communication infrastructure theory as a guide for the pilot project's design and evaluation. From late 2017 to early 2018, we followed their efforts: observing their activities; conducting eighteen interviews with journalists, participating residents, and community stakeholders;[62] and analyzing their project start and end online surveys.[63] I wanted to learn whether their participatory journalism efforts were affecting local storytelling networks. To what extent were they attempting to address issues of trust between media and residents by giving residents agency over community narratives and self-representation, and how were they leveraging existing community assets?

We were particularly curious about two efforts to reimagine rural community traditions as engagement activities—through a community contributors[64] program and a "liars table tour." The *Ohio County Monitor* refashioned the tradition of "society columnists,"[65] where, in the pre-Facebook past, a resident would write, in exchange for a free subscription, an accounting of his or her particular corner of the county—births, out-of-town visitors, accomplishments of local youth, and the like. Building on this tradition, the Bratchers invited a new cadre of residents to join them as community contributors, seeking representatives from different parts of the sprawling county with different interests and perspectives. They also began an exploration of the "liars tables" tradition,[66] where groups of farmers, coal miners, retirees, and other locals gathered to discuss the news of the day over coffee or breakfast in rural convenience stores. While these spaces represented some of the only public venues for sharing hyperlocal information, they were also problematic given they were exclusively white and male. Despite this, the Bratchers conducted a tour of several area liars tables to listen to citizens' concerns and develop ideas for how their coverage could connect with participants.

Reimagining Society Columns as Citizen Journalism

Much of the work the *Ohio County Monitor* does online sets it apart from the traditions of rural print journalism in the area. The county is also home to one print newspaper with a limited online presence. This weekly paper continues to run a society column, which shares hyperlocal updates from only one of the many small communities in the county. The *Ohio County Monitor* has not historically run society columns. It spends much of its time focused on accountability journalism and covering stories that would be dated by the time the print newspaper published on its weekly schedule. The two editors (the only two staffers) also act as reporters, attending and sharing updates from local government meetings, as well as providing announcements about community events. They lamented that a considerable amount of their traffic came from crime stories and obituaries.

For this reason, the Bratchers were initially unsure how stories written by community contributors would be received. The *Ohio County Monitor* conducted an online survey of residents in 2017 to gauge interest in the idea of a revival and reinterpretation of the society column tradition, as well as to seek input on the news site and its activities more broadly, and 110 residents responded to open-ended questions, offering a range of suggestions regarding approaches to society columns. Some were fairly traditional, suggesting columnists write about local events and personal announcements in their areas. Several referenced a desire for stories that featured more positive developments or for information about how people could respond constructively when negative things happened. However, some critiqued the traditional model, suggesting it led to an insular focus that favored the friends and family of the writer and spent too much time on "who visited with whom." They suggested that a new model could include more viewpoints and offer more substantial coverage of community events, achievements of community members, and local government efforts to address problems. In addition, several respondents said they would like to see more historical features about the county's past.

The *Monitor* then put out a call for community contributors. Contributors were invited to write on any subject matter, "as long as your focus is on this community or has a community tie of some sort—and it might be that the only tie to the community is that you are from the community."[67] Setting out to recruit five contributors, they settled on a cohort of seven, though only five completed their stories in the first round. Contributors who volunteered shared a variety of motivations, though most expressed being drawn by some combination of a creative interest in writing and a desire to contribute to the community. None of the contributors had a professional background in journalism, but several confided that they had always harbored an interest in writing more creatively or more publicly, possibly even writing a book. Others spoke of their interest in community issues around civic engagement and health. Two of the contributors (who took different positions on Trump) had been participants in our research study.

Over the course of a couple of months, the contributors went through a process of brainstorming story ideas, getting feedback, writing, and sharing the stories for editing. For many, the starting point was one of uncertainty. One contributor, Martha, said she really wasn't sure "what you're supposed to put in the newspaper."[68] She recounted how they had held an initial brainstorming workshop at a local restaurant to share ideas. She had been struggling with her story idea and credited one of the other contributors for helping her think through her focus. Jenny, another contributor, explained how this workshop helped her and the others to develop confidence as writers: "I think collectively, we felt in the beginning that we weren't going to be very good writers, and there was a couple of people that really felt like what they wrote about was not even what they were looking for. Come to find out, even though all five of our pieces were completely different, they were all good reads, and . . . you know, people have different opinions and thoughts."[69]

For their actual articles, most contributors drew on personal experiences, though several wove in interviews they did with other county residents. The resulting stories varied in topic and style. One column focused on tips for healthy alternatives to sugary drinks, highlighting the strategies of fellow Ohio County residents. Another contributor also drew on a background in health, offering guidance on smoking cessation but also cautioning against stigmatizing smokers, telling a personal story of a friend who had died of lung cancer. A woman who was herself very civically active shared her experience of how she first got involved in community issues and offered tips for getting more engaged. There were also profiles of community members, as well as personal reflections—like a retired woman who told about encountering a bluegrass celebrity from the area and how she came to think of the county as home after moving from another region.

At a meeting following their first round of articles, the initial cohort of contributors was joined by two additional residents interested in becoming contributors. As they shared their story ideas, one contributor related how she was grappling with writing about school shootings. She wanted to connect this national issue to some of her observations as a parent witnessing what she saw to be negative and bullying behaviors by other parents at sporting events.

This led to a vibrant conversation about the history of gun ownership in the area and the reaction to the youth-led gun control movement following the February 2018 Parkland shooting. From there, discussion turned to how young people in Ohio County have been engaged in community life in the past and in the present. Group members suggested that they explore ways to reach out to area youth to ask what issues concerned them and invite them to share their perspectives as contributors as well. Throughout this conversation, participants returned to the idea that they wanted to use their forum to offer an alternative to polarized national discourse—like the one around gun control. Responding to a contributor who complained about political divides, one of the editors, Lee Bratcher, agreed that "today we're so bogged down by nonsense."[70]

When discussing their stories, several participants talked about deliberately choosing those that showcased positive elements of their community. One contributor, Tom, said his story featured a "local hero." Tom explained how he profiled a retired band teacher because he wanted to highlight a good man overcoming adversity: "I chose it because I felt like it would leave a good taste in people's mouth."[71] The story apparently did. It garnered some nine hundred page views over two days, which was even more than most crime stories on the site. Lee said he was relieved to see all of the stories get a positive reception: "When I put their stories out, I'm more protective over what they've put out than even my own stuff because I want everybody to like their stuff because they're kind of like . . . a guest in my home, and I want everybody to treat them right."[72] Beyond his sense of hospitality, he explained that these were the sorts of stories the *Ohio County Monitor* wanted to publish to build its connection with residents.

As they assessed their initial piloting of the community contributor initiatives, contributors reflected on how to strengthen and continue the project. Heather had signed up as a contributor after complaining as a study participant about how her community was represented and how it needed more community involvement in local media. Now as a contributor, she suggested that they find ways to connect with residents in distant parts of the county who had information and ideas but were not comfortable writing: "I think there's a lot of people who . . . love the content, they love to read it, they just don't think they have the ability to actually write down something coherent and well enough to get published."[73] She suggested the *Monitor* find a way to connect with these people to crowdsource story ideas. According to her idea, community contributors could play the role that professional reporters play in engagement models such as Hearken[74]—following up with members of the public who nominate ideas for stories. Another contributor also mentioned possibly becoming a writing buddy for a would-be contributor who needed writing support. At least one community member, who responded to the Bratchers' project-end online survey, seemed to support this need for alternate engagement paths: "Do you have resources for someone in the community who would like to contribute but may not be the best writer? Are there polls where people can submit ideas or opinions that can be incorporated into someone else's work, or they can be helped into developing their own piece?" Several contributors suggested that the *Ohio County Monitor* was on the cusp of developing a genuine community resource with the potential to help people get involved in community issues and to "keep people tied to the county."

By sharing ideas to problem-solve and strengthen the *Monitor* in their meetings and interviews, participants demonstrated a sense of investment in the success of the initiative. Studies of participatory journalism initiatives have referenced challenges that can arise when participants feel their goals and expectations are not matched by the journalists'. Merel Borger, Anita van Hoof, and Jose Sanders outline how participants in citizen journalism projects go through stages—anticipation, participation, evaluation, and reconsideration.[75] One challenge that they found was when expectations for reciprocal relationships with journalists were not shared. It is still too early to know whether *Ohio County Monitor* community contributors will make it through these stages successfully. However, one dynamic that may assist them is a comparative lack of distance between the rural journalists of the news site and residents. The *Monitor*'s editors do not see themselves as apart from the community but rather as part of it. Given that they themselves did not come from traditional journalism backgrounds (though one of the brothers worked as a photographer for the rural weekly paper in the past), the Bratchers were more open to contributors telling stories that may vary from journalistic norms. As a result, participants spoke freely in meetings, giving advice and making recommendations for the editors in a way that would be difficult to imagine in more hierarchical, formal editorial structures.

Reimagining Liars Tables as Listening Posts

The "liars table" at the McHenry store in Ohio County was actually a collection of several small tables along the wall at the back of a convenience store. Arriving at 6 a.m., we were greeted by several men waiting for their breakfasts to be made to order, biscuits and gravy being a popular choice. We overheard one man explain to another that he had injured his face because he had a dream where he got into a fight with his brother and fell out of bed. When asked about the name "liars table" in an interview, one of the participants explained, "We've got a man down there, and he likes to tell good tales, and he said it's only a lie if you believe it. And anything anybody says, we don't believe it, so it's not a lie."

The *Ohio County Monitor* initiated its "liars table tour" as a way to connect with these groups of men who gathered at stores all around the sprawling county. While the men did their share of swapping tall tales, including fishing and hunting stories, they also talked about the news of the day. On that day, the *Monitor*'s second visit to McHenry, conversation meandered from joking about the latest Trump scandal (participants seemed to be a mix of supporters and critics) to conversations about concerns over Kentucky cutting the pensions of teachers. In a separate interview, Walter explained that these liars tables were a hub of local information. He recounted how in his community and others in the area, there used to be more places to gather, like the local post office. Now many post offices had closed or reduced their hours. This led residents—from farmers and miners to local politicians wanting to take the pulse of the community—to seek information, and camaraderie, in local stores. "Wherever you go there's certain places . . . that if you really want to get to know anything, that's where you go to find out," Walter said.[76]

This was part of the reason the *Monitor* wanted to connect with these liars tables. But the Bratchers were concerned that a pair of reporters would not be welcome: "They're used to each other, and they all know each other. They can joke around with each other. They probably don't have to hold back from each other, and then you have two or three guys just out of the blue showing up and sitting down, and you're just sitting there." Lee's worries were not entirely unfounded. One regular participant, Terry, said, "They're taking up somebody's seat." Still, he conceded, "If they get there early enough to get them a spot, then yeah, they're welcome."[77]

Of course, it is not clear that the Bratchers would have been so welcome if they were not also white men. While their county was 94 percent non-Latinx white, there of course were other residents, particularly people of color and women, who would be unlikely to feel comfortable joining in liars table conversations. It is important not to uncritically equate these groups of white men as "the public." Nevertheless, the editors were interested in connecting with the liars tables to put them in conversation with the broader community.

As the Bratchers visited the different spots on their tour, their interactions illustrated some of the challenges that come with engaged journalism. Initiatives like this one call on journalists to deploy new skills, such as facilitation. The editors seemed to intuitively attempt to build trust by listening to these groups. But there was a tradeoff in that conversations were not focused and at times did not go deeply into substantive local issues. The Bratchers observed that some groups were more receptive than others. They discussed how different groups may require different approaches, and they tried to think of a variety of strategies that might match the interests of those at the liars tables. The McHenry store was one of the most welcoming and dynamic. The editors suggested that the next time they visited, they would explore possible activities like doing a podcast with participants. But they noted that they would do such an activity only with buy-in from the groups themselves.

As the Bratchers continue, the *Ohio County Monitor* may find itself needing to negotiate expectations with residents at the various liars table sites. At McHenry, regulars said in separate interviews that they thought the first visit of the *Monitor* had already led to a positive development. They had complained when they met earlier about some coal trucks driving too fast and worried they posed a danger to school buses and others. But after their chat with the *Monitor*, "somebody must have got ahold of somebody because they've slowed down." The Bratchers, however, said while they remember discussing the issue of the coal trucks, they had not reported it to any officials or on the website. Nevertheless, liars table participants perceived their conversation with reporters to have led to solving a local problem. Be it a placebo affect or coincidence, this incident underlines how limited interaction with local media can raise expectations when encounters do take place.

"We'll see what the results are three to six months from now about what their visit was and issues we talked about," explained Mike, a regular at the Horse Branch general store in another part of the county. At his liars table, the conversation centered on challenges with the Internet and attempts to bring a dollar store to the area. Mike said he wasn't interested in talking with the *Monitor* editors if they were just there to visit. He wanted to see them "put an effort to help with what we need in this community."[78] For Lee, these substantial expectations were seen as more of a motivator than a deterrent. He pointed out that in the rural context, "one person really can make a difference."[79] One or two calls to a magistrate could lead to changes, such as slowing down the speed of passing coal trucks.

Following their initial pilot visits, the Bratchers plan to continue to explore ways to engage with liars tables. This may mean a regular series of columns drawing from liars table tours. The monthly *Monitor* columns will aim to connect readers in different parts of the county (and those who might not feel welcome in these exclusionary spaces) by letting them know about issues on the table in other small communities scattered throughout the area. Given that many liars table regulars were not online (though several mentioned other people in their family, often women, reading the *Monitor*), the *Monitor* may also experiment with other offline ways to stay connected, such as newsletters or text messaging services.

Strengthening the Ohio County Storytelling Network?

The *Ohio County Monitor* has been running the community contributors and liars table outreach efforts for only a limited time. However, even in this pilot phase of the intervention, observations of project activities, meetings, online discussion boards, and follow-up interviews suggest some preliminary impact on ties within the local storytelling network.

Both the community contributors and liars table projects have attempted to build connections between the *Ohio County Monitor* as a local media site and residents. In the case of community contributors, this connection has required a fairly substantial investment of time and energy. Residents working with the *Monitor* to produce stories ended up discussing a range of issues with the editors in meetings, often trying to help them strategize or offering suggestions that drew upon their interpersonal networks. When they held an event at the public library to talk about the community contributors project, several contributors asked others they knew to join. The contributors even encouraged the editors to plan more public-facing activities—such as a public ribbon cutting, which they then helped to organize. Most contributors talked about sharing their stories through online and interpersonal networks. Several successfully inspired other new contributors to start writing, or at least to show up to meetings. This included contributors making connections across partisan lines, suggesting the focus on local issues was helping to make at least small repairs in interpersonal networks.

Liars table tours have attempted to connect with residents who had largely been unaware of the *Monitor*'s existence. The editors of the *Monitor* have tried to build upon existing communication assets by going to communication hotspots where residents already gathered. By going to convenience stores, they were using the communication action context to encourage interaction between actors in the storytelling network. However, to date, the *Monitor* has primarily played a role of listening rather than facilitating dialogue that may not have otherwise occurred. Going forward, if they wish to promote interaction, the editors may need to take a more active role in facilitating and intervening.

For the *Ohio County Monitor*, one of the ongoing barriers to strengthening storytelling network connections with residents has been a sense of distrust toward media. Many residents referred to the trustworthiness factors[80] of representation and the perceived motives of journalists. Many did not see news media as representing their community fairly, having their best interests at heart, or being responsive and relevant to their lives. This was evident particularly at liars tables. Regulars expressed appreciation that local reporters were showing up but remained skeptical about media and media practices. For example, Jake suggested that media coverage was biased and depended on whom you knew: "It hasn't changed in fifty years, so I don't see it changing for another fifty years."[81] Others stated that what made the local news usually didn't really affect them, or if it did, they would "hear it really quick the next morning at the store."[82] Clearly, liars tables spaces were areas that rarely had visitors from elsewhere in the county, let alone reporters. It was unsurprising, then, that coverage rarely felt resonant to the lives of those at the tables. Distrust this deep would take more than a few visits to overcome.

A related theme discussed by both community contributors and liars table participants was an appreciation of efforts to ensure that the stories circulating were not exclusively negative and shared a fuller picture of their communities. "The only time you ever hear anything in these small communities is something bad happened," Walter, a liars table regular, explained. He welcomed an alternative to negative news that he felt stigmatized his area: "In Ohio County people say, 'Well, you don't want to go up there. This place . . . it's drug-infested. It's this or it's that.' You know? And it's good to hear some of the good stuff that's going on in the communities."[83] This desire for more constructive coverage was a recurring theme in many conversations. As Jean, a participant in an event at the library said, "I think that it can be really frustrating to see portrayals of rural Kentucky in the media, you know, and not feel like that's reflective of who we really are."[84] Many participants from the *Monitor*'s outreach activities expressed pride in where they lived in spite of the reputation it may have.

As referenced in their meeting, some community contributors took it upon themselves to offer a more positive representation of Ohio County. "Sometimes we don't represent ourselves to the rest of the world, you know, and we kind of put on a mask and we stand idly by and let the world just think we're a bunch of dummies," said Tom. Countering this was important to Tom, even if he also felt a burden of representation when he thought about how outsiders may see his stories online. He lamented finding grammatical errors in his story because he didn't want "somebody in Rhode Island" to stumble across the errors: "That just gives them more fodder to say, 'Well, yeah, they can tell a story, but they sure as hell can't write.'"[85]

Tom emphasized that constructive representations in local media were even more important to reshape narratives the community tells about itself. He stressed the need for local writers who could say, "Look, you're a lot smarter than you look. Give yourself credit. And when you start giving yourself credit then maybe the rest of the world will look at us a little bit better."

Notably, we did not use the term "solutions journalism" in our conversations with contributors. And, indeed, what residents were proposing generally would not fit the definition the Solutions Journalism Network puts forward of "rigorous and compelling reporting on responses to social problems."[86] Residents did express a desire for solutions-oriented reporting on local problems. But for community contributors, most of whom had no journalism training, the "rigorous reporting" part of that definition was often beyond their reach. Nevertheless, they made the case that offering more positive representations of fellow community members was in itself an intervention with the potential to change the narrative circulating both within the community and externally about the community.

Residents at times directly made the connection between representation and trust. Library attendee Jean noted that negative representations made people distrust media and "feel like they're getting the story wrong." Offering a more nuanced range that included more constructive representations offered a step in the direction of building trust. Like Tom, she saw community contributors as a way to move in this direction: "Right now there's such a distrust of media, and I think that the more participatory we can make local media, the more support folks will have for it and the less distrust of the media we'll find."[87]

The *Monitor*'s efforts primarily focused on the storytelling network link between residents and media (see figure 5). The community contributors initiative in particular had taken steps to address trustworthiness factors and create a space for two-way dialogue between the *Monitor* and residents. However, there was also some secondary influence on the link between residents and community organizations. Community contributors' stories often referenced organizations. For example, after Heather wrote a column encouraging people to "stop complaining" and become more active in the community, another contributor noticed an uptick of clicks and likes to a community organization's Facebook page that Heather's column had linked to. Given it was the off-season for that organization, she concluded that the column had driven readers to connect with the organization online. Other contributors mentioned that they themselves had wanted to get more involved after reading and discussing each other's pieces. For instance, Martha said she had since started volunteering at a local organization.

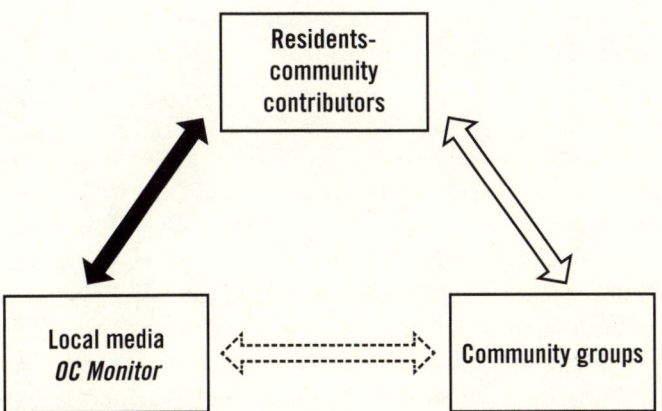

Figure 5. Communication Infrastructure Theory's "Storytelling Network": *Ohio County Monitor*

At the same time, there were limits, as liars table participants from more distant corners of the county noted. Mike explained that for a lot of people, there were historical reasons they didn't feel motivated to get involved: "This is in a rural area, and you know, there's been so many things promised around here about things that haven't come true for the community."[88] Building connections through that element of the *Monitor*'s intervention would take more time and consistent effort before there was likely to be noticeable changes—including trust—in the local storytelling network.

Paths Forward and Process Models

The *Ohio County Monitor*'s efforts to reimagine community traditions are still nascent, and there are limits to what claims can be made regarding the new site's influence on the local storytelling network. Initial observations and reflections from participants suggest that network ties between local media and residents have been strengthened at a micro level. That is, the project has deepened connections between participating community contributors and the *Monitor*. Through an intervention informed by communication infrastructure theory, the *Monitor*'s efforts made the processes of journalism more participatory, allowed residents to represent and share their own stories, and covered a wider range of stories that are not exclusively negative. Critically, the *Monitor* has worked to share ownership of the project with the community members themselves, who have subsequently taken the lead on several initiatives and activities, from an oral history project to a series of videos on local health concerns. Through this project, the *Monitor*'s editors has done some work to build trust and strengthen ties between their outlet and community members. The Bratchers are currently exploring how they may continue to work with the pilot cohort of contributors while expanding to bring in some additional participants—including from the immigrant and refugee community in the area.

With liars tables, the *Ohio County Monitor* has a steeper road ahead. Given that liars table participants mostly started without a shared understanding of what the *Monitor* was, the process of building trust will likely take a greater investment of time and energy. The sites of the liars tables, however, are some of the few public place-based communication hotspots remaining in many of these rural communities. For this reason, the Bratchers will do well to continue to explore how they may facilitate dialogue and an exchange of information and ideas. Critically, it will be challenging to grapple with how to makes these spaces more inclusive—if not in the physical spaces, then through other types of exchange.

Of course, none of these engagement initiatives will be sustainable if the *Monitor* itself does not become financially sustainable. Over the course of this pilot phase, the news site tracked its subscription rate to see if there was a correlation with its engagement initiatives. It found no impact from efforts such as Facebook ads, podcasts, or livestreaming. However, the editors attributed a small but noticeable bump to the launch of its community contributor stories. In addition, the *Monitor* received a micro-grant from a foundation supporting engaged journalism to continue its pilot initiative. Going forward, there remain more questions than answers around how a hyperlocal in a community with limited income can support itself—even when it attempts deep engagement practices.

The *Ohio County Monitor* is, of course, not alone in exploring the link between engaging communities and people's willingness to pay for journalism. So far, most studies of this question have been conducted by organizations with a vested interest in showing a link between engagement and financial benefit. For example, Hearken has put forth several case examples that argued that people who engaged with media outlets through their participatory process were more likely to become subscribers.[89] The *Monitor*'s experience is also in line with recent discourse around nonmonetary ways publics can contribute to or become members in news organizations. The Membership Puzzle Project has explored various models for this,[90] though some of these have also offered cautionary tales for what can go wrong when trust is violated, as it was with the start-up of the U.S. version of the Dutch *De Correspondent* outlet.[91] Overall questions around a possible link between engaged journalism and the pursuit of more sustainable business models offer an area ripe for additional research.

The *Monitor* may still be far from any engagement holy grail to guarantee sustainability by building trust, but the news site's work, particularly with community contributors, suggests these efforts offer promise. In the long run, the *Monitor*'s initiatives to strengthen the local storytelling network may depend on its ability to deepen and normalize the relationships it has begun to build with community members. The Bratchers hope the investment of community members who see value in sustaining a hyperlocal news outlet will ripple out to broader circles of would-be subscribers, readers, and participants. But assessing this will require tracking their efforts over a longer period of time.

This Western Kentucky case illustrates how communication infrastructure theory can be used to assess local storytelling networks, design interventions to strengthen them, and inform evaluations of progress. In Bowling Green and Ohio County, our research revealed how connections between residents, community groups, and media had been weakened by partisan divides that contributed to sentiments of mistrust. However, it also revealed communication assets and opportunities—such as local media outlets that were shared across party lines; a receptiveness to exploring community issues through nonpartisan, solutions-oriented frames; and an interest by some residents to be more active participants in shaping community narratives. CIT's attention to place and the communication action context pointed to the potential for communication hotspots to connect residents to storytelling networks. This helped to underline the potential of community spaces, even if those were to be found inside convenience stores and gas stations.

This chapter shows how findings can inform a participatory project design process where stakeholders in local storytelling networks brainstorm intervention ideas to strengthen the network. In this case, intervention ideas were piloted through cases like the Bowling Green Civic Assembly and the *Ohio County Monitor*'s rural journalism innovation lab. While it is still early to draw conclusions about these projects' effect on local storytelling networks, it is encouraging that participants like Heather, who complained of the media painting everyone as hillbillies, are now collaborating with other residents, including those who voted differently from them, to document community stories. Heather likes that these efforts can highlight local voices with a range of views and offer more varied insights on "what's going on, and how people can get involved."[92]

Through a case using CIT-based research, followed by participatory brainstorming, followed by pilot interventions informed by the research, this chapter also offers a process model. It illustrates how diagnosing weaknesses in local storytelling networks can assist community stakeholders in collaboratively developing responses that address key trustworthiness factors and account for the needs and assets of local places. The projects that grow from this process in Ohio County, Kentucky, are unlikely to be effectively transposed into another community in New York or Nebraska. But, could the process be portable—could it offer a way for other communities to diagnose the state of their storytelling networks and design interventions to strengthen them? How might interventions look different in other contexts? What would it look like for these projects to be led not by news organizations but by community members? In the following chapter, I will examine what happens when this process is transported from Kentucky to a neighborhood and a suburb of Philadelphia.

CHAPTER 4

The Process Is Portable

Toward a Community-Driven Intervention

It's a familiar story: a claim of a large crowd, a huge crowd, packing the National Mall in Washington, D.C.—a claim later contradicted by news media and analysts. The crowd actually wasn't that big, they say. Then, angry responses flood in. The media is lying, they argue. The media does not respect us and our experiences.

This story could have been about Donald Trump's claim of having the largest inauguration attendance ever[1] and the subsequent genesis of the concept of "alternative facts."[2] But for Brandon, this narrative refers to a much earlier instance of media mistrust.

In a group discussion in Philadelphia's historically Black Germantown neighborhood, African American residents strained to remember the first moment they lost faith in news media. For Brandon it was the 1995 Million Man March, a gathering organized by the Nation of Islam and civil rights organizations aiming to unite Black men in addressing economic and social ills: "I think it might have been *Time* magazine that said that there weren't a million African Americans in D.C. And I was like, that's not true. I was there. I saw them with my own eyes."[3] As Brandon recalled, the march was quickly followed by controversy. The National Parks Department estimated the crowd at only 400,000. Organizers and supporters protested, and a later study by Boston University suggested the crowd included over 800,000 people, with a margin of error that could have put the crowd at over a million.[4]

For Brandon, this controversy cemented his sense that the media did not fairly represent his experience. Brandon, who is Black, went to a well-known private high school where many of his classmates were white. "I remember being in high school arguing with kids—like, all the white kids in my school—arguing with them about how the *Time* magazine was wrong. Like, I was there. There's no way."

In post-2016 election discourse in the United States, concerns over media and trust are often associated with political polarization. As we learned from residents of Western Kentucky, partisan mistrust can take a toll on the relationships between media and publics and how information circulates in interpersonal networks. But this mistrust often intersects with older underlying power dynamics and damage done to the relationship between publics and media. In Western Kentucky, that meant dynamics of class and geography. In Germantown, as in South Los Angeles or the South Side of Chicago, relationships between residents and media are intertwined with a history of racist power structures and disproportionately negative media coverage. For residents like Brandon, distrust of media is not a new problem.

As attention turns to "rebuilding" trust between journalism and publics, it is important to acknowledge that attention is also due to publics where trust has always been in short supply. A considerable amount of hope has been pinned on the possibility of local media to act as a beacon of comparative trustworthiness.[5] As our exploration in Western Kentucky showed, local news is less likely to cover polarizing political content or to be seen as a distant elite "parachuting in."[6] But trust has different meanings in different locales, with differing dynamics of power, place, and history. The way Philadelphia metro area news outlets have historically reported on the Germantown neighborhood may be very different from how they have reported on the downtown business district or on suburban communities.

In this chapter, I explore how place and proximity to power affect the communication infrastructure theory–based intervention model piloted in the Western Kentucky case. Shifting to the Philadelphia region, I look at how CIT can be applied in different communities to assess their communication health and to design interventions in response. In doing this, I demonstrate the critical role played by place—and how the layers of history and power dynamics embedded in places can determine how storytelling networks function and who connects to them. The chapter further illustrates the importance of looking not just at the needs and weaknesses in local storytelling networks but also at existing assets and communication resources and how they can inform any possible intervention. These place-based differences cast doubt on any one-size-fits-all solution to building trust between journalism and publics. But through these cases we can explore what it would look like to transport the *process model* we developed in Kentucky to a neighborhood or a suburb in Philly.

Working with colleagues,[7] I undertook a similar process of assessing both local information needs and assets in two different Philadelphia areas. As part of this venture, we invited residents to explore how they might imagine an alternative and more trust-filled relationship with media. Following our research study, we gathered community stakeholders and local journalists in workshops to brainstorm possible measures to strengthen local storytelling networks. The project ideas that emerged illustrate how even when following a similar process, the interventions generated will take different forms based on both local needs and assets.

Taking Stock of Urban and Suburban Storytelling Networks

Since October 2017, I have been working with colleagues to research local communication infrastructures and design interventions to strengthen them in two areas served by the same Philadelphia metro media market: Germantown, a majority African American neighborhood in Northwest Philadelphia, and Montgomery County, a majority white suburb where nearly half of voters who participated in the 2016 election supported Donald Trump. The distance between Germantown and Montgomery County is less than five miles at their closer points. Both places sit within the Philadelphia metro news coverage area. But their contexts and the challenges they face with local news and information vary vastly when their hyperlocal storytelling networks are considered. Montgomery County residents participating in our study complained about a reduction in original local reporting due to the consolidation of newspapers. Meanwhile in Germantown, residents grumbled that reporters came to their neighborhood only when a crime was reported. Exploring how participants in these respective places navigated their relationships with news and information outlets offers a more nuanced understanding of the complexity of what to some may be one "local" news market.

In order to grapple with public perspectives in these areas, we followed a similar triangulated research process as in Western Kentucky. From October 2017 to February 2018, we conducted a series of seven focus groups with forty residents from Germantown and Montgomery County. A convenience sample of participants was recruited through a combination of online postings and snowball sampling, with an effort to form groups that roughly reflected the demographics and partisan patterns of the surrounding communities.[8] Each ninety-minute discussion was moderated by myself and one of two co-facilitators.[9] We employed a series of semi-structured activities, similar to the way we did in Western Kentucky, exploring information diets and attitudes toward local news outlets and imagining alternative relationships with news media. Participants then kept "story diaries" for a week, which were used as conversation starters for more in-depth, one-on-one follow-up interviews. The research case studies were followed by workshops in March and April 2018. Here, as researchers, we acted as "interstitial actors"[10] connecting storytelling network actors—study participants, community leaders, local media, and engaged journalism stakeholders. After discussing our findings, workshop participants brainstormed possible next steps to strengthen the local storytelling network.

Germantown: Covering Crime at the Expense of Community

I met longtime Germantown resident Donna a week later than planned to discuss her diary of news stories. Around the time she had originally intended to keep her diary, she hit a wall. She said she felt overwhelmed by the negativity and intensity of the news cycle: "I was like, 'You know what, I need a news break.' So, I didn't listen to any news for a whole week."[11] Donna, like a number of participants in the study, explained that she periodically allowed herself a news "cleanse." From time to time, since the 2016 election season, when she felt that she was becoming overly "saturated" and "bombarded" with negative or political news from the twenty-four-hour news cycle, she would take a break. As in Kentucky, this meant her feelings about the national news cycle led her to adjust how she used or avoided communication resources in her local storytelling network. When she sought to avoid all news outlets, she didn't access local news, either.

Once she made her way back to her normal news routines, Donna's diary contained more national and international news stories than local ones. She explained that she was frustrated with local coverage, dominated by crime and violence: "It's always a murder, a killing, or something and usually, typically, somebody of color." Donna raised a refrain common among participants: "I think it's slanted, biased in how they report it." She said she knew there were problems in the community, but "they never balance it with anything positive." This, she argued, was a phenomenon that affected Germantown and other communities of color disproportionately: "The stories are slanted according to the zip code."

When asked about their local news use, nearly every study participant shared this sentiment that Germantown was unfairly stigmatized by media coverage. In one of the focus group discussions, Celeste offered a view expressed by many: "So, it seems like they only report on crime in certain neighborhoods, and I'm pretty sure crime goes on all over Philadelphia. They tend to focus more on certain areas like predominantly Black neighborhoods." Participants worried that narratives circulating about Germantown could have material consequences, making outsiders less likely to visit or invest in their community. "I think when they spend so much time talking about crimes in certain neighborhoods, then people will automatically get the perception that this neighborhood is bad or what have you," Celeste worried.[12]

This was not to say that participants did not want any crime coverage. In one focus group, participants pointed out that there were some crimes, namely crimes against residents in the name of neighborhood development, that seemed to get very little coverage:

> **MARTHA**: Yeah, what's underreported is people that rip us off.
> **KATHY**: Yeah.
> **MARTHA**: Not at the end of a draw on the street, but . . .
> **KATHY**: Yeah.
> **MARTHA**: . . . our landlords who raise the rent $300 a month, you know.
> **KATHY**: Yeah, those kinds of crimes.[13]

News coverage's emphasis on violent crime meant that crimes that were more commonly felt in daily life were not explored. The group gave examples, such as the dumping of commercial tires in the neighborhood that residents bore the burden of cleaning up.

Numerous participants argued that local news would be more valuable if it focused less on violent crime and more on community issues—both challenges in the community and positive developments. Their wish list for coverage included areas such as housing and development, the state of local schools and activities for young people, jobs and wages, transportation, and the state of the business district in terms of shopping and parking amenities. Several participants noted they wanted more investigative coverage, particularly around topics such as development and gentrification. But participants also called for more positive representations of Germantown and its people. As Celeste noted, they wanted news coverage to reflect "the good things that's going on in the community." Donna echoed this wish and offered the example of a story she had recently read in a historically African American local newspaper about a man who had adopted three children. She said she had shared the story on Facebook "because I think it was a feel-good story and I just always feel like . . . we're saturated with so much stuff that's not always so positive and good, and I feel like sometimes we just need to have some good energy flowing."[14]

As in Kentucky, we did not introduce the concept of "solutions journalism" in our initial conversations with residents. Despite this, Germantown residents also expressed interest in more solutions-oriented coverage of local concerns.

But, like Western Kentucky participants, they also wanted stories that simply offered more constructive narratives about their fellow residents.

Trustworthiness Factors

As we heard earlier from Brandon, a distrust of media was not a new phenomenon for many Germantown residents. In the focus groups and interviews, participants mentioned the trustworthiness factors[15] of perceived accuracy and credibility, respectful and equitable representations, and benevolence of motives. These were almost always referenced in terms of how media outlets were seen as falling short—and the factors were often intertwined. As residents like Donna and Celeste noted, there was a perception that local news outlets disproportionately reported on crime and negative stories about Germantown and other communities of color in Philadelphia. Variations on this came up in nearly every conversation.

Regarding assessments of accuracy or credibility, several residents suggested that local reporting often had factual errors due to a lack of knowledge about the community. As an example, in one focus group, participants discussed how the Germantown neighborhood was often tarred with crimes that happened elsewhere:

> **KATHY**: Even though Germantown Avenue runs through many neighborhoods, they report things have happened in Germantown because it was somewhere near Germantown Avenue.
> **JAMAL**: Yeah.
> **KATHY**: So, I see the misreporting of neighborhood . . .
> **JAMAL**: It'll be like something, like she just said, something that happened on Germantown Avenue. You're like, "That was North Philadelphia."[16]

Kathy suggested having more "homegrown journalists" with local knowledge and context would make such inaccuracies less likely. Here, as with the resident of the South Side of Chicago mentioned in chapter 2 who complained about local news outlets incorrectly saying a crime happened in her neighborhood, local journalists were failing to establish what Nikki Usher calls "place trust"—a concept to describe "how journalists legitimate their specialized knowledge by knowing places."[17] This example also illustrates that for residents like Kathy and Jamal, the problem is not merely a lack of local news but rather a lack of local news that is community-centered.

Participants ascribed a range of motives to the shortcomings they perceived in local coverage—from accidental sloppiness to the more sinister and intentional. In every focus group and most interviews, participants expressed concern over financial motives for biased or sensational frames in stories. For some this meant emphasizing dynamics such as violence and sex because they were perceived to "sell." But others suggested that the media acted deliberately on behalf of private business and political interests. For example, Jamal suggested that news outlets sometimes covered an area in a negative light to keep property costs low for developers.[18] When sharing in her focus group what a healthier relationship with news media might look like, Donna explained that she wished the profit motive could be removed by publicly funding news: "I think all the money that is behind all these big news sources is why they get reported the way that they do." Responding to her, Raheem agreed, "I think the news must be independent and have no connection to companies at all. And each section of the community needs to tell its own story."[19]

Overall, as participants reflected on their relationship with local media and the stories circulating about their neighborhood, they revealed weaknesses in this link in the local storytelling network. A lack of trust had damaged ties between local media and residents. For some, perceptions of negative narratives circulating in local news led them to disengage from the network. And even those who continued to stay connected expressed frustration with the gap between the issues they deemed important and what was actually covered.

Montgomery County: No News Not Always Good News

Brenda's story diary included a fair amount about Prince Harry and the royal wedding in the UK. "It was nice to see something positive," she explained. Sitting in a booth at McDonald's in Montgomery County, we reviewed what stories had caught her eye. There wasn't much local news about her suburban area. "Down in Philadelphia, there's always something going on," she said. "It never seems like anything positive. You know? There's always some kind of shooting or some kind of depressing news." Brenda said she wished there was more positive news coverage. But because she associated "news" with negativity, she was somewhat pleased that there wasn't much news about her particular corner of the county: "We don't really have any commotion here in Collegeville, you know. I mean, it's a peaceful place, so you don't really hear much."[20]

Not everyone saw this absence of local news as a sign that all was well. Mark viewed it as a consequence of several of the small local papers in the area being bought by the same large corporation: "Go to each of them, and go into the search and put in 'Collegeville,' and you'll get the exact same articles because there are just a handful of articles, and there are fewer people writing, fewer people going out and investigating." For Mark, this had civic consequences. With fewer people devoted to original local coverage, it was harder to find out what was going on in local government: "A really important aspect of a local paper, to me, is to go to local council meetings, township meetings, and planning commission meetings. That's how people know what's going on in their town. That's how they know who voted for what, and whether they're going to re-elect that guy. That's how they're going to know who is building a development and if they should come speak up on it." Mark lamented that "all that is gone."[21] Shrinking reporting capacity also meant it was harder for community groups to get coverage of local issues and events. And even if a reporter covered something, the overall decline in content had led to a decline in readership and reach.

Anne shared a similar sentiment that local news coverage, especially in local newspapers, had become "thin and not really well written." Because of dwindling resources, "you don't get that community kind of news that you once did that was important in communities." For her this contributed to a lack of a shared community story: "In some ways, I think we've become disconnected in our communities. You have neighbors that we don't talk to, things like that. There was a day when somebody would say, 'Oh, I saw you in the paper,' and say, 'Oh, hey, great job.' That was part of the discussion in the smaller community. You don't have that anymore." These days, she explained, you at best heard about kids participating in sports or "a snippet of how many cars are broken into this past week." Without a point of comparison, it is difficult to verify differences in the quality of coverage, but at least in Anne's recollection, there was a sense of loss. She missed what she remembered to be "really good stories about what was happening amongst our community."[22]

Alternative Sources in a Suburban News Desert

Anne and Mark identified with different sides of the political spectrum. In Montgomery County, where residents were nearly evenly divided along political lines, mistrust of national media was often expressed in partisan frames. But when it came to local news, as in Western Kentucky, residents from across the spectrum attributed shortcomings to a lack of financial and human resources rather than to partisan motives. Overall, participants' critiques of local news centered on similar concerns over shrinking coverage and a lack of positive coverage of community efforts, as well as a lack of substantive investigative coverage. Because of these concerns, many reported turning away from traditional local news outlets and often seeking out alternative communication resources such as word of mouth, Facebook groups for neighborhoods or schools, or area e-newsletters. Participants suggested that many of these networks were stage-of-life dependent—for example, several referenced feeling disconnected when they no longer had school-age children. As a result, these networks could be influential but not necessarily accessible to all, as Emily explained in one of the focus groups: "My neighborhood Facebook group, there is actually one person who has become almost a reporter to the neighborhood. She goes to all the township meetings, the school board meetings, reports back her findings, and I think it's been really interesting to see how that group has changed from kind of like a mommy-and-me kind of group to more social issues."[23] In this way, while links between media and residents were weakening in the local storytelling network, links between residents were at times picking up slack, albeit unevenly, in an attempt to fill information voids.

Compared with Germantown, Montgomery County residents' concerns were rooted more around an absence of news outlets than around a distrust of them, though there was a lack of confidence in local legacy outlets due to concerns over resource gaps.

Storytelling Network Intervention: From Workshop to Pilot

After exploring the state of local storytelling networks in Germantown and Montgomery County, particularly weaknesses in links between residents and local media, we organized workshops in each location. The goal for each was to discuss ideas residents had shared about what they wanted to see improved and to brainstorm interventions aiming to strengthen the local communication infrastructure. For each workshop, we invited residents who had participated in the study, community leaders, local business associations, local journalists, representatives from area universities, and engaged journalism specialists.

As in Western Kentucky, workshops began with a presentation and discussion of key findings from our focus groups, story diaries, and interviews around the state of local storytelling networks. As discussed, the needs and assets in Germantown and Montgomery County varied considerably. However, when study participants were asked about their wish lists for what a better relationship with media would look like, there were some common elements. Participants spoke of a desire for more constructive, less negative coverage of local news. They also spoke of opportunities for media to work with communities to cocreate coverage and for media to facilitate discussions on community issues.

Our goal from the workshops was to begin to outline ideas for how items on these wish lists could be operationalized in the context of each location. To do this, in each session, participants were organized into small groups containing a mix of residents, local journalists, community leaders, and engagement specialists.[24] Groups were invited to brainstorm how they might design a project or series of responses to address concerns and move toward an intervention that would strengthen the storytelling network by deepening connections between journalists, residents, and community groups. From this brainstorming, themes emerged—some place-specific and some resonant in both locations.

Hyperlocal Communication Assets

In both Germantown and Montgomery County, conversations around what could be done differently to develop more trust-filled networks often started with an acknowledgment of what was already being done through existing informal networks. In both locations there was an emphasis on recognizing and building on communication assets already present—be they neighborhood Facebook groups or e-newsletters organized by community groups or private citizens, as well as community groups, churches, or historical societies.

Participants in both areas suggested that journalists would improve their coverage if they paid more attention to what one Germantown participant called the "value of connectors": "A lot of news goes on underground. There are people who know about it, but it doesn't get distributed in ways that those of us who are actually working in the media see, and how do we get plugged into those networks? How do those networks plug into us?"[25] In Montgomery County another participant shared a similar call to journalists. She proposed that journalists covering challenging issues like food security or homelessness should consider connecting with people and groups who had on-the-ground experiences offering support in these areas, such as local churches. "There are people who know what the issues are that the journalists could connect with, and they already have that deep knowledge," she said.[26]

Many of these local connectors actually had organized their own communication networks to circulate hyperlocal information. One participant had developed a 4,000-person-strong email newsletter with her community group. "Our newsletter focuses on events and things, or families in the town, and just what's happening in general," she explained. She had been able to grow her following by tabling at the local farmers' market.[27]

In Germantown, newsletters and nontraditional media were also referenced. This included electronic mailing lists and Facebook groups. Most participants followed or were at least familiar with two popular Germantown Facebook groups—a general community group and another focused primarily on development issues. Germantown residents also spoke about how in some ways there was a glut of hyperlocal information coming out of "community organizations and overlapping community development councils all over the place."[28] Participants spoke of a need for curation of information—and ways to connect these informal networks to a broader pool of residents, to each other, and to local media. Residents appreciated that their local storytelling network had many active community organizations. But they hoped local media could help them navigate this abundance and connect them to other residents beyond the most frequent and vocal meeting participants.

Potential Assets: Community Reporters?

Beyond these existing assets, participants in both locations raised the question of how community members could potentially be mobilized to cocreate content with local media. In Germantown, residents expressed a desire for citizen journalists, as well as what one group called "assistant journalists" consisting of a core of youth reporters. In Montgomery County, one of the concerns raised was gaps in local coverage of civic issues, and residents wondered how they might be able to help.

One Montgomery County newspaper reporter openly shared the challenges of covering the area's many local council and school board meetings. He worked for an outlet with a shrinking newsroom but a large geographic scope of coverage. It was impossible to be at every meeting, he explained. Participants discussed whether area residents could help to fill this gap by reporting on some of these meetings and sharing the information with media. Ideas offered included collaborating with an area college and its journalism program or working with local civic groups such as the Rotary Club. Participants suggested a variety of models to train local residents and students, including the Documenters model offered by the Chicago-based organization City Bureau, which pays residents to document local civic meetings.[29] While not all participants believed payment would be required in Montgomery County, a majority thought some version of training, support, and networking would be appreciated: "You have to support residents. Maybe that's giving them information so that . . . they know that there even is an issue in their community. Enable them so that they can work towards solutions. Connect them with media and with other folks who would be interested."[30]

While ideas varied regarding what it might look like for residents to participate in the media-making process, there was a consensus that citizens did offer a critical potential resource in areas where media coverage had been limited or lacking. Of course, it is worth noting that previous studies of citizen journalism initiatives have had at best a mixed record. Researchers observing initiatives have noted the challenges of sustaining such projects[31] and of maintaining the expectations of participants.[32] Nevertheless, workshop participants' ideas included a range of approaches to participation that differed from traditional citizen journalism models by drawing on existing structures—be they community groups, Facebook pages, or the resources of local influencers. In all of these ideas, participants pointed to the importance of recognizing community assets and involving them in the process of strengthening the local communication environment.

Beyond the Hyperlocal: Narratives about Communities

Both Germantown and Montgomery County participants discussed possibilities for helping residents connect with each other to access community information needs. But in the case of Germantown there was a recognition that the local storytelling network would never be healthy if larger regional media outlets continued to portray the neighborhood in a stigmatized light. As one participant explained, "Hyperlocal news can do a lot about trying to change those perceptions, but it is legacy media that shapes the narrative."[33]

Participants outlined key ways legacy outlets like the daily *Philadelphia Inquirer* newspaper, local television networks, the public radio station WHYY, and other citywide outlets could realign their coverage to begin to build trust. These included questioning habits of sourcing, recognizing historical context, and establishing two-way channels of communication.

As participants lamented a lack of representation that adequately reflected their community, a common refrain from residents was that journalists tended to talk to the same limited number of people. "There are people who kind of appoint themselves or become the spokesperson," explained one journalist. She said she worried that when you see the same people story after story, "everybody is rolling their eyes like, 'I can't believe they talked to that person.'" Journalists had a responsibility to develop alternative banks of sources: "We have to keep going deeper in terms of our sources."[34]

KNOW THE HISTORY. Beyond highlighting a broader range of voices in stories, Germantown workshop participants pointed to the need for stories to acknowledge history and context: "Journalists should have more understanding of American history and how a place became what it is today.... I don't want to hear about gentrification. Tell me about the context. Write me a good story in WHYY about how we got here.... Because a journalist should step correct when they come to Germantown."[35]

Neighborhood change and gentrification was a critical issue in Germantown. Because of this, several participants shared the example of how stories about development should also include context regarding how the neighborhood came to be the way it is through redlining and other racist practices: "We can't talk about where we're going now and what we're going to do in the future without always grounding ourselves in the history. Because if you do that ... you're starting in the middle without the context."[36]

Journalists participating in the workshop acknowledged that their practices were not always conducive to integrating historical perspective:

> Journalists sometimes have a habit of going and talking to sources because we know what side they're on. We don't leave room for that person to share the

perspective for history. . . . We say, "But we hear you're against this. What are your thoughts on this issue?" So, just by that approach to reporting, we've already created a gap as opposed to giving someone an opportunity to tell their story.[37]

Even when there had been reporters who were mindful of neighborhood history, for many newsrooms there was the challenge of turnover. Participants discussed possible strategies to address this, including connecting new reporters to existing community groups and historical centers, holding community history roundtables, and getting personal stories from elders at local senior centers.

ACCOUNTABILITY CONVERSATIONS. Ultimately, what participants expressed was needed was infrastructure to support two-way conversations between legacy outlets and communities. As one participant suggested about legacy outlets, "I think they need to do a better job of telling people that and sort of explaining that they're on this road, and they understand that they, you know, kind of need to repair relationships particularly in communities like Germantown." Taking steps in this direction could include setting up regular accountability conversations between communities and journalists: "So, talking, getting feedback, trying to do your reporting better. Then coming back again, you know, six months later and saying, 'How did we do? What can we do better? Where did we screw up?' So, having that kind of continuous dialogue."[38]

A Neighborhood Information Hub

These workshops were just an initial step in generating ideas for interventions into the local storytelling networks in Germantown and Montgomery County. Following these, conversations between area journalists and community members have led to some preliminary piloting in the Germantown neighborhood and planning discussions in Montgomery County.

In Montgomery County, where an absence of local news due to shrinking local news resources has been the primary issue, workshop participants have explored designing and seeking funding for a pilot project that would connect a local university's journalism program with community organizations and local media. Of course, the idea of journalism schools attempting to fill local news voids is not new.[39] Nevertheless, this proposed project would respond directly to needs and assets raised by community members in the study and workshop. It would entail students working on a solutions journalism course contributing content for local newspapers, which have ostensibly become "ghost newspapers,"[40] as well as their campus publication, and would involve other community stakeholders. While they have not yet secured funding to fully launch the project, they have begun piloting elements of it.

In Germantown, workshop participants had called for a community forum where residents "talk and meet each other and report out—and, you know, begin to come together under some unified voices."[41] Following this mandate, a pilot intervention has begun initial work, under the guidance of an eight-person community advisory group with representatives of local community groups, businesses, and unaffiliated residents. The Germantown Information Hub has been launched as a collaboration between this advisory group, researchers from two Philadelphia universities,[42] community and student journalists, and both citywide and hyperlocal media partners. The intervention has two primary goals, which came from our research and workshops: (1) improve the circulation of hyperlocal information by facilitating connections between existing groups and extending information access to residents who were not already connected to these networks, and (2) strengthen relationships between the community and citywide media to improve narratives circulating about Germantown.

In order to attempt to address these goals, the Info Hub has undertaken a number of different activities, in which I have played a role co-organizing as a participant observer. Core activities include outreach and crowdsourcing story ideas to share with community/student journalists and media partners, developing community stories and profiles, and community discussions and accountability conversations with media partners.

In an attempt to strengthen connections between residents, and between residents and local media, Info Hub team members have conducted face-to-face outreach via tabling. Here, similar to *Curious City*'s efforts in chapter 2, they have focused on setting up informational tables and interactive displays in locations community members frequent—from flea markets and thrift stores to libraries and grocery stores. Participants at the tables invite residents to respond to prompts to crowdsource ideas for stories or community discussions. For example, they may ask what questions people have about Germantown that they would like a reporter to investigate. Or they may invite people to nominate a neighbor they think contributes to the community in some way. This weekly face-to-face outreach is complemented by outreach via text messaging using the GroundSource digital engagement platform, which allows residents to opt into a weekly text message announcement of local events and stories and to share their ideas for stories or discussions. All of the ideas gathered are shared with student and community journalists for potential follow-up stories and with the Info Hub team to consider for planning community discussions. We have also shared community-generated ideas with citywide media partners to encourage them to develop reporting that more directly connects with the priorities of residents, though we plan to make this process more systematic.

The Info Hub has also begun piloting the production of occasional stories on community issues, profiles of community members, and a multimedia community asset map, shared online and via social media. Here the goal has been to offer coverage of stories that community members have expressed an interest in (often accountability questions around local development issues) and that respond to the desire expressed in this study for more positive and solutions-oriented stories. These have primarily been gathered and written by a combination of community and student journalists. In the fall of 2018, we organized a class with a mix of university students and community members who worked together to coproduce solutions journalism stories about the neighborhood. Following this, two of the community members from the course have continued on to join the Info Hub team as part-time paid staff, conducting outreach and writing occasional stories.

Perhaps the project's most promising elements to date have been community discussions and accountability sessions with media partners. Ideas for these sessions have come from project outreach and input from community advisory group members. For community discussions, the goal has been to convene residents to talk about an issue they have raised, connecting a range of stakeholders as well as local journalists. For example, residents expressed concern over the problem of trash in the neighborhood and shared suggestions of a number of people who were taking action on the issue. At the discussion,[43] after an initial introduction, the thirty-something community members who came broke into small groups to discuss efforts to respond to various dimensions of the problem, such as trash collection in the business district, stopping illegal dumping in vacant lots, block cleanups, and litter prevention. Community members who did not know each other prior to the event were able to connect and learn about initiatives they had not been aware of—for example, small grants offered by the Environmental Protection Agency and a city program that gave citations for litter. Other discussions have covered issues ranging from gun violence prevention to the future of a local high school that had been closed. In addition to residents and local journalists, representatives of various formal and informal community organizations have also attended these conversations—everyone from local cultural organizations to an informal group of former gang members who mentor young people. By providing time for small group discussion and informal networking, these different actors in the local storytelling network are encouraged to interact.

In addition to community discussions, accountability conversations have brought media partners into the community to get feedback on coverage they have done about Germantown. For example, a session with the public radio station WHYY invited residents to weigh in on reporting the station did about the planned redevelopment of a section of the neighborhood's commercial corridor.[44] The nearly forty residents who came had the opportunity to work in smaller groups to discuss the news story in question, what they would have done differently, and what other community issues they would like to see covered. The reporter of the WHYY story as well as WHYY editors and the newsroom manager participated. This meant at times getting difficult feedback. Perhaps one of the most charged and revealing moments came during the larger group discussion, when a community member asked why reporters tended to always feature the same community spokespeople—including a representative of a community group who was in the room. The woman who had been quoted agreed that she was often contacted by reporters and that she had tried to suggest that reporters call others. But when someone asked the reporter why he still contacted her, he justified it by saying, "She gives good quotes." This statement resulted in an animated conversation around what that meant and what that might reveal about the shortcomings of journalistic deadline habits and norms around how voices are valued and edited. Despite facing difficult questions, WHYY expressed an appreciation for the opportunity and a desire to hold follow-up discussions. We have also discussed the possibility of planning workshops with WHYY reporters to critically explore their implicit biases around what makes a "good quote" or "source" and how to work with a broader range of community members in their reporting practice. Likewise, the Info Hub has begun to build an alternative local knowledge source bank (to share with media partners) that highlights residents who may offer valuable perspectives to media, beyond the traditional cast of local experts and community leaders. Through these activities, the Info Hub has attempted to strengthen the storytelling network link between citywide media and residents in hopes that the narratives that result may offer a more nuanced reflection of the community.

Of course, none of this has been without difficulties. The initial pilot phase of the Germantown Info Hub intervention was a largely volunteer operation, with all the limitations that a lack of resources brings. Transitioning from a pilot project to a sustainable, ongoing intervention has led the project to seek philanthropic support, as have the projects featured in other chapters. For the Info Hub, this meant receiving initial seed funding in early 2019, which allowed three community members to receive a stipend for outreach work. Then in mid-2019, it received more substantial support, which will allow it to hire several staff members and fund activities over a two-year period. While the project attempts to maintain a light footprint in terms of resource needs, like so many projects, it will likely continue to rely on philanthropic support.

Apart from funding, the intervention grapples with a range of complications—for example, the considerable investment of time required to train and edit community journalists, or the need to navigate political fault lines in the community that occasionally crop up in public discussions or even within our community advisory group. It has also been challenging to engage residents from parts of the neighborhood away from the commercial corridor, particularly in East Germantown, who tend to be less represented in community organizations and meetings. Likewise, while the neighborhood is majority Black, white residents have at times been overrepresented in community discussions, which also sometimes privilege issues of concern to property owners (for example, development or trash). Our community outreach team plans to use such community organizing strategies as tabling, one-on-one meetings, and door-knocking to build relationships with underrepresented areas of the community. To support this effort, the Info Hub undertook a project in collaboration with the national organization Free Press News Voices to receive mentorship in community organizing skills for journalists.

Finally, the deep mistrust some community members feel toward media initiatives occasionally bubbles to the surface. I and others have had conversations where we attempted to explain the concept of the Info Hub only to be schooled in the history of media, nonprofit, and university initiatives that came and went in the neighborhood before. We must grapple with perceptions and realities of who we as a collaborative are associated with in terms of both institutions and individuals. And we must work to maintain a consistent presence that remains accessible to and welcoming of community input—tasks that can be challenging when working with limited resources. Building trust with community members will not be a short-term process.

It is much too early to assess outcomes of the Germantown Info Hub's efforts. Ongoing research will seek to understand whether this intervention has any impact on local storytelling networks—including residents' access to hyperlocal information, their sense of trust in local media, and how communities are portrayed in metro area media. It will look not only at how the intervention may facilitate residents in connecting with journalists in local storytelling networks but also at how residents may be connecting with each other and with community organizations. Navigating resource issues facing local journalism and historical power dynamics will likely make quick change or linear progress highly unlikely. Nevertheless, if the investment of community and media stakeholders can be maintained, participants have acknowledged that they may be "on the same team," despite a history of difficult interaction and what promises to be a complicated path forward.

Portable, not Scalable

What then can be gleaned from looking at these hyperlocal nodes in a larger metro network? Montgomery County and Germantown were selected to explore variation within a metro region, as well as to offer a sister case to our work in Western Kentucky. Despite differences between the sites, the studies have followed a nearly identical process model consisting of a research study to examine the state of local storytelling networks, followed by workshops and then by collaboratively designing engaged journalism interventions and piloting them.

The projects that have begun to emerge illustrate how the character of place can shape the dimensions of interventions when communities are involved in the process. Differences between pilot projects highlight the importance of looking not only at local needs but also at local assets. For example, there were some similarities between needs in the Western Kentucky case and the two Philadelphia sites. Both the rural Ohio County site and the suburban Montgomery County site were on the verge of becoming news deserts with very limited local news resources. At the same time, both the Western Kentucky and Germantown sites grappled with perceptions of being stigmatized by outsiders coming in to cover their areas (be they national or regional press in the Kentucky case, or metro-wide press in the Germantown case).

The assets in each location, however, were substantially different. Indeed, it has been the assets that seem to offer form to the intervention ideas generated by participants through this process. In the Ohio County case, local traditions were the assets. There was already a history of "society columnists" who had functioned as reporters of community news and announcements through newspaper columns in the pre-digital era. This legacy gave the community contributor pilot project a framework for residents to reference and to reimagine. The project built upon this historical asset to serve multiple needs, offering perspectives from distant communities that are difficult for the tiny hyperlocal staff to reach and positive representations created by community members who had complained of being portrayed by external media as "hillbillies." Likewise, while the availability of public spaces in their rural community was generally framed in terms of deficit, the *Ohio County Monitor*'s liars table tours were grappling with how to reimagine the few remaining gathering spaces for sharing information. Liars tables are imperfect assets—white male spaces where many would not feel welcome. But through their project these hyperlocal journalists were exploring how they could reimagine these assets and make connections between these spaces and their larger public.

In Germantown and Montgomery County, the set of hyperlocal communication assets available in their local storytelling networks is different. For example, in one Montgomery County town, there is a college with a small journalism program and an interest in solutions journalism. Residents have potential human resources to channel toward a project connecting student journalists to local media to supplement their limited reporting resources. In Germantown, there are numerous community organizations and a community radio station but also a sense of fragmentation between different parts of the community and different information sources. For this reason, the intervention piloted in Germantown focused on bringing existing groups together to create a network to curate information, coordinate outreach, and facilitate dialogue. As a collaboration led by community members and researchers rather than by a media outlet, the Germantown Info Hub focuses more on the process of connecting community members rather than media products or outputs. In this way it directly works as an intervention to make connections between different parts of the local storytelling network—community members, community organizations, and local media.

In terms of place-based assets, Philadelphia was also home to several collaborative public service reporting initiatives, which included both legacy and community news organizations and involved community outreach. These experiences meant there were larger news organizations, like the public radio station, that had come to see it as part of their mission to strengthen ties with communities. As a result, the Germantown project has been able to incorporate media partners and set up accountability relationships as part of its pilot intervention. Philadelphia as a city is also on the radar of media funders[45] in a way even the suburb of Montgomery County is not. This combination of collaborative partners and funders has contributed to the Germantown Info Hub intervention being able to launch more fully while the Montgomery County intervention idea has not gotten past a pilot phase.

These engaged research interventions cannot claim to offer exact models for other hyperlocal sites to build trust between media and communities and to strengthen communication infrastructures. Such interventions are, by their nature, not scalable. Rather, this series of projects offers a *portable* process model—a research-based, participatory process to design with communities an intervention that best fits the needs and assets of their particular context. By comparing what has been generated by these processes to date, this still-preliminary research suggests that projects would benefit from an assets-based approach to designing community-centered journalism interventions. Shrinking resources for local news or a lack of coverage that represents community issues is a real and serious challenge in many communities. But even in the face of great deficits and needs, every community has assets in its residents, their networks, and their historical traditions—even if they need to be reimagined to be more inclusive. By respecting and acknowledging these, local media, community stakeholders, and engaged researchers may inch closer to strengthening local storytelling networks.

How, though, does this process model for community-centered journalism compare with the larger field of engaged journalism and solutions journalism practitioners? And how does or doesn't it push against norms of how journalists do their work? Even from these very preliminary pilots we have seen glimpses of clashes—where, for example, a journalist's habits around sourcing conflict with practices of community engagement and relationship building. In the final chapter I will explore how some of the early adopters of engaged journalism and solutions journalism have attempted to challenge some journalistic conventions and where their work does or does not intersect with efforts to strengthen local storytelling networks.

CHAPTER 5

A New Kind of Journalist?

Competencies for Community-Centered Journalism

Mike Rispoli,[1] the director of the Free Press News Voices project, was leading a workshop for journalists in Philadelphia, including several community journalists working with the Germantown Info Hub. He had just identified himself as a "former journalist." Appropriately for a workshop on community organizing strategies for journalism, Rispoli explained that while he still works in the field of journalism, his primary professional identity now was as an organizer. He told the group how he adapted organizing strategies to develop outreach plans and build relationships, working to shift how journalists and community members interacted with each other and how journalists thought about their jobs. Engaging with communities meant more than just "good reporting," he argued. "It's about understanding power dynamics."[2]

At the beginning of this book, I asked whether we need a new kind of journalist to do the work of strengthening local storytelling networks—that is, to build ties between local news, residents, and community groups and to circulate more nuanced narratives within this network. In this chapter, I return to this question and argue that the answer is a resounding yes. If people who identify as journalists are going to play a role in building connections with community stakeholders, weaving a fabric to share and discuss community issues, they need new competencies beyond "good reporting." Journalism has the potential to be a more constructive actor contributing to the health of communities—something that is particularly critical in communities that have been marginalized or divided. But to do so, we need *community-centered journalists*. While these journalists will still require bread-and-butter reporting skills, they will also need to reimagine some habits of journalism. They will have to question norms like objectivity that can, even if unintentionally, reinforce racist and classist power structures. And they will need to question how they make determinations about what makes journalism "good," looking beyond awards or other markers of prestige journalism to focus on the needs and priorities of community members. Community-centered journalists will have to challenge taken-for-granted norms and practices in order to work more effectively as relationship builders and to share power.

The cases I have highlighted in Los Angeles, Chicago, Bowling Green, and Philadelphia arose at a moment when engaged journalism and solutions journalism projects have blossomed in many parts of the United States and internationally. In order to contextualize these cases and offer some variations on the process model for community-centered journalism that they have generated, in this chapter I share experiences from early adopters of engaged journalism and solutions journalism. I draw on interviews with twelve representatives of nine organizations: Resolve Philadelphia, the Discourse, Your Voice Ohio, Listening Post Collective, Outlier Media, Free Press News Voices, City Bureau, Capital Public Radio, and the Center for Investigative Reporting. They are intended not to reflect a comprehensive sampling of initiatives but rather to illustrate a range of more community-centered approaches that focus on various elements of local storytelling networks.

Some common themes emerge in these initiatives' efforts that sit in conversation with the process model piloted in Western Kentucky and Philadelphia. For many of these organizations, projects begin with assessing the information needs of communities, in some cases convening communities and journalists to discuss these needs. In terms of local storytelling networks, most groups centered their energies on connecting with residents and circulating more solutions-oriented narratives. Several also involved community organizations to varying degrees. All of the groups challenged at least some journalistic norms and practices, and all relied on philanthropic support to do this work. By looking at these efforts, I explore more fully the question of how journalists see themselves adapting their roles and how they view their processes and methods. To what extent do they perceive themselves building connections between media, community members, and community organizations? Rather than feature full case studies incorporating community perspectives, here I focus on *journalists' perspectives* on their own efforts within local communication infrastructures. I also outline areas that would benefit from additional research.

While most of these projects are led by people who identify as "journalists" (or at least as "former journalists"), each is involved in evolving the boundaries of journalistic roles and norms in various ways. In particular, I concentrate here on projects that move beyond newsroom-centered engagement and solutions journalism. The labor involved in these projects differs, for example, from the work of audience engagement editors primarily concerned with social media interactions on behalf of their newsroom.[3] While community engagement and solutions journalism reporting offer great value to newsrooms, journalism that centers more explicitly on communities has greater potential for the more radical change needed to build trust and strengthen storytelling network relationships in marginalized communities. As I discussed in chapters 1 and 2, for historically stigmatized communities like South Los Angeles or Chicago's South Side, stories about communities (solutions-oriented or otherwise) are unlikely to connect with residents of those communities if they are not combined with community-centered outreach.

In the pages that follow I look first at projects that are shifting solutions journalism practice toward communities. I next discuss several engaged journalism projects that work to varying degrees to decenter the newsroom in how they deploy engagement platforms and convenings. In these mini-cases, I focus on journalists' perspectives on the strategies they are using to strengthen relationships with community stakeholders and to assess the information needs and assets of communities. But I also look at the difficulties many of these initiatives have had negotiating the storytelling network link between news outlets and community organizations and grappling with journalism practices that default to detached objectivity. Finally, I outline how some of these projects reflect on the challenges of securing philanthropic support and evaluating their own success, particularly given an emphasis among potential funders on quantitative metrics and short project lifespans.

Community-Centered Solutions Journalism

As I outlined in chapter 1, it is possible to do solutions journalism without engaging communities. Simply reporting on responses to social problems alone may offer value, particularly when investigating national and international issues. However, as residents in South Los Angeles suggested, they were unlikely to find out about this reporting or connect with it without community outreach and engagement. The following solutions journalism initiatives have embraced engaged journalism practices alongside their solutions journalism approach.

Resolve Philadelphia

"I think there's an underused power that media organizations have to be conveners of conversations," founder and co-executive director of Resolve

Philadelphia Jean Friedman-Rudovsky explained.[4] Resolve grew out of an initiative of the Solutions Journalism Network in 2016. Resolve's flagship project is a collaboration between twenty-two partner newsrooms—ranging from the city's largest daily newspaper to local television to community media.[5] After spending a year covering the issue of prisoner reentry, the project continued with a new focus on solutions to poverty and economic mobility.

Resolve has gone beyond SJN's mandate to offer "rigorous and compelling reporting on responses to social problems." As a third-party organization working with newsroom partners, Resolve has been able to facilitate a range of approaches to community engagement. Some of these have remained close to the newsroom-centered model, for example using the Hearken engagement tool to crowdsource questions to ask city hall candidates. But Resolve has gone beyond this, developing community partnerships with a variety of organizations and facilitating discussions between community stakeholders, government officials, and journalists. Resolve's mission of advancing journalism "built on equity, collaboration and the elevation of community voices and solutions"[6] has led it to work to share ownership with community partners in a variety of ways. For example, at an event for its series on prisoner reentry, Resolve staffers collaborated with a group run by formerly incarcerated citizens to design, plan, and host the program. Through this work they have attempted to strengthen storytelling network ties not only between different newsrooms of local journalists and residents but also with community organizations. They have also repeatedly worked to activate and boost participation in the storytelling network so that actors in it can more effectively communicate with policy makers and power holders. This was a goal of the crowdsourced questions for city hall candidates but also was part of their series on reentry. In fact, the mayor attended the session organized by formerly incarcerated citizens, and several stories from the project led to changes of policy in area prisons.[7]

Beyond its outreach and engagement work, Resolve has brought solutions journalism narratives into a community-centered journalism framework. This has included questioning the forms that solutions journalism can take. As Friedman-Rudovsky explained, the emphasis in solutions journalism on including data and evidence to back up reporting on responses means that solutions stories can at times "come off as kind of wonky." This can also create a disparity in what groups or projects are featured in stories, as not everybody has the funding or capacity to gather data to show the impact of their work. Because of this, "certain stories are being told more than others." Friedman-Rudovsky said while those can be important stories, "there is a real value to solutions reporting on what's happening at a very neighborhood and grassroots level." She said Resolve hopes to do more of this kind of reporting: "In my mind those are the stories that... on a local level, could have the most impact. Because then it's like seeing, 'Oh, someone like me could do this, or folks like us.'" In this way Resolve's approach to solutions journalism seeks to change the narrative circulating in the local storytelling network in a way that aspires to increase collective efficacy among readers and viewers.

Resolve is also planning an initiative, called the "Reframe," that aims to encourage more community-centered journalistic practices. Through a combination of resources, training, and tools, it will offer a "scaffolding" to help newsrooms engage people-centered language and more accurately reflect communities by using the terms they identify with. As Friedman-Rudovsky explained, for reporting on identity, gun violence, sexual violence, or any number of other issues, Resolve staffers want to "assist newsrooms who are interested in changing their practices." While the framework is still in development, it may involve elements such as style guide tools, training to ensure the entire newsroom infrastructure is on board, and eventually supporting community members to act as "co-reporters" on stories where newsroom staff lack direct experience or perspective. Speaking of the latter, co-executive director Cassie Haynes described co-reporters as a potential pipeline for "nontraditional journalists to do journalism." This will be critical, she explained, as, "if we're looking at our vision for a newsroom of the future, the people who are working in that newsroom look different than people who are working in most newsrooms now." Resolve's efforts to reimagine what a newsroom can be, and how it is positioned with respect to communities, mean it is often pushing boundaries—and occasionally faces push-back and questions from journalists and funders. As Friedman-Rudovsky said, "I feel like our very existence is brushing up against traditional norms."

The Discourse

Resolve Philadelphia is not the only project attempting to deploy solutions journalism in ways that are more community-centered. I met Anita Li at SJN's annual Solutions Journalism Summit. Li is the director of communities at the Canadian startup media company the Discourse. Its website describes the Discourse as "reimagining the community newspaper to better represent all of us."[8] Li explained that the Discourse produces "solutions-focused stories."[9] But similar to Resolve's efforts to "elevate community voices" and encourage people-centered language, the Discourse also prioritizes the trustworthiness factor[10] of representation, focusing on communities that have historically been marginalized.

The Discourse has identified three communities to test its "community-powered journalism model." One of these is the eastern suburb of Toronto that

Li grew up in: "Scarborough is a place that has historically been associated with crime and grime. That's, like, the only narrative that outsiders know." Li explained how her colleagues did a data analysis of the Greater Toronto Area to identify underserved communities and found that Scarborough was one of the largest underserved areas.[11] "It's basically a news desert," she said. It was also an area that was a flashpoint in municipal elections and home to considerable controversy over transportation. Adding to this, over the years, journalists and others have been critiqued for contributing to negative and racialized narratives of the community, including by calling it "Scarlem" and "Scarberia."[12]

Once Discourse staffers settled on Scarborough, they undertook their own version of a community information needs and assets assessment, as we did in Western Kentucky and Philadelphia. They identified a minimum of twenty local stakeholders across multiple industries—a mix of community, arts, business, nonprofit, education, and other leaders. For each person, they asked the same set of sixteen questions, including some that focused on assets: "The questions include everything from 'What do you love about your community?' Because that's rarely asked. That's also informative because that tells you about the way they view their relationship to their community. What kind of issues are you concerned about in your community? What issues are your friends and family concerned about? Where do you get your source of local news?"

Li explained that once they had data on the themes stakeholders were most concerned about, she worked with a reporter who also had long-standing ties to Scarborough to list the most frequently mentioned themes as broad story topics. They then put these to a community vote on their closed Facebook page of Scarborough residents, as well as on their weekly newsletter and website. Out of this, the Discourse has been producing a series of solutions-focused stories about the community-nominated topics, posting progress and updates on the group's Facebook page and in its newsletter.

The Discourse's approach offers an alternative for groups that may have limited resources to sample community members on their information needs. Using a two-part approach, staffers were able to first survey community leaders to get their perspective. While this was a small sample of twenty people, by using a second phase of discussion and voting on a closed Facebook group with over four hundred people, they were able to gain input and additional feedback from a broader spectrum of residents. There are of course limitations and trade-offs with online outreach and assessments. Nevertheless, as they have followed up with additional offline outreach and pop-up events,[13] their two-part assessment of needs and assets seems to have helped them establish a baseline understanding to inform the development of their programming.

Discourse staffers have also worked to ensure that their online presence retains a connection to place and that they build and maintain trust through transparency online. Their closed Facebook group screens all would-be participants. Li explained that she is "only approving requests from people who are connected to Scarborough." In addition, Li said they "constantly consult with the community." For example, they invited residents in the closed Facebook group to vote before they admitted anyone they thought could disturb the balance of trust with the community. Li recalled how they encouraged participants to comment before admitting a police officer who was organizing a "Coffee with a Cop" community engagement initiative. In a community with a history of distrust toward police, "we weren't just going to go in there and then destroy that trust," she explained.

Your Voice Ohio

On its website, Your Voice Ohio describes itself as a collaboration between more than fifty Ohio news organizations that embraces "representative and solutions-oriented news coverage on the issues that matter most to Ohioans." This solutions journalism project positions itself as responding to a need to repair relationships: "We use engaging, authentic, and accessible solutions-driven community conversation to rebuild trust between Ohioans and Ohio media."[14] Your Voice Ohio operates primarily at the state level with occasional emphasis on particular cities or regions. But similar to Resolve Philadelphia and the Discourse, this solutions journalism initiative also pushes to center its focus outside the newsroom.

Doug Oplinger, a longtime newspaper editor and the director of Your Voice Ohio, was sitting in what the Jefferson Center calls a "Citizens Jury" when he had what he describes as a "holy schnikes"[15] moment.[16] The Jefferson Center is a nonprofit organization that promotes civic participation through public deliberation processes like Citizens Juries. For this Citizens Jury, the center brought together just over twenty Ohio residents who represented the demographics of the state to participate in a series of three-day sessions. The goal of the sessions was to figure out what people wanted from local news media, assessing and discussing not just the information people wanted but also how they wanted it delivered. At the end of each Citizens Jury, after days of deliberation, participants made recommendations for next steps.[17]

Your Voice Ohio's first Citizens Jury session was largely spent airing grievances community members had about journalists. But after this venting, the facilitators from the Jefferson Center worked with participants to develop an understanding of how journalists did their work. This meant things like how they filed, and were sometimes denied, public record requests. Oplinger shared,

"They said they didn't realize journalism was so difficult, so we needed to tell people more detail about . . . how we did our stories. They were fascinated by that. It's like a whodunit, like, you know, Sherlock Holmes." Oplinger concluded from participants' feedback that journalists should be more transparent about how they did their work. His takeaway resonates with what a number of actors in the journalism innovation community have been saying: transparency builds trust.[18]

After discussing the journalistic process, the second Citizens Jury session focused on content, particularly on what people wanted from election coverage. Because the process was deliberative, it went beyond criticizing media and invited the public to imagine what the news media could be (not unlike the approach we used in our Kentucky and Philadelphia focus groups). Participants asked for a number of things—like connecting election issues to people's experiences so they could know "if we do this, who's affected this way." They also asked for a list of solutions proposed by each candidate. This reinforced Oplinger's belief in the value of solutions journalism: "To me, that was really important because it confirmed a suspicion that I had, that ever since Watergate, journalists have been looking for the 'gotcha.' 'Here's something that's wrong.' We're always telling people what's wrong, and they're sick of that. They don't want to hear that they're going to die over and over. They want to know, 'How do I survive?'" Here, Oplinger's conclusions resonate with the Solutions Journalism Network's argument, discussed in the introduction, that the watchdog model's theory of change is insufficient without highlighting responses to a problem.[19] Oplinger concluded from what participants told him that it was critical not only to build trust-filled links between communities and journalists through transparency but also to change the narratives circulating between media and the public by offering content with a solutions orientation.

But the big revelation to Oplinger came at the Citizens Jury's third session when the Your Voice Ohio team gave examples of stories to get feedback from residents. After discussing an AP story on immigration, they shared a story the Your Voice Ohio collaboration had done about immigration in Ohio that incorporated feedback from the previous sessions. That meant it included graphs illustrating the situation (which participants in the second session had requested), as well as solutions proposed by the two candidates. Participants loved it. This was Oplinger's "holy schnikes" moment: "If we just listen to the people, there's an answer for us."

Oplinger's observation highlights the value of constructing feedback loops. In this case, Your Voice Ohio had created an opportunity for residents to weigh in with what and how they wanted news covered, the media partners responded to this input in their coverage, and they subsequently circled back for feedback.

In different ways, each of these cases—Resolve Philadelphia, the Discourse, and Your Voice Ohio—offers examples of a sort of solutions journalism 2.0. Each combines coverage of responses to social problems with a focus on community voices and priorities. In this way, each is potentially changing the valence of stories being circulated in local storytelling networks—*and* changing who is connecting to these networks. Because of their dual focus on solutions and engagement, the projects potentially go beyond the South LA case explored in chapter 1 by bringing community members and organizations into the solutions journalism process. Each case also raises the need for additional research. Future studies could explore whether Resolve's intervention in the Philadelphia media system has shaped attitudes toward journalism norms, or whether Resolve or the Discourse has affected narratives circulating about stigmatized populations. Likewise, additional research would be needed to track whether and how Your Voice Ohio did or did not maintain feedback loops with residents. Following these more community-centered solutions journalism efforts may offer insights on their potential to build trust in storytelling networks and ensure that more representative, solutions-oriented narratives are part of community conversations.

Community-Centered Platforms and Assessments

Assessing the information needs and assets of communities is a critical first step in informing the design of any engaged journalism project. As we learned in the Western Kentucky and Philadelphia cases, conversations with community members may reveal not only areas of concern or gaps but also strengths and assets in local storytelling networks. Understanding both an area's needs and its assets can be pivotal to designing place-based interventions. Along these lines, the projects that follow took a range of approaches to discover what information residents wanted, as well as where and how it could be effectively shared.

The Listening Post Collective

"What's missing in New Orleans?" read a sign stuck to a utility pole in New Orleans's Central City neighborhood. The sign listed a phone number to text above the project's name, "The Listening Post."[20] The person getting those text messages was Jesse Hardman, the founder of the Listening Post project. Hardman was a radio reporter who had spent time working on international humanitarian information projects, a field where assessing information needs of communities was a standard practice. He went to New Orleans in 2013 and decided to adapt this approach to assess the information needs of New Orleans residents. At that time, many of the majority Black neighborhoods had yet to completely recover from 2005's Hurricane Katrina, but at the same time they were having to deal with encroaching gentrification pressures. Hardman spent six weeks going to community events, meetings, and church services with a clipboard and a short survey asking some four hundred people how and where they accessed and shared local news and what issues they wanted to explore more.

Hardman used what he learned to develop the Listening Post project.[21] This project used engagement platforms and tools, but its real emphasis was on a process that centered communities. Just as we saw from the example of *Curious City* and Hearken, an engagement tool or platform on its own can be applied in many ways (which is why Hearken now identifies as both a platform and a consulting service).[22] In the case of the Listening Post, Hardman focused on a process that first established where people gathered and shared information, or what communication infrastructure theory would call communication hotspots.[23] Once he determined these community assets, be they grocery stores, libraries, or community events, he might set up an audio recording station, or "listening post." People could walk up to the recorder, read a prompt, and then record their own response. In this way, Hardman shifted the engagement platform away from the confines of the newsroom, or the online and offline spaces of a newsroom's existing audience, to the places where New Orleans residents, particularly from communities of color, frequented.

Hardman also used a mobile messaging platform called GroundSource[24] that allows organizations to set up two-way communication, sending and receiving text or voice messages. Hardman used this to text some fifteen hundred people around the city, sending them news and asking them questions. But critically, he would adapt how he disseminated this platform based on residents' existing communication habits, such as using the tradition of advertisements on signs posted to utility poles. Hardman would take this new platform to the places people were already gathering—for example, going to neighborhood meetings and events with a sandwich board indicating how people could text him.

"The goal is always, 'Let's start a conversation so people feel included,'" he explained.[25] When Hardman asked residents what was missing in New Orleans, crowdsourced responses ranged from "reliable public transportation" to "opportunity equality for the Black and poor" to a children's hospital to glass recycling.[26] Hardman then followed up on some of the ideas, investigating details and corresponding with residents to get deeper anecdotes and to record their viewpoints. He synthesized this information to produce radio stories for the local public radio station, a station with almost no full-time reporters to cover local news. But he also looked for opportunities to share these stories in spaces that were seen as more welcoming and accessible to communities of color than the public radio station.

Under the auspices of the media development organization Internews, which has historically focused on projects outside the United States, the Listening Post project has been adapted to become the Listening Post Collective. The Listening Post Collective has expanded to work with a range of local outlets in several U.S. cities, including Oakland and Omaha, sharing needs assessment strategies in an online "playbook."[27] The collective is also part of what seems to be a growing trend and financial sustainability strategy among engaged journalism specialists, offering consulting for existing organizations hoping to deepen their community engagement. This has partly been spurred by initiatives such as the Community Listening and Engagement Fund, where foundations subsidize applicants from media outlets to pay for engagement tools and consulting services (such as Hearken and GroundSource). The form the resulting Listening Post partners have chosen to engage with residents varies (and there is a need for research to follow how these projects affect local storytelling networks), but the step of assessing information needs has been a consistent starting point.

Outlier Media

The Listening Post is not alone in combining engagement platforms such as GroundSource with information needs assessments.

"Imagine if any news organizations were investigating the information needs of Flint residents in the years and months before state and national stories broke." Sarah Alvarez, the founder of Outlier Media, wrote this somewhat painful what-if in a guide to information needs inquiry for news organizations.[28] Her thought was prompted by a Pew Research Center study that showed that long before the news story became prominent, residents were googling information about the water supply.[29]

For Alvarez, Flint's information gap illustrated the need for news organizations to shift from "post hoc" analysis of info needs, or reliance on "proxies like press releases or other news organizations."[30] She outlined, in her guide for newsrooms, a "better way" to determine information needs. Alvarez adapted an experience sampling method,[31] an intensive longitudinal research method. It used text messages to prompt study participants to log their responses, similar to asking people to keep a diary of their activities. Alvarez explained that Google had been using a variation of this to design its algorithm for anticipating the needs of its users. In her guide, she recommended that newsrooms aim to text a group of thirty to forty people four times a day for three to five days. In these texts they could ask questions like, "What do you need to know or better understand right now?" These would be followed up with questions about whether and where people were able to find this information and whether they got the information they wanted from news sources.

Alvarez teamed up with the founder of the GroundSource texting platform, Andrew Haeg, to test this model, which they called Pulse.[32] Together, they worked with three news outlets in California, Michigan, and North Carolina. Like the Listening Post's needs assessment, Pulse's method went directly to community members. At the same time, like the Discourse, it relied upon a relatively small sample. However, because Pulse asked participants to answer questions several times during the day, it improved the likelihood participants would recall more granular information needs and information-seeking habits in a way that can be difficult to gather after the fact. This granular level can be particularly valuable for initiatives seeking not just to provide coverage *about* community issues but to offer coverage *for* communities, responding to specific needs and interests. What remains to be seen is how effectively media outlets who use this strategy will be able to synthesize the rich data they may potentially gather and how they will act upon it. What they can claim to understand from their assessment will also vary based on the range of the participants sampled—for example, whether they sampled from their existing audiences or by buying random phone numbers, which may give them more insights on community members beyond those they already have a relationship with.

Alvarez is a proponent of the latter in Detroit, where she is based. In her own work with Outlier Media, she has been buying lists of phone numbers to connect directly with Detroit residents. "I just kind of started from scratch and was like, if you're going to build a news service for a low-income news audience, how would you do it?" Alvarez took a very direct approach to filling information gaps for members of the public. She decided to focus on two of the biggest issues in Detroit: housing and utilities. Then she bought a list of cell phone numbers and texted them using the GroundSource platform. "This is Outlier Media, a free journalism service for Detroit," the text message introduced. "You can use these txts to check if your home is on the auction list or if your landlord has blight tickets. You can also talk to a journalist about your housing and utility questions this way."[33] The messages would invite those who received them to enter an address in Detroit. She set up a program that used city and county databases to automatically reply with information before asking text recipients if they had other questions that they wanted to talk to a journalist about.

Instead of trying to juggle reporting *about* a community with reporting *for* a community, Alvarez did each separately. Alvarez emphasized that her goal was to provide actionable information that furthered accountability. She did this through her texting service, providing responses to individuals and connecting them to resources for assistance. But occasionally, through texting with residents and researching the issues they raised, she uncovered more systemic problems. She offered the example of how residents would get high water bills, not because they were using more water but because the city imposed a drainage fee based on how much rainwater went into the sewers (which was based on how much concrete was on the property). In cases like that, she saw the best path to accountability as reporting narrative stories that would run in news outlets like the public radio station. But while she occasionally shared with a resident who had a relevant question the basic information she learned while reporting on a story, she never shared the full news stories back with the residents she was texting: "The people that I have really worked with on stories do not care about the story. What they do care about is, like, someone is continuing to follow up and using their energy so that this person doesn't have to use all their energy to just fight with the water department."

The residents Alvarez texted with wanted answers to their questions. But she said they didn't have time to read a long story, and they didn't see a benefit in being featured in a news story: "Some people have even asked me, 'How is this going to help me if I'm doing a story?' I'm like, 'It doesn't.'" While news coverage about communities that grew from this project could and did deliver accountability wins, her priority was to directly deliver to people the information they told her they wanted. For this reason, using Alvarez's very direct approach to information needs assessment, Outlier Media tailored both the information and the way the organization delivered it in two separate ways for two groups of stakeholders. Through both of these approaches, Outlier Media was attempting to further an accountability mission. Either it was sharing narrative stories through channels such as public radio that would directly reach power brokers, or it was giving residents the information they needed to contact authorities themselves. Alvarez's work is a reminder that intervening to strengthen local storytelling networks is not an end in itself but rather a means to achieving larger goals like greater participation and a sense of efficacy, so that actors in the network may do things like advocate for change.

These different approaches to assessing the information needs and assets of communities illustrate just some of the many possibilities news organizations interested in engagement have been trying. These and other efforts underline the importance of the argument made by City Bureau's Harry Backlund for an "information hierarchy of needs." This concept, developed with Alvarez and others, calls for a rebalancing of journalists' priorities, from abstract analysis that serves a comfortable elite to focusing on information that fills basic needs.[34] While the Outlier Media and Listening Post Collective examples have strengths and weaknesses, each takes a different approach to community-centered journalism. Outlier Media completely decenters the newsroom by focusing on the needs of individual community members. And Alvarez's information needs assessment strategy may offer the most potentially representative sample by buying phone numbers. However, it focuses on a narrow set of issues and does not attempt to bridge between local storytelling networks. In other words, it does not create a shared space for exchanging and discussing stories between the residents its texts serve and the media outlets that host its narrative journalism. Given the project's mandate, this may be the most appropriate tactic.

However, there is also value to assessments that look more broadly at how residents connect to community organizations or public spaces, as the Listening Post does. The Listening Post's assessment strategy takes a holistic account of local storytelling networks. But at the same time, this strategy on its own does not ensure a community-centered outcome if it is deployed by a newsroom without a community-centered production and distribution plan. Ultimately, design of any assessment will likely come down to a combination of resource availability and the context in which a given project or news organization is operating.

Community-Centered Convenings

For a number of groups, exploring the needs and assets of communities takes place face-to-face around an assortment of tables. While these public convenings may not replace more formal information needs assessments, they can act as a step to strengthen relationships between local media and community stakeholders. From New Jersey to North Carolina, Illinois to California, a number of projects have been working to build shared spaces for exchange between local news media and community members.

News Voices

"I think the more that journalists or newsrooms are in the community listening to people, listening without being defensive . . . I think that that is a greater path than ever to local news," Mike Rispoli explained.[35] Rispoli directs News Voices, a project of the nonprofit group Free Press, which advocates for communities to have stronger voices in local news. For Rispoli, listening to communities was a necessary, if insufficient, step to build links between journalists and communities. News Voices came to a similar conclusion to what I had learned from projects in South LA, Bowling Green, and Philadelphia: while determining the information needs and assets of a community was a necessary first step, getting residents and journalists into the same room was often key in order to understand these needs deeply and to start to chart a path forward. This not only allowed for a greater understanding of a community's needs but was often an opportunity to strengthen relationships between residents and local media and sometimes even community groups—key actors in local storytelling networks.

Like Your Voice Ohio, News Voices also undertakes projects that bring residents and journalists into shared spaces to listen to each other. News Voices comes to the process as a third party, as part of Free Press, a nonprofit group that advocates for media reform and local journalism. News Voices tends to storytelling network ties as interstitial actors,[36] not unlike the role played by researchers in the Western Kentucky and Philadelphia projects I shared in chapters 3 and 4.

Explaining how the nonprofit group developed its method, Free Press's former journalism program director Fiona Morgan recalled thinking, "What if we situated ourselves in the community and then reached out to the community and the newsroom simultaneously?"[37] Focusing on communities in New Jersey and North Carolina, Morgan explained how Free Press's News Voices would first try to understand "what's the story about the place." Staffers would look at narratives circulating about the community and people's information needs and involve community stakeholders in the planning process.

In Charlotte, North Carolina, News Voices' community organizer Alicia Bell worked to bridge the gap between the *Charlotte Observer* newspaper and community members. The *Observer* realized the value of relationship building after a local trans woman was killed, an incident that required rapid response. In the process of covering the story, the *Observer* misidentified the woman, in part due to the newsroom's lack of relationships with the trans community. "They [the *Observer*] had seen over and over again how rapid response moments had pushed community members and the paper further away from each other," Bell explained.[38] Responding to this, the *Observer* took steps to open channels of communication with community members, working with News Voices to do so. For example, the *Observer* staff hosted a breakfast at their newsroom, and News Voices put together the guest list of community members who were not already connected to the paper and didn't necessarily trust it. This grew into a series of monthly meetings between *Observer* staff and small groups of residents, followed by a series of larger public conversations.[39]

Morgan noted that one of the most meaningful parts of that first breakfast was having journalists sitting at the table with non-journalists: "If you're actually sitting next to someone, and both of you are speaking in turn, it changes the power dynamic, and it opens up all these possibilities. It says to the person who is not a journalist that what they have to say matters."[40] For News Voices, which has a commitment to racial justice, attention to the dynamics of power and place has been baked into its operations. Morgan and Bell said that through the process of discussions, they have seen journalists not only gain knowledge about various communities and their information needs but also learn how to benefit from feedback loops.

City Bureau

Like News Voices, getting people together to talk about journalism is core to the work of City Bureau, which describes itself as a nonprofit civic journalism lab. Based in the South Side of Chicago, City Bureau has several projects that involve the public at various stages of gathering and sharing civic information and news.

Unlike News Voices, City Bureau also does its own reporting. It creates content through its fellowship program, which pays and mentors less-experienced reporters, pairing them with veteran team leaders to cover South and West Side communities. This reporting then runs in a variety of news outlets. But City Bureau is not itself a media outlet. This gives it a sort of interstitial role[41] like News Voices', where it can focus energy on shifting journalism away from exclusionary journalistic spaces into community-centered spaces where community members can share ownership.

This includes making journalistic spaces, like the newsroom, feel more relevant and welcoming. As discussed in chapter 2, relations between Chicago's South and West Side communities and mainstream news media have not historically been characterized by openness or trust. City Bureau's Public Newsrooms program attempts to create new relationships between community members and journalists from multiple news outlets by inviting both groups for weekly discussions. Public Newsrooms explores a range of media and civic issues, from Freedom of Information Act requests, to better education coverage, to racial equity voter guides, to traffic tickets.

For these discussions, City Bureau opens up its own South Side newsroom to the community, but staffers also go to other communities, hosting meetings in galleries, community centers, and even ice cream shops.[42] The discussions have attracted a consistent crowd of participants to talk about issues. Cofounder and editorial director Bettina Chang explained that these Public Newsrooms function as spaces to connect community members with the reporting City Bureau fellows have been doing and reporting that's being planned and to follow up on stories they have reported on in the past. They also embrace transparency and critical feedback. Chang recalled a Public Newsroom they held on restorative justice where the reporters showed a slide about the negative feedback they had received. Some of the people who shared that feedback were in the room: "So, you have this conversation about what does it mean to be reporting on this vulnerable population, and people are upset about it."[43] Chang said these kinds of accountability conversations were not easy, but they engaged community members and journalists in meaningful conversations.

The Public Newsrooms program has also tackled the issue of local news needs head on, inviting residents in different neighborhoods to work with the

City Bureau team to develop a "local news contract." As cofounder and News Lab director Darryl Holliday explained, "A new contract is needed: a commitment that reframes the traditional consumer-producer relationship into one of co-creation, with journalists and communities working together to produce this essential public good. . . . The new contract between journalists and the public will frame journalism as an act of citizenship rather than an entity for and separate from citizens."[44]

At the time of writing, City Bureau was organizing meetings around the city and inviting resident to share declarations, many of which challenged journalism norms. For example:

> We would like more opportunities for community members to come to local newsrooms to talk about what to cover—more opportunities for bottom-up feedback not top-down feedback.
> Media outlets and reporters must be accountable to their own racial biases.
> Media outlets need to stop striving for objectivity, and instead focus on nuanced realities.
> When covering marginalized groups and people, do not be afraid to let them propose solutions to the problems they are facing. Too often, news features let real people tell stories about their own suffering, then pivot to experts to propose constructive solutions. People living inside problems are often the best experts on those problems.[45]

City Bureau planned to compile these declarations and to work with partner outlets and residents to "reimagine local news and put those ideas into action, either individually or as coordinated campaigns."[46]

Through its Public Newsrooms, City Bureau works as a connector not only building relationships between the public and its own reporters but also encouraging other media outlets to use collaborative practices. Different public newsrooms fall at different points along the process, from developing to reporting to distributing stories. But by creating a culture of exchange between members of the public and journalists, City Bureau aims to create points of access.

Capital Public Radio

Relationship building through community-centered convening is at the center of jesikah maria ross's[47] work at Capital Public Radio in Sacramento, California. She sees her job as connecting news media and communities for mutual benefit through what she calls an "engaged documentary convening process." In this process, community convenings take place at the beginning and end of larger documentary projects, bringing together community stakeholders and newsroom reporters to explore issues and solutions. She describes one of her events: "125 people in a beautiful hall with late afternoon sunlight. . . . There are tables and it's kind of set up kind of like a wedding."[48] She is a proponent of what she calls radical hospitality; ross wants participants to feel welcome and appreciated. That means she makes the effort to have flowers and candles on tables. And it means ross ensures that everyone who comes, including journalists, are there as participants to share personal stories and to listen to each other.

Unlike most of the engaged journalism specialists in this chapter, ross sits within a news outlet, working as a senior community engagement strategist at the public radio station. There, she has organized engaged documentary projects to explore a number of issues, including hunger, the lack of affordable housing, and suicide and mental health. For each project, ross undertakes a cycle that includes developing relationships with key stakeholders building up to the actual events. For example, in a project where she held "Story Circles," ross led participants, who came from a range of backgrounds relevant to the project, through a facilitated process of sharing their experiences with the issue in the form of a personal story. Her convenings are not broadcast, but afterward participants often can document their experience and views at a "story booth" recording station or talk to someone about what local organizations are doing to address the issue.

For ross, separating the process of listening and being heard from the work of reporting stories for broadcast has value. She explained that the crush of daily news deadlines means for many reporters that "there's not room for them to actually really pay attention to other people's needs, which is weird because you'd think that's what journalism is." For reporters, listening often means trying to hear what they're "going to use": "I'm already making the narrative in my head of what the person is saying because they fit a formula that I can put together." She argued that building relationships with community stakeholders requires a deeper, slower form of listening: "listening not to fill in a formula but actually, like, getting to know each other." She explained that all this took time—at least two months of showing up to community meetings and arranging one-on-one meetings, "which is glacial for a newsroom, fast for me." But all this relationship development and trust building was necessary to strengthen links between ross's media outlet and communities. Before ross could count on people to show up for her events, she needed to do her part to show that "I'm here, I'm listening, I'm learning for reals."

From News Voices community discussions to City Bureau's Public Newsrooms to Capital Public Radio's engaged documentaries, engagement specialists have embraced the idea of connecting with and convening publics to meet their information needs. Each of these also offers fertile ground for additional research. The News Voices team has noted that outcomes of their work often develop slowly over time, long after initial conversations between journalists and community stakeholders. Because of this, assessing impact requires a longer lens. Likewise, City Bureau's Public Newsrooms program would benefit from research on whether and how it is affecting the residents who participate in the program or the broader circles of residents who may encounter news stories that grow out of this process.

As I will explore more below, ross undertook a robust process of evaluating her engaged documentary efforts, working with multiple external consultants. This included, among other things, surveys with participants that sought to assess "changes in knowledge, empathy, connection, emotions, and intent to take action."[49] To explore whether and how the engaged documentary projects may have affected storytelling network links between local news and residents, this research could be supplemented by follow-up interviews or discussions with participants. Checking in with participants over time would offer insights into how the behavioral intentions they expressed were or were not realized and how their experience has shaped their perceptions of and connection with Capital Public Radio.

While additional research is needed, these community-centered convenings seem likely to be moving in the direction of strengthening ties between news media and community members. But what about the other node in local storytelling networks—community organizations?

Storytelling Network Links: Connecting Journalists to Community Organizations

As explored in chapters 1 and 2, many journalists have reservations about collaborating with community organizations. And it turns out many journalists specializing in engagement were not exceptions. "I don't want to work with a community group. That's weird," Alvarez of Outlier Media said. She then conceded that she actually did work with such groups but had to "keep my eye on them too." Alvarez explained how when she was sharing information with people about tax foreclosures, she would tell them about an initiative to help residents that was run by a nonprofit. But then she would try to hold those organizations accountable by instructing people, "Let me know if they don't help you. Let me know if they don't take your calls." Alvarez said she wanted to avoid blurring the lines between the information provision she did and what organizations did. "I don't want to do outreach for nonprofits."[50] Alvarez's hesitance to do anything that blurred into outreach for nonprofits echoes the views of the *Curious City* outreach producer who didn't want to "carry water" for organizations.[51]

At Your Voice Ohio events, Doug Oplinger similarly saw a need to create some boundaries with community organizations. He explained that Your Voice Ohio would invite these groups to its events, "but if we see a community organization getting a little bit active, we ask them to chill a little bit." He said that often he had to tell them they could not distribute pamphlets or make a statement at the end: "We say no, this is about regular folks coming together in real life and trying to come to grips with the issue from shared experiences. This is not an opportunity for someone to try to steer the conversation."[52]

While both Alvarez and Oplinger sought to center their journalistic work to respond to the needs and interests of community members, they adhered to dominant journalism norms when it came to community organizations. Here their rhetoric suggested concerns about retaining independence and objectivity.

Community engagement consultant Cole Goins, the former director of community engagement at the Center for Investigative Reporting's Reveal, said that in his work he has collaborated with community groups, but he concedes that it is easier for most newsrooms to collaborate with a library or a technology group than with an activist organization. "I'm not saying that there can't be a partnership, but . . . it's a tricky line to walk when you have an organization that's specifically advocating for X." But Goins emphasized "tricky" did not mean impossible: "I think there's education on both sides about how one another operates, and how we can better form collaborations and partnerships."[53]

Goins shared an example of how input and collaboration with organizations and advocates not only can help outlets tell better stories but also can ensure that their outreach initiatives don't have unintended consequences. To complement investigative reporting on the sexual abuse of farmworkers in California, Goins and his team put together a toolkit for women working in the fields; the folder contained a hotline number and resources in case they were abused. He gave the folder to an advocate to see if she could share it at a conference for women farmworkers. "She's like, 'Yeah, we're happy to do that, except . . . can you take your logo off of this and really make these as discreet as possible?'" Goins explained that the advocate was concerned women could be put at risk or stigmatized if the materials were seen by their partners: "How we designed it was well intentioned but not optimized for how people were actually going to use it. So, journalists do this all the time. Like, 'Oh, people are going to love it if we do X.' And then you talk to the people who work with those communities, and they're like, 'Well, no, that's not going to work, and here's why.'" This experience offered an important design lesson for Goins. Especially when looking for nontraditional paths to serve the needs of communities, involving the people closest to the issues from the beginning of the process is key.

Other initiatives underlined the value in developing relationships with community organizations that set shared expectations from the beginning. For jesikah maria ross, community partners, including organizations, were at the heart of her engaged documentary projects. She explained how she would start the project by forming an advisory group. For the Hidden Hunger project, she had ten community partners on the advisory group, and they gathered every month for two hours. At the very beginning they were involved in meetings to shape the direction of the reporting that would be done for the project. They also helped plan community activities: "I asked them to help me design a community engagement plan and it's like an MOU [memorandum of understanding] but it's very detailed. So, 'Here's activities, here's your role, here's our role.'" Ross worked with these partners so that they would feel invested and heard: "They're all involved from the get-go, not just as an afterthought, and it's set up so that while people can kind of participate to the level that works for them, they're clear on how it's going to benefit them and how they have some say."[54]

After the initial planning, community partners would help recruit participants for the events and also run the "info zones" after the events where they could share with participants resources and follow-up opportunities. By involving community groups with deep community ties, ross was able to orchestrate events that included participants who came from vulnerable backgrounds, like those dealing with hunger. As she worked to earn the trust of these partners, the partners then extended the trust they had with community members to ross's events. Here, trust seemed to mean a sense of benevolent motives, a jumping-off point from which the news organization could prove that it was committed to fair representations and accurate coverage of the community.

"Initially all of them were like, 'No, we don't want to work with these organizations,'" said Mike Rispoli from News Voices, sharing some of the challenges of getting journalists to work with community groups.[55] News Voices was working on a collaborative project where journalists were meant to identify community members to talk about economic hardship. From the start, News Voices encouraged the reporters to connect with community organizations. The reporters resisted, using a familiar skeptical, journalistic logic: "They're going to give us people who are going to tell us stories that these organizations want to hear."

Rispoli cautioned them that they would have difficulty talking with vulnerable people about a stigmatizing issue, but the organizations "can vouch for you and allow for you to have trust going into that interview or that relationship." Indeed, after a month, the reporters relented. "They're like, 'Oh, this is really hard.'" He explained that being open to work with community groups required a shift in journalistic practices: "I think a journalist's natural inclination is to call up an organization for a quote for that organization, so they're not going to call up an organization and say, 'Hey, I need you to help me find a story.'" Doing this was tough because it required journalists essentially to acknowledge "I need your help in order for me to do my job."

While strengthening the link between journalists and community members is seen as the bread and butter of engaged journalism practice, the connection between journalists and community organizations remains more fraught. In chapter 1, I shared some of the reservations community organizations had about journalists in South Los Angeles. Some questioned journalists' motives and their commitment to representing the community and its issues fairly. These cases of engaged journalism projects suggest that the skepticism between journalists and community organizations often can be mutual. Like their counterparts affiliated with organizations, many journalists question the interests of community organizations and attempt to create and maintain professional distance. This reticence seems to be rooted in a combination of journalistic norms of objectivity and independence, as well as a skepticism of the role organizations play at times in facilitating connections to community members but also curating and potentially blocking said connections. At the same time, other practitioners of community-centered journalism have found that great value can come from strengthening links with community groups. But even for these practitioners, as they work to strengthen local storytelling networks, they often have to navigate fundamental questions: Is this work the job of journalists? How are these practices boundary challenges[56] to journalistic norms and roles?

Navigating Newsrooms and Journalism Roles

Most of the engaged journalism practitioners I spoke with shared moments of grappling with the skepticism of colleagues and collaborators as they attempted to strengthen ties between their news outlets, residents, and community groups.

Shortly after Doug Oplinger had his "holy schnikes" moment at the Your Voice Ohio Citizens Jury, he stumbled into the reality of trying to implement new approaches based on participants' preferences. Back in his newsroom, he asked a reporter doing a story about gerrymandering to include a chart to illustrate the issue. "She said, 'Oh God, people don't like charts.' And I said, 'Yes, they do.' And she said, 'Who says?' I said, 'Well, I just listened to three weekend conversations.' She said, 'I just don't believe it. Who were these people?' And that's the challenge. There're so many freaking journalists out there who refuse to give regular people credibility."[57] While the issue of whether or not to use a chart may seem relatively minor, Oplinger says it illustrates a fairly pervasive resistance to changing practices and conceptions of what role the public should play in the process of making journalism.

Oplinger said one of the ways he has been able to see journalists open up to different possibilities has been for them to participate in the Jefferson Center–run discussions. As with News Voices community discussions, just getting journalists and community members to sit at the same table to listen to each other can shift perspectives. Oplinger said he still had to "crack a couple knuckles" with some journalists who took out laptops and started doing interviews when they were supposed to be engaged in discussion at small tables: "I said, 'Close the laptop. You can take a few notes on a piece of paper but I want you to share with these people as professionals and as regular people so that they see you as caring and also like them.' And when they did that, they became better listeners." Oplinger's experience highlights how difficult it can be to shift journalists away from transactional relationships where the goal is to extract content. He said in his work in Ohio it has taken time to find colleagues "willing to take some risks in journalism." For him, journalistic practices need to change, to become more solutions-oriented and responsive to public input. Finding other journalists who share his vision and his discontent with the journalistic status quo has been difficult but rewarding: "You find them and you just fall in love with them. When you find those people, you feel so energized. It makes you want to keep going. There is hope. And there are a lot of journalists who want to try, [who] understand that we've got a problem and they want to try."

Capital Public Radio's jesikah maria ross is also often looking for likeminded journalists for her community engagement work. She explained that when she first ventured into the world of journalism in the 1990s, she felt "kicked out of the club" for wanting to work with communities: "I kind of saw myself in the world of journalism but as a new type or new breed, and it was this kind of group of people who were really trying to find ways to bring community voices into the mix in an equitable and kind of mutually beneficial way."[58]

Drawing from her graduate work and background in community development principles, ross engages with communities. She sees her work as part of a community development process, using a cycle of one-on-one meetings and power mapping, leading up to convenings. For many years, she found the most enthusiasm for her work in the worlds of alternative or independent journalism. When she joined Capital Public Radio, she felt a bit like "the experiment," bringing new tactics into their newsroom: "You're, like, trying to shift the culture, but you're also trying to embody having feet in two worlds."[59]

Her experience highlights the challenges that can arise from designating a staff member as *the* engagement person. The work she does requires competencies that are not traditionally part of a journalist's toolkit—things like facilitation, organizing, partnership management, and the like. She sees value in her role as a specialist who is able to act as a bridge between communities and reporters. But it also means she becomes the keeper of relationships. For example, she does the groundwork in building and nurturing relationships, and reporters see the end result in the convenings she organizes. This, she said, was the most efficient process for the reporters, but "it contributes to the problem that I think a lot of people in my role are in, which is we become the go-to person of, 'Hey, do you have somebody I can talk to about blah?' And then I do. But then [when] I give you that . . . if you don't treat them well, it's a problem." It would be more effective for her and others to maintain long-term relationships with community stakeholders if principles of managing community relationships were woven into the culture across the newsroom. Tapping one person as the point person for engagement runs the risk of others feeling that it is not a dish that they need to include on their plate.

In her experience, ross says, newsrooms have been cautious about the kind of work she does due to fears of "advocacy" and an allegiance to "objectivity." But for her, the journalistic norm of objectivity has always been problematic:

> Our newsrooms are very subjective and they don't recognize it. . . . It's either the reporter who is mostly white [and] middle-class or a managing editor who decides what our public wants to know, needs to know, or will benefit from knowing. . . . I think that there's a lot of subjectivity, and I'm okay with subjectivity. I just think you have to call it out and then be open to how do we broaden it out.

This perspective resonates with Sue Robinson and Kathleen Culver's argument that journalistic practices associated with objectivity reinforce white supremacy.[60] For example, maintaining distance from communities or using only named sources means the voices that will be heard or seen in media will be more likely to be white and relatively privileged—people who either have a professional reason to be interviewed as authorities or who have social capital to protect them if they go on the record to say something that may be controversial. Robinson and Culver put forward Stephen Ward's concept of "pragmatic" or "active" objectivity as an alternative,[61] which recognizes the interpretive nature of journalism and "privileges citizens as the recipient of media loyalty and emphasizes community trust building as an essential part of news gathering."[62] This concept aligns with ross's argument that public media journalists are "not neutral" and should see themselves as advocates for democracy, "trying to make healthier communities."

Through their work in New Jersey and North Carolina, News Voices has similarly been challenging traditional objectivity norms. The group has also been pushing journalists to consider approaches similar to ross's in Sacramento, particularly focusing on community organizing strategies.

"Journalists aren't organizers, but what if they could be? What would that look like?" These questions inspired News Voices projects, says Fiona Morgan.[63] The group was attempting to do what Cole Goins complained journalism did too rarely—look to other fields for ideas and ways to evaluate and improve outreach and engagement practices: "When we do arrive at some kind of idea of, like, well, no one has ever thought of this before . . . it's like, no, no, no. . . . Public health was doing that in the early '90s, you know, or community organizers have been doing this literally forever."[64]

For News Voices, organizing strategies have been the bread and butter of staffers' work to connect communities and newsrooms. They use a number of classic organizing strategies like one-on-one meetings with community stakeholders and mapping assets and power in a community. But to make organizing strategies work for journalism, they did have to make some adjustments. As Morgan explained, "Conventional organizing in the Saul Alinsky mold tends to have a combative, transactional relationship with professional journalism."[65] It didn't recognize the potential for alignment between journalism and community organizing. Morgan explained that she married some of the more traditional organizing strategies with a "more generative kind of organizing,"[66] borrowing from groups like Journalism that Matters[67] as well as from deliberative dialogue models like the World Café method.[68] "The main thing with organizing journalism is that it's about building relationships and building *with* people rather than *for* them," Morgan points out, not "going into the community and saying, 'What news do you need? What did you want?' I'm here to build this with you and hav[e] that be the guiding force rather than thinking of people as consumers. Think . . . of them as constituents of your work."

The News Voices team mapped out principles and strategies of organizing for journalism not only for their own work in North Carolina and New Jersey but also to share with other journalists and communities. They put together guides on organizing strategies and tactics.[69] And they have offered workshops and trainings for other media outlets and journalists, from community-driven efforts to more conventional newsrooms. For example, in Philadelphia they have offered training and guidance not only to the community-based Germantown Info Hub project but also to WHYY, a major public radio station.

Similar to what ross experienced, Morgan and Rispoli encountered skepticism toward the idea that this kind of community outreach should be the work of journalists, largely due to concerns around objectivity norms. As Rispoli recalled, "Initially a few years ago when we first started preaching this gospel of organizing for journalists, I think the first thing that came into the journalist's mind was activism, but that's not what organizing is."[70] Morgan experienced similar reactions: "Usually when someone balks at the idea of, like, 'I can't be an organizer; I'm a journalist,' it doesn't mean that you're advocating for a specific outcome or a specific policy."

Rispoli starts many of his workshops by inviting participants, usually journalists, to think about a relationship that they value and to share what qualities they value in that relationship. He uses this thought exercise to encourage journalists to think about how they build relationships with publics. He notes that another thing different in organizing for journalism rather than organizing for activism is that where, traditionally, organizing is about building power from the ground up, journalists already have power. Journalists have access to information, relationships with people in positions of power, and a platform. So organizing for journalism is less building power than sharing power: "Sharing power really starts with shifting away from that transactional relationship building that most journalists have with community members. 'I need a quote. Can you help me with the story?' . . . And so, it's really about a kind of culture that prioritizes just being in collaboration to build relationships that are multidirectional or reciprocal."

Here too Rispoli's conception of a journalist's ideal role is more compatible with active/pragmatic objectivity than with traditional journalism norms. Rispoli acknowledged that the drive to encourage journalists to use organizing strategies to build relationships comes from a critique of dominant journalistic practices: "There's an inherent criticism of journalism in the work that we do by pointing out how traditional ways of doing things have actually led to the erosion of trust or decline in journalism." This element of critique explains the defensiveness of journalists who see these efforts to strengthen relationships between news outlets and community stakeholders as a challenge to their ways of working.

City Bureau in Chicago shares a similar ethos as News Voices. "We want to live right at the intersection of organizing and local news," News Lab director Darryl Holliday explained.[71] He said City Bureau often worked with community groups to enable "a mutual exchange of local news information done right, and really good ground organizing done right." It was through such efforts that he and his team have been able to recruit participants for their Documenters project, which offers paid opportunities for community members to do things like attend and document public governance meetings and get skills training. Through the project they learn things like note-taking, interviewing, audio/video recording, live tweeting, or how to enter data into Excel spreadsheets—all skills they can use to gather and organize civic data. While some Documenters do take on more traditional citizen journalist functions like writing a blog post, their training also allows them, among other things, to compile databases that can be searched by professional journalists or any interested citizen.

City Bureau's Documenters program also grows from a critique of journalism norms. Where its public newsrooms project challenges norms of secrecy among journalists, its Documenters program challenges the idea that certain acts of gathering and recording information should be the work of journalists as opposed to the work of citizens. "We rely too much on journalists to do work that impacts local communities," said Holliday. "People begin to think that they can't do it." Holliday said that he regularly gets questions from people who didn't know that they were allowed to go to a public meeting of a city council: "We have that question all the time. 'Can I go?' I'm just, like, wow, if we've come to that point where you're not even sure if you can go to a city council meeting, this is bad news. So, we find ourselves in this position of really wanting to redistribute skills."

Holliday says City Bureau's work takes the skills of journalism and trains community members in how to use them to make information "actionable" for civic engagement. Through this, these citizen documenters can provide accountability of civic processes that otherwise would not be possible and that Holliday argues should not just be within the purview of journalists. Through the Documenters project, City Bureau makes a clear boundary challenge in advocating for "non-journalistic informational actors,"[72] aka community members, to take on responsibilities associated with professional journalists.

Each of these initiatives present boundary challenges to journalistic norms and practices. For Your Voice Ohio and Capital Public Radio's community engagement work, there are the challenges of navigating inside news outlets with ingrained norms around objectivity and editorial control and of structures designed to prioritize serving audiences over communities. News Voices also confronts journalistic practice norms with its organizing principles, but it does so from the outside as an interstitial actor connecting community stakeholders and newsrooms. City Bureau at times plays this connector role with its public newsroom work, but it also questions who gets to provide community news and information through its Documenters program (as does Resolve Philadelphia's plan for co-reporters). In combination, these initiatives offer the field a menu of strategies to shift journalism toward communities. They address the information needs of communities, challenge problematic objectivity norms that can weaken ties between journalists and communities, and, while more research is needed, potentially contribute to stronger links between storytelling network actors.

Accessing Funds and Assessing Impact

How, though, do these projects access the resources they need to be implemented, and how do they know if what they are doing "works"? While it is unlikely to be a long-term solution, philanthropic support is currently the primary lifeline of these and many similar projects. Within the context of market failure, there are interesting experiments exploring alternative funding models, particularly around public funding and community crowdfunding. But at present, a number of initiatives have found that simply producing engaged, solutions-oriented work alone does not guarantee communities will pay for it.[73] Because of this, all of the engaged journalism projects mentioned in this chapter have received foundation support, primarily from the same handful of funders (the Democracy Fund, the Knight Foundation, the Lenfest Institute, the MacArthur Foundation, the News Integrity Initiative, the Wyncote Foundation, and so on). Following the 2016 elections in the United States, donor interest in funding media grew in what some have called a "Trump bump."[74] Several years in, funding support has continued, with participation in the Knight Media Forum growing from 2018 to 2019.[75]

This philanthropic support itself has in many ways enabled boundary challenges to journalism. Engaged journalism specialists are given leverage to make their case to more traditional newsrooms when they can demonstrate that such projects have the potential to bring in much-needed capital. But this also means that funders can act as potential blockers or limiters to boundary challenges, something that groups like Resolve Philadelphia have experienced from funders who have been hesitant to challenge notions of objectivity.[76] Philanthropic dollars additionally have the potential to perpetuate gaps and inequities by supporting engagement specialists with social capital, while smaller local or hyperlocal outlets that lack access to social capital are largely unable to get their foot in the door. For example, I have seen all the practitioners mentioned in this chapter at a circuit of national engaged journalism and solutions journalism conferences. Meanwhile, were it not for our serendipitous intervention project in Western Kentucky, Dustin Bratcher of the *Ohio County Monitor* likely would never have been invited to participate in a national journalism conference. There are many more would-be *Ohio County Monitor*s or would-be Germantown Info Hubs that do not currently have pathways to make the necessary connections with potential funders. The patterns of this lack of access to social capital largely fall along lines of race, class, and geography.

Even for those media organizations that are able to access donors, the structures of foundation funding can be problematic. Donors almost all prioritize funding "new" projects over general operating budgets, let alone community-based design processes. Nonprofit outlets and start-ups are more likely to receive funding than the legacy commercial outlets where the majority of Americans get their news, making projects more likely to super-serve an information elite. Funding periods are often short—rarely more than one year—and yet projects are often required to follow substantial donor reporting schedules and demonstrate "impact."

There are a small number of funders attempting to raise these and other issues within the philanthropy field. In an open letter informed by anonymous grantee input, media funders Jessica Clark and Molly de Aguiar discussed matters affecting the engaged journalism and broader journalism funding world.[77] This ranged from procedural challenges, like the length of time and amount of work required to even apply for funding, to how to create more equitable power dynamics between grantor and grantee. Clark and de Aguiar went beyond procedural correctives to advocate for a more radical rethinking of processes to "share control of grantmaking funds and decisions with the communities you serve." As de Aguiar explained in an interview, "It just strikes me that we have to practice what we preach. If we are asking journalism to be more participatory, then philanthropy itself also needs to be participatory." This included working to get beyond "circles of who I know"—something that de Aguiar acknowledged was particularly challenging for national funders.[78]

At least in the short to medium term, community-centered journalism initiatives seeking philanthropic funding must continue to navigate funders' requirements. One of the most challenging of these can be the need to demonstrate the "impact" of their work. This raises the question of how these projects determine what they are doing works. And what does "working" mean? As Jacob Nelson has pointed out, assessing the return on investment of engaged journalism projects like Hearken can be complicated due to a lack of clear metrics to measure engagement.[79]

This question of measuring community engagement efforts is a messy and frustrating one for many of the practitioners in this chapter. As News Voices' Mike Rispoli explains, "I get frustrated with the belief that . . . because we can't see the value of community engagement, . . . therefore it's not valuable. If we can't measure it, it's not valuable." Rispoli argues that the work News Voices and other engagement practitioners do is fundamentally about shifting culture. It's not possible to boil the work of relationship building down to story views and subscriber rates. "A lot of these feelings that people have towards local media have been built up over decades," he explains. Building relationships may down the line lead to outcomes that are measurable. But untangling, repairing, and weaving together connections between communities and local media is not a short-term fix. Interventions that steer the ship in this direction have great value, he argues; "it's just your metrics dashboard may not be able to measure it quite yet."[80]

Others have maintained that measurement can have value, so long as projects are measuring the right thing. De Aguiar notes that as a funder, she does not see value in a standardized approach to metrics, but this doesn't mean projects should abandon all measurement: "It's OK to dismiss the stuff you know is meaningless, but you have to create a framework that is meaningful and hold yourself accountable to that framework."[81] For some, this has meant seeking out alternative evaluation strategies. Capital Public Radio's jesikah maria ross considers herself an "evaluation nerd." She outlined in a Medium post the evaluation process she used to assess the community-engaged documentary model she designed for her Place and Privilege project exploring housing affordability and residential segregation.[82] From the beginning, ross involved station management in the process of brainstorming an evaluation plan. To help them, they used an "impact pack" media strategy card deck developed by consultants at Dot Connector Studio, which included cards for tactics and goals—from "podcasts" and "SMS text" to "amplification" and "culture shift."[83] Once they developed their plan, ross sought outside help from several evaluation consultants through a combination of pro bono support and philanthropic funding. With this team, the evaluation looked not only at traditional measures of reach, like podcast downloads and web traffic, but also at numbers of community members participating in face-to-face activities. The evaluation also assessed how different components of the project contributed to impact goals like "increased empathy" and "new/strengthened relationships." From this, Place and Privilege team were able to make conclusions and recommendations about various parts of the project—for example, how some elements were effective at building relationships but had a small reach, or vice versa.

Ross's experience highlights the small but growing number of consultants in the engaged journalism world collaborating with newsrooms on project design and evaluation. Over the course of this one project she worked with four different consultants/groups. Many of these consultants and the strategies they practice draw from interdisciplinary backgrounds beyond journalism. For example, the Agora Journalism Center's Andrew DeVigal and Regina Lawrence worked with Eric Gordon of Emerson University's Engagement Lab to design what they call a "Reflective Practice Guide." Drawing from the tradition of empowerment evaluation,[84] a participatory approach to evaluation, the guide charts progress on goals that are key to community engagement: network building, holding space for discussion, distributing ownership, and persistent input. They piloted the guide on seven projects[85] that received Finding Common Ground microgrants (which included both ross's project and the *Ohio County Monitor*'s project featured in chapter 3).[86] Each project team was asked to have guided conversations, sometimes involving community stakeholders, answering questions that related to each goal over the course of the project. The discussion guide included questions such as, "Are there people in your network communicating with each other (without you) who weren't before?," and, "How have you created opportunities for a diversity of participants to connect with each other through your project?" After the open-ended conversation, a team point-person rated members' progress on each area through a brief survey to track changes. The process allows project teams to reflect on their progress at various points in the project, which in theory encourages adjustments and course corrections along the way.

These are just some of many evaluation strategies that offer promise in understanding how interventions affect relationships within community storytelling networks more than media metrics alone do. Our projects in Western Kentucky and Philadelphia also have been experimenting with using focus groups to not only gain feedback on project outputs but also to look at relationship ties between community members and media and to track the presence or absence of trustworthiness factors in the storytelling network. We have found value in adapting a communication infrastructure theory framework for evaluation as well as for project design. As Garrett Broad has outlined, CIT offers three main questions that interventions and evaluations may seek to address.[87] To paraphrase, these include (1) does an intervention strengthen the local storytelling network by building connections between and among local residents, local media, and community-based organizations? (2) Does an intervention successfully produce stor(ies) that motivate change at the individual and/or community level? (3) Does an intervention enhance the ability of local places to promote discursive interaction between and among actors in the local storytelling network? Using these questions to inform the design of an evaluation increases the probability of understanding progress toward, and barriers to, complex goals like improving the communicative health of a community.

Just as there may be no one-size-fits-all intervention to strengthen storytelling networks, each intervention may need to adapt these questions to ensure its evaluation plan responds to local place and power dynamics—as well as to constraints of logistics and budgets. For example, to address the first question, about storytelling network ties, a project could track connections built over time between storytelling actors who participate in the project. This is something we have begun to do in the Western Kentucky and Germantown cases and something that would offer valuable insights for so many of the projects discussed in this chapter. Question two would require defining goals for change and what they would look like in the context of the project. For example, for an organization such as Resolve, it might involve getting more key stakeholders in communities and newsrooms to use people-centered language around issues such as economic mobility or prisoner reentry. Or in the Germantown case, motivating change might mean a group of community members connect at a community discussion and decide to take action on a community issue. It may also be as direct as a story, by a project like Outlier Media, that leads to a policy change. Or it could be the production of stories that motivate individuals to take action in their communities. Finally, the third question about facilitating interaction in local places could be explored for many of these projects through observations of interactions that grow from the project in places such as community events or pop-up newsrooms. What is key is that interventions decide upon what success looks like at the outset of projects, such as stronger and more trust-filled relationships between residents, community groups, and local media. Then, based on the local context, a combination of qualitative and quantitative measures can be outlined to track what "progress" looks like for such community-centered initiatives.

While some funders have been receptive to the kinds of qualitative or mixed-methods evaluation strategies discussed here, many continue to rely on standard quantitative reporting metrics. And even funders with the best intentions struggle to get beyond their networks of social capital that tend not to extend to many geographic regions or marginalized communities. Additional education and advocacy targeting those who hold purse strings is needed if engaged and solutions journalism projects are to be funded and evaluated in a way that reflects their principles of inclusivity and community participation.

Community-Centered Journalists: Learning Skills, Unlearning Norms

The early adopters of community-centered journalism featured in this chapter all presented themselves as challenging the boundaries of journalistic norms and roles in some ways. Of course, these are only their self-reported perspectives. It would be valuable to conduct additional research to analyze the content that circulates in storytelling networks as a result of their efforts. Would stories produced by these organizations or their media partners offer alternate narratives of marginalized communities? How would the voices featured vary from the voices that saturate news outlets following more conventional journalistic habits? And how is their work experienced and felt from the perspective of community members?

Likewise, while each project suggested that they varied from dominant practices, there were some areas where traditional practices persisted. For example, when it came to building relationships with community groups, many reported either feeling or observing reticence. In some areas, norms of objectivity and keeping a professional distance seemed to linger. While there is much to be said for a healthy dose of journalistic skepticism, for marginalized communities, the stickiness of these norms may pose obstacles to deepening ties between journalists and community stakeholders. And while boundary challenges were facilitated by philanthropic support, this same support also constrained where these projects came from—stacking the odds against projects that were socially or geographically distant from funders. Likewise, because funders generally funded projects, not processes, even most of the relatively community-centered projects featured in this chapter grew from the ideas of organization leaders rather than from a community-centered process, such as what we undertook in Western Kentucky or Philadelphia.

These examples illustrate how the role of a community-centered journalist requires a variety of skills and strategies to assess information needs, organize communities, and build relationships. But adopting the mantle of community-centered journalist also potentially involves unlearning some traditional journalism norms and practices. The cases explored here were already largely community-centered. Many more efforts use engaged journalism and solutions journalism practices on a continuum between community and newsroom—and many of those fall closer to newsroom-centered vantage points. The lessons of these community-centered cases may also offer insights for journalists undertaking more newsroom-centered cases but interested in inching closer to communities.

Addressing the communication health of communities is a messy business for journalists. The priorities of communities, particularly marginalized communities, are not always aligned with what have traditionally been the priorities of journalism. As the case studies of earlier chapters and the mini-case examples offered here demonstrate, communities may want something different from just more local news. As Cole Goins concluded from his interactions with marginalized communities, journalists may want to question their default assumption of what they can offer a community: "My community needs a lot of things. Maybe it's not a story about who we are. We know who we are."[88] For community-centered journalists, this means a more expansive toolkit is required—one that may include information needs assessments, facilitation skills, and community organizing strategies. These practices offer value because each in some way is premised on sharing power—a prerequisite to building trust between links in the storytelling network.

While undertaking these practices requires challenging some boundaries and norms of journalism, the community-centered journalism this can yield offers what may be the best hope for building relationships of trust with communities where this has long been in short supply. In the conclusion, I will reflect on what solutions journalism and engaged journalism offer as reforms for the larger field of journalism—and for communities—as well as on what these case studies contribute to communication infrastructure theory. Finally, for both engaged scholars and practitioners, I will offer a summary of a community-centered process model that may be adapted in different contexts to understand community needs and to design interventions in response.

CONCLUSION

To Repair, or to Burn It Down?

In the corridors of many a conference exploring engaged journalism or solutions journalism, I have heard some variation of the following questions: "With so many communities where news outlets have never established relationships of trust, is it worth trying to repair journalistic institutions? Particularly when those institutions are often mired in norms that prop up racist and classist structures? Or should we just try to burn it all down and start over?"

The response I have come to after listening to many such questions and exploring the topics in this book is "both, and."

Yes, there are instances where starting new initiatives makes sense. In some communities, the outlets that do exist are so problematic that it would be placing an unfair burden on marginalized groups to expect them to help improve what is already there.

But also, yes, repairing and collaborating with existing institutions is critical because this is often the most effective way to meet many people where they are. New start-up initiatives often serve a relatively engaged elite. Despite the reservations many have toward existing legacy outlets, residents of numerous communities continue to rely on these same outlets—rural newspapers whose reporting staffs have been gutted, or local television stations that devote a disproportionate amount of airtime to crime. While national polls do not account for differences between communities that have been historically stigmatized and those that have not, they continue to show local television as not only frequently viewed but also highly trusted (though what factors are referred to by "trust" are not specified).[1] Even when residents see these local legacy sources as problematic, they may be the only way to learn about local job prospects or a community meeting. And in some communities, finding out about local crime can be a matter of survival and harm prevention. News avoidance is a luxury not all can afford.

Because this book has been less concerned with strengthening journalism for journalism's sake than with strengthening the communication health of communities, I argue that considering ways forward must be answered in and with communities. Solutions will vary depending on the needs and assets of each and on local dynamics of place and power, but we can use a shared community-centered process model to grapple with them.

From South Los Angeles to Bowling Green, over the course of researching this book I encountered people with a range of life experiences and histories with news media. Journalism was not the focal point of their day-to-day lives. It was but one element of how they gathered information and made sense of issues facing their communities and often took a back seat to a conversation with a neighbor or a friend's Facebook post. But, particularly in communities with a history of marginalization, local news represented power and control over narratives—stories that circulated within communities and externally about communities.

In concluding this book, I reflect back on a key question woven throughout. How can communities access some of the power of journalism to shift narratives from exclusively negative to solutions-oriented ones and to find a variety of ways to be involved in the process of making and circulating community stories? To map a path in this direction, I've drawn from a communication infrastructure theory framework. Through these case studies, I have shown that CIT can offer a guide for assessing the state of communities, then for designing and evaluating interventions that attempt to strengthen local storytelling networks—particularly in communities that have been stigmatized or marginalized.

After considering projects that had limited but not insignificant roles in connecting local media with community organizations in South Los Angeles and connecting the public radio station with residents of underrepresented communities in Chicago, I worked with colleagues, first in Western Kentucky and then in Philadelphia, to develop a process model for intervening in local storytelling networks (see figure 6). When the goal is serving the needs and respecting the assets of communities, dynamics of power and place mean we should not be looking for one-size-fits-all, scalable project models. What worked in Western Kentucky was not what worked in a neighborhood of Philadelphia. However, my colleagues and I have found value in a process model that seeks to engage both community stakeholders and journalists in designing and implementing interventions in the storytelling network.

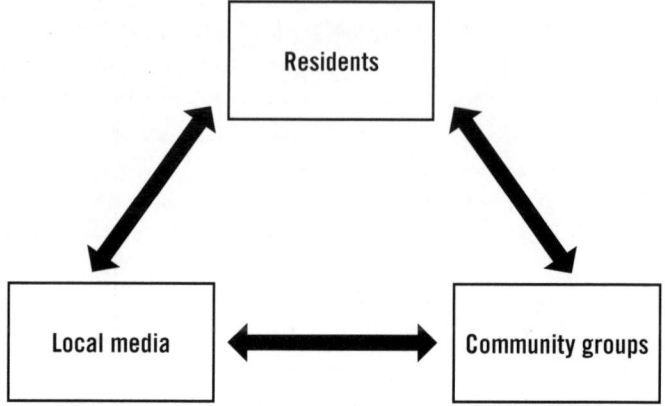

Figure 6. Communication Infrastructure Theory's "Storytelling Network"

The projects that grow from this process will vary, but the *community-centered process model* comprises the following steps:

1. Assess the community's *information needs and assets*, accounting for power and place dynamics along the way. (In our cases we used focus groups, story diaries, and interviews—but as cases mentioned in chapter 5 illustrate, a variety of methods could be used.) Consider how barriers to trust (perceptions of unfairly negative representation, partisan polarization, and the like) may be weakening links in the storytelling network.
2. Share the results of these studies in a *convening* that includes study participants, key community stakeholders (including representatives of community organizations and institutions), local journalists (from both legacy outlets and new initiatives if present), and engagement specialists who can give examples of possible project tactics and approaches. Invite workshop participants to brainstorm possible pilot interventions.
3. Circle back with community stakeholders and journalists to further develop and launch *pilot interventions* designed in convenings.
4. *Monitor and evaluate* pilot projects to understand their impact on relationships between local media, residents, and community groups. Assess progress at multiple points along the way and plan course corrections or additional phases accordingly.

As part of this process, particularly in the assessment and convening stages, our case studies illustrate the value of paying attention to the kinds of stories that circulate about a community. For communities that have been stigmatized, strengthening links between local media, residents, and community groups means assessing whether community stakeholders perceive coverage to be disproportionately negative. While the concept of solutions journalism is unlikely to be familiar, residents may describe the concept in their own words when sharing wish lists for local news coverage, as they did in Kentucky and Philadelphia—though for many, countering overly negative representations also included a desire for more positive stories that did not necessarily meet the formal criteria of solutions journalism. This desire for a fuller spectrum of stories, including positive stories, supports the push that groups like Resolve Philadelphia are making, as discussed in chapter 5, for more grassroots solutions reporting—even when stories may lack the rich data that have traditionally been hallmarks of solutions journalism. In combination, these cases add to the findings of previous researchers[2] that suggest the valence of content circulating in a storytelling network matter.

Perceptions of the positivity or negativity of media also contribute to how trust operates within storytelling networks. While discussions of the word "trust" can be so broad as to be unhelpful, the cases in this book have illustrated the relevance of particular trustworthiness factors.[3] In communities that feel marginalized, trust may refer not only to how people sense *accuracy* and credibility but also to perceptions of how a media outlet *represents* a community and to the benevolence of perceived *motives* behind their coverage. Understanding these perceptions requires attention to how dynamics of power and place-identity have operated through these communities' histories. These cases have shown how, particularly in marginalized communities, barriers to trust can weaken discursive links between actors in local storytelling networks (see figure 7). These barriers may include perceived negative/inaccurate coverage, polarization, or objectivity norms that create distance between journalists and communities. For example, when residents may occasionally read a news story they encounter on social media from an outlet they don't think represents their community fairly, they might process that story through a lens of distrust and be skeptical of the story's accuracy or the journalist's motives. Likewise, journalists who lack relationships of trust with community groups or residents (perhaps because they are deterred from building them due to objectivity norms) may find it difficult to access voices and perspectives outside a narrow group of institutionalized sources, exacerbating perceptions that the community is not represented fully by their reporting. And as we saw in places like Western Kentucky, political polarization can lead residents to adapt how they move through their community—affecting what groups and people they seek out and what and whom they avoid. The cases explored in this book, then, add to communication infrastructure theory by illustrating how trust, and the factors that contribute to it, can play a role in modifying the strength and efficacy of discursive links in the storytelling network. Interventions that grow from the community-centered process model seek to strengthen trust in those network links. But because the process of building trust is a long-term effort, additional longitudinal research

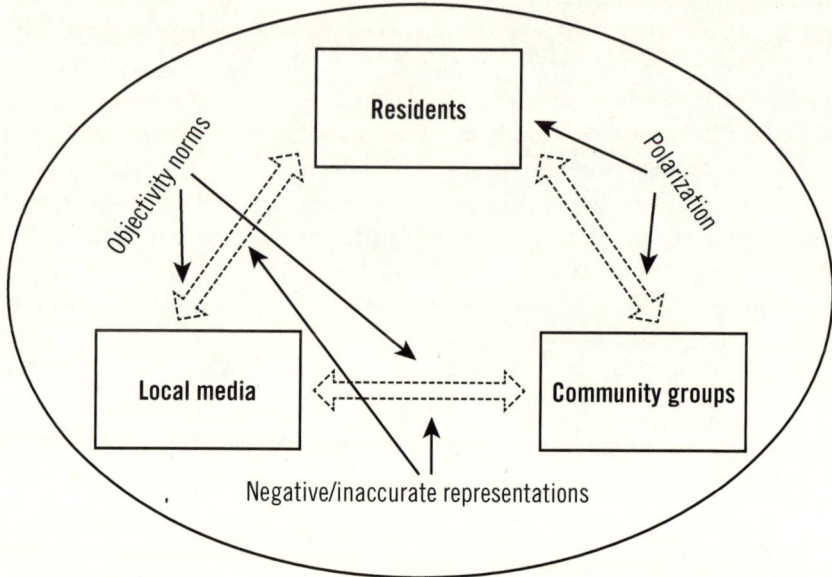

Figure 7. Barriers to Trust That Weaken Communication Infrastructure Theory's "Storytelling Network"

will be needed to fully track the extent that interventions such as these are able to affect the communication health of these communities.

While I have focused on interventions to strengthen communities, this process of incorporating solutions-oriented and engaged journalism practices will also have the effect of strengthening journalism. Building links between local media, residents, and community organizations requires expanding journalistic norms and practices to create space for a new kind of journalist. As practitioners such as Doug Oplinger of Your Voice Ohio demonstrated in chapter 5, solutions journalism requires rethinking journalism's watchdog theory of change.[4] Shining a spotlight on social ills is only one part of a journalist's responsibility. As such, practitioners and those who support them may wish to consider the following:

- Engaged journalism practices that effectively connect community members to local storytelling networks require journalists to let go of their expectations that interactions take place exclusively on their own terms. For power to be shared, the newsroom cannot remain at the center with community members at the periphery, interacting according to the newsroom's requirements and norms around what makes a good quote or a good question. Rather, journalists must find opportunities for more equitable interactions and mutual exchange for mutual benefit.
- Likewise, engaged journalism practices that are community-centered push against boundaries of detached objectivity norms. If projects like City

Bureau, Capital Public Radio's Story Circles, or the Germantown Info Hub are to effectively use community organizing strategies and create feedback and accountability loops, they must challenge taken-for-granted objectivity norms that have historically privileged whiteness and authority.

- Projects that shift from a newsroom-centered approach to a community-centered approach need journalists who are willing to combine these engaged and solutions-oriented practices in a way that pushes the boundaries of dominant journalism practices. As noted above, boundary challenges to objectivity norms are needed in order for journalists to build relationships of trust with residents and organizations, a prerequisite to strengthening local storytelling networks.
- As discussed in chapter 5, empowering the boundary work of these journalists is likely to require continued philanthropic support, at least in the short and medium term. This is why a new kind of engaged philanthropy that is open to community-led grant-making, and the funding of processes as well as projects, offers promise. This kind of philanthropy has the potential to reinforce new engaged journalism principles through grant-making that makes room for and incentivizes participatory and community-led project design and participatory evaluation.

The Solutions Journalism Network cautions journalists to not fall prey to the temptation of "silver bullet" stories that overhype an innovation as a cure-all. Likewise, even the best designed and best intentioned of these interventions offer no guarantees of success. Building relationships between media and communities is only a first step. As I can attest from personal experience, those relationships require constant, at times exhausting, care, maintenance, attention, and resources. A small conflict or misunderstanding between personalities in the community, a complaint by someone who was interviewed but not quoted in a story—such things, when left to fester, can derail colossal efforts to build trust. As Sue Robinson warned, trust "can be gained and lost fluidly."[5]

At the same time, even if they offer only incremental steps, these interventions can be important moves toward creating shared spaces for discourse so communities can grapple with the challenges they face. When Your Voice Ohio brought together residents and journalists from Youngstown to talk about efforts to address the opioid crisis, a community member thanked Doug Oplinger, the project manager, and said, "We had no idea the news media cared." One editor added, "I've never felt this kind of goodwill in the community before."[6]

The stakes for shifting to a more community-centered journalism are substantial. Facilitating this move will require a pivot away from questions of how to "save journalism" or how to restore journalism to profitability. It is of course critical to wrestle with questions of financial sustainability, and there are reasons to believe engaged and solutions journalism may be part of an equation that contributes to profitability. Establishing a link between increased trust and financial sustainability would require additional research to follow these projects over a longer period of time. However, framing these questions in a lens of restoration assumes that there was a mythical golden age of journalism, which for many marginalized communities never existed. Furthermore, even when there are no market solutions, the health of local storytelling networks should be recognized as a public good. This is a critical point, as prioritizing transactional engagement as pathway to securing financial investment is sometimes in tension with prioritizing relational engagement that shares power with communities with an aim of strengthening their communication health. While these goals at times can be complementary, the CIT framework centers around the health of communities rather than on the financial health of specific journalistic outlets. In order to avoid increasingly fragmented communities—divided along lines of race, class, and politics—it is critical to engage communities in reimagining and redesigning how news and information is gathered, shared, and funded.

Rolling back decades of distrust, which are often intertwined with unequal dynamics of power, race, class, and politics, will not be a tidy or efficient project. As the residents we met at the beginning of this book, Gwen and Steph, would attest, there are layers of bad feelings due to a sense of unfair and inaccurate representations and suspicions about journalistic motives. Those taking on the hard work of building community-centered relationships will have to be attuned to these trustworthiness factors to build or repair relationships within local storytelling networks. In an era of community-centered journalism, Gwen and Steph will need to feel like their reality is reflected in local news in a way that is respectful, even as the news grapples with stories that tackle difficult issues and challenges. They or their neighbors may take an active role in shaping how the multiplicity of their community is represented, sharing ideas with journalists, contributing stories of their own, or participating in community dialogues. Even if they have limited time to contribute to this community-centered journalism, they may start to feel that people outside their community understand them more fairly as a result of how this journalism represents them. Or the narratives circulating in their strengthened storytelling networks may give them a shared understanding of community issues, allowing them to talk with other residents and community groups about how they may take action to address issues in their community. Getting to this point will require a process of trust-building. But the openness of these women, and countless others, to at least considering solutions-oriented efforts to engage communities offers some room for optimism—that local journalists have the potential to contribute to the civic health of communities and to become more inclusive and accountable communicators along the way.

APPENDIX

Methods for a Process Model

The questions at the heart of this book center on the communication health of communities. For this reason, rather than focusing exclusively on the insides of newsrooms—for example, by using a method such as newsroom ethnography—the methods used to explore these questions draw from communication infrastructure theory,[1] a framework that looks at journalists as just one part of a larger network of local storytellers. As discussed in the introduction, CIT holds that every community has key "storytelling network" actors—residents, community organizations, and local and ethnic media—which are each involved in circulating stories about the community. Each storytelling network is situated within a "communication action context," which includes places in the community (for example, clinics, barbershops, parks) that may facilitate or constrain connection to the storytelling network. When common stories are shared in the storytelling network, residents are more likely to have a shared sense of identity and a shared understanding of community issues, including which issues may call for community-level action.

CIT is particularly well-suited to grapple with contemporary challenges of trust in today's journalism landscape because it (1) centers on multiple actors within communities rather than just on media outlets (reflecting today's more decentralized and participatory communication landscape), (2) looks at the content of stories rather than just at the quantity (a factor that is particularly relevant in historically stigmatized communities), (3) is place-based, and (4) offers a framework for assessment and, when necessary, for the design of interventions to strengthen the communicative health of communities.

In this appendix, I detail how I have adapted CIT for case studies that assess the state of local communication infrastructure and how media interventions are and are not strengthening it. I also offer an overview of how CIT can be used to codesign interventions with local stakeholders and to monitor the progress of those interventions. I share this as a way both to explain the methods I have used and to offer a model for how these methods may be adapted by researchers exploring related questions.

CIT and the Value of Qualitative Inquiry

Past CIT research studies have employed a range of both quantitative and qualitative methods to analyze the state of local storytelling networks. Here, I use qualitative methods (interviews, focus groups, ethnographic observation, and story diaries) to explore, at the meso and micro level (for example, residents, community groups, local media), issues raised by large-scale quantitative measures at the macro level (such as national surveys). As Ruth Palmer has pointed out, while public opinion surveys leave little doubt that people do not trust media, "they leave many questions unanswered."[2] Qualitative methods such as interviews and focus groups add granular shading to our understanding of national trends.

In this book, I adapted the CIT framework to design studies relevant to cases in South Los Angeles, Chicago, Western Kentucky, and Philadelphia. Research sites within each area were chosen not only to offer a range of demographic compositions and political and place identities but also because each shared an experience of marginalization or perceived stigmatization by news media. Each site also had news outlets in its area that had the potential to be part of an intervention responding to local needs and assets. Potential outlets were identified through initial consultations with local collaborators and then approached after assessing their role in local storytelling networks.

In chapters, 1, 3, and 4, I used CIT to first assess local storytelling networks. Data were collected and analyzed before the information was shared with local journalists and community stakeholders, involving them in the process of designing an intervention aimed at strengthening links in the storytelling network. In chapter 2, *Curious City*'s outreach intervention was designed and implemented by the media outlet WBEZ, so I used CIT as a framework to assess the intervention's impact using ethnographic observation and interviews. With the exception of chapter 5, which focuses on journalists' perspectives (those in the engaged and solutions journalism fields) on journalism norms, all other chapters include the perceptions of both journalists and community stakeholders. In all cases, CIT guided my research questions, how they were operationalized, and how the resulting data were interpreted and analyzed.

Exploring a variety of cases allows researchers to illustrate how different dynamics work across geographies with different place and power dynamics and different scales. The cases in South Los Angeles (chapter 1) and Chicago (chapter 2) were used to focus on CIT's storytelling network links between local news, community groups, and residents with marginalized communities. Then, the cases in Western Kentucky (chapter 3) and Philadelphia (chapter 4) built on lessons learned from chapters 1 and 2 to develop and pilot a process model. This community-centered journalism process model includes a research study, followed by participatory project design, followed by piloting and assessing impact. Below I detail the methods used to develop this model.

Assessing the Storytelling Network

The first step in the community-centered journalism process model was to assess the state of the local storytelling network, including communication needs and assets. In chapters 3 and 4, I undertook methodological triangulation using a combination of focus groups, story diaries, and interviews. Triangulating data from multiple methods enables comparisons between the data, generating stronger and more contextualized analysis.

FOCUS GROUPS

For Western Kentucky and Philadelphia sites, the initial assessment of the storytelling network began with a series of at least three focus group discussions, with most groups having between six and eight people. Participants were recruited through a combination of online postings (for example, on neighborhood Facebook groups) and snowball sampling. Applicants completed a screener questionnaire to gather basic demographic information, political identity, length of residence in the area, and availability. Participants from this pool were chosen to roughly reflect the demographics of the surrounding area in terms of ethnicity/race, gender, age, partisan affiliation, and residential tenure. Each group had two co-moderators, myself and one of three other researchers.[3] At each location, at least one of the moderators shared the same racial/ethnic background as the majority demographic group in the area. For example, for focus groups in the majority Black Germantown neighborhood, one of the co-moderators identified as Black. This was important to "establish confidence more quickly"[4] and make it more likely that participants would feel comfortable sharing experiences that connected to issues of race that otherwise would be likely to go unvoiced.

The ninety-minute semi-structured discussion included two card-based focusing exercises.[5] The first explored how participants used communication resources—not only news outlets like newspapers or television but also social media, word of mouth, and what CIT calls "communication hot spots,"[6] where information was exchanged (for example, the gym, cafés, barbershops). Participants discussed how and why they used the various sources and platforms and their order of importance. The moderators encouraged participants to discuss their choices and habits but avoided direct prompts referencing concepts such as trust, disinformation, or solutions journalism so as to allow participants to discuss their practices and views using their own terms.

The second exercise presented participants with a series of statements about news media and invited them to place the statements on a continuum from "strongly agree" to "strongly disagree" (for example, "News outlets have a good understanding of the issues most important to people in my community"). This section ensured that participants directly addressed issues that may or may not have emerged unprompted in the first section.

Finally, participants were asked to complete a brief visioning exercise, sketching or jotting notes individually about how they would imagine a future news environment in which they felt they and their community had a healthy relationship with the news.

These visions were then discussed with the larger group to elicit a better understanding of current barriers to trust as well as possible pathways forward.

Focus groups were used because of their track record in CIT research as well as in exploring news and information needs. Researching news needs in New Jersey, Kathleen McCollough, Jessica K. Crowell, and Philip M. Napoli used focus groups to elicit "perceptions of the news and sources available to them and the means by which they go about trying to meet their news and information needs."[7] Focus groups added value by documenting interactions among participants: "In the process of discussing and reacting to other participants' ideas, a richer and more deeply refined set of findings may emerge than would be possible through individual discussion alone."[8] Focus groups cannot be used to generalize about a population,[9] but the method allows participants to reflect on how they understand and make meaning of communication resources within their news ecosystems.

STORY DIARIES AND INTERVIEWS

At the conclusion of the focus groups, participants were given "story diaries" to complete (either electronic or hard copy forms, depending on their preference). These diaries invited participants to log for one week up to five stories a day that resonated with them. They noted not only what a story was about and how they found out about it (through either mediated or interpersonal channels) but also why it interested them, how it related to their life, and whether they shared the story or attempted to find out more about it. Rather than a traditional media diary where researchers attempt to capture a comprehensive picture of media use, I used story diaries to seek insights into how narratives circulated in participants' storytelling networks. Participants also noted whom they interacted with that day and where the interaction took place, offering a picture of how residents were was connected to other residents and community groups in the storytelling network.

These diaries were then used as jumping-off points for one-on-one follow-up interviews (usually about forty-five minutes), where participants discussed in greater detail how they did and did not interact with a local storytelling network (local media, organizations, fellow residents, and so on). The semi-structured interviews offered an opportunity to clarify points in the story diaries (for example, if the week was atypical for any reason) and to discuss in greater depth examples of stories they noted and whom they shared them with. The interview protocol also included questions about participants' opinions toward media outlets and what it would look like for them to do a better job, how they felt their community was represented, and how they thought about the role of news media.

INTERVIEWS WITH LOCAL MEDIA

In addition to interviews with community members, I also conducted interviews with editors, publishers, and reporters from local media outlets in order to get a better understanding of the local media environment. These journalists were asked about their outlets, what challenges they faced, how they conceived of their audiences, and any outreach or engagement they attempted. Gathering data from both community members and journalists allows researchers to reflect on how each group perceives the other and its practices and to contextualize the relationship between the two.

THE BENEFITS OF TRIANGULATION

Methodological triangulation adds value as it allows the strength of one method to counterbalance the weakness of another.[10] The different methods can act as a sort of check on each other, yielding more than the sum of their parts.

One of the biggest vulnerabilities of these methods is that they all rely on self-reported data. Researchers have found that self-reported data on how much and what media people use tend to be skewed due to social desirability and overreporting.[11] This study has not focused on claims of how much or how often participants engage with particular sources, in part for this reason. However, interviews and focus groups have offered an opportunity to gain textured data on how participants make meaning from and assign trust to various sources—and (in focus groups) how they present and defend their practices and interpretations among peers.

Researchers have found triangulation to be particularly helpful when incorporating methods such as diaries.[12] In the cases presented in this book, I also found this to be true. For many participants, the practice of keeping a diary prompted self-reflection. By logging stories throughout the day, participants were often left with a different picture of their media habits from the one they had previously conceived of. For example, several participants who expressed during focus groups that they got news from multiple ideological perspectives shared during our interview about their diaries that they had been surprised to see all or almost all of their stories came from one source. And for participants who were less reflexive, the diaries themselves offered an additional layer of data that could be checked against participants' statements elsewhere.

To synthesize this data, transcripts of focus group discussions and interviews were thematically coded and analyzed[13] using the NVivo coding platform. Thematic categories were developed in response to research questions. Subthemes were then added and refined based on initial coding of recurring or theoretically relevant moments.

Participatory Design Process

As discussed earlier in the book, I take a normative stance that a healthy and inclusive local communication infrastructure is a goal that can and should be pursued through academic scholarship and practice. For this reason, once case studies analyzing local storytelling networks were complete, I worked with colleagues and local stakeholders in a participatory process to design potential interventions based on research findings.

To do this, when focus groups, story diaries, and interviews were completed, preliminary reports were circulated to study participants and other community and media stakeholders. I then worked with colleagues to organize workshops with community members (including some study participants), community organization representatives, local journalists, and representatives of various engaged and solutions journalism initiatives from elsewhere in the United States. At these workshops we discussed findings and shared examples of solutions journalism and engaged journalism projects from elsewhere. We then broke up into small groups to brainstorm possible initiatives that would respond to local needs and assets identified in each study and could perhaps strengthen the local storytelling network. Here, as researchers, my colleagues and I acted as "interstitial actors"[14] connecting storytelling network actors and working with them to design an intervention.

Piloting Interventions

The interventions that grew out of each participatory design process varied based on local needs and assets and the perspectives of the various stakeholders involved in the process. I offer more detail on the pilot interventions we developed in Western Kentucky and the Philadelphia region in chapters 3 and 4. Despite their differences, there are some shared logistical considerations. In each case, following the workshops was a cycle of follow-up to further develop and seek feedback on the intervention ideas outlined at the workshops. This process of eliciting input, clarification, and feedback was also an opportunity to build investment in the project idea and to begin to form shared expectations between potential partners. The more detailed the project ideas became, the more critical it was for us to ensure that partners—from media outlets to community members—had a clear understanding of their goals, their responsibilities, and the resources they needed to implement the pilot intervention. Once we had concepts and budgets drafted, we were able to seek out seed funding with our partners to pilot the projects and conduct additional research. Depending on the situation, it may alternatively be possible to hand over the plans that have been developed to media or community stakeholders, allowing them to seek additional support separately. This may be more likely in cases where project partners come from larger organizations with more institutional capacity than was the case here.

Part of designing interventions, of course, is also determining how they may be effectively monitored and evaluated. As discussed in chapter 5, there is a range of approaches possible to measure what a successful intervention would look like. For the cases explored in Western Kentucky and Philadelphia's Germantown neighborhood, the pilot interventions are still in early stages. However, plans are underway to monitor and assess the extent the projects are or are not strengthening ties between local news media, residents, and community groups.

Because these projects are designed using a CIT framework, they adapt Garrett Broad's CIT-based evaluation questions:

- Does an intervention or program strengthen the neighborhood storytelling network by building networked connections between and among local residents, geo-ethnic media, and community-based organizations?
- Does an intervention or program enhance the ability of the communication action context to promote discursive interaction between and among community storytellers?

Broad offers a third evaluation question that may cause projects attached to dominant journalism norms to bristle:

- Does an intervention or program successfully disseminate a story that motivates change at the individual and/or community level?[15]

Whether this third question is applicable would depend upon the details of the project that has been designed.

For these cases, some early research has been conducted in Western Kentucky via observation and interviews, and observation, interviews, and focus groups will take place in Germantown. Both projects also either have used the Reflective Practice Guide[16] referenced in chapter 5 or plan to adapt it. The guide allows projects to measure their progress against goals including network building, holding space for discussion, distributing ownership, and persistent input. Periodically tracking progress through such a process enables projects to make course corrections through the project rather than evaluating only at the end.

A Portable and Adaptable Process

The CIT-based methods used in this book were selected to fit the project's particular needs and research questions. Triangulating focus groups, story diaries, and interviews allowed me to assess local storytelling networks in marginalized communities. Including the perspectives of community members and journalists allowed me to put both news and information use practices and journalistic practices into context. Working with colleagues in Western Kentucky and Philadelphia, I then followed these studies with a process of participatory intervention design and piloting, adapting to local needs, assets, and dynamics of power and place. Because the study emphasized a process rather than a particular intervention project, it was possible to apply the process to these two very different places. Likewise, I believe this process model has the potential to assess local storytelling networks and design follow-up interventions in a number of other communities with different dynamics and complications.

This process model for designing research-based, community-centered journalism interventions is, of course, adaptable. There are other methodological options to diagnose the state of local storytelling networks and to design and evaluate interventions attempting to strengthen links between local media, residents, and community groups. Researchers could weave in a survey or additional ethnographic observation or conduct focus groups segmented by type of storytelling network actor (local media, resident, community organization representative). The possibilities vary greatly depending on the local context and, of course, the availability of resources. The cases referenced in chapter 5 offer numerous additional examples for assessing information needs and assets and involving community members in the process. Regardless, particularly for researchers interested in playing an interstitial role in facilitating community-centered journalism, CIT offers a framework that can inform a range of options in the methodological toolbox.

Notes

Preface

1. AEP has since become an independent Afghan NGO called Afghan Education Production Organization.

2. The research process supporting AEP's work was initially designed in consultation with Gerry Power, who previously directed the Research and Learning team for BBC Media Action (at the time BBC World Service Trust). Power was a former student of Dr. Sandra Ball-Rokeach, the scholar who, along with her Metamorphosis research group, developed communication infrastructure theory—a framework I return to throughout this book. I learned about this only years later after I coincidentally had also become Dr. Ball-Rokeach's student.

Introduction

1. Names of interview and focus group participants from the four locations (Chicago, South Los Angeles, Western Kentucky, and the Philadelphia region) highlighted in the book have been changed unless otherwise noted.

2. Interview with Gwen, Chicago, May 31, 2016. Quotes in the next few paragraphs are from this interview. All interviews in the book were conducted by the author unless otherwise noted.

3. Interview with Steph, Beaver Dam, KY, May 19, 2017. Quotes in the next few paragraphs are from this interview.

4. Solutions Journalism Network, https://www.solutionsjournalism.org/who-we-are/mission (accessed January 17, 2019).

5. See the section below for more discussion of communication infrastructure theory. See also Ball-Rokeach, Kim, and Matei, "Storytelling Neighborhood"; and Kim and Ball-Rokeach, "Civic Engagement."

6. WBEZ Worldview's Global Activism series was started in 2004 and ran for fifteen years until the show ended in 2019; see https://www.wbez.org/playlists/global-activism/c6a33cd5-5138-4e1a-8fe7-1b0dc7b44835.

7. Knight Foundation, *American Views: Trust, Media and Democracy*, Gallup/Knight Foundation Survey, 2018, https://kf-site-production.s3.amazonaws.com/publications/pdfs/000/000/242/original/KnightFoundation_AmericansViews_Client_Report_010917_Final_Updated.pdf (accessed January 17, 2019).

8. Zuckerman, "Mistrust."

9. Schudson and Tift, "American Journalism."

10. Ladd, *Why Americans Hate the Media*, 203.

11. Konieczna, *Journalism without Profit*.

12. See Michelle Ferrier's work for a discussion of media deserts on the Media Deserts Project website, https://mediadeserts.wordpress.com.

13. Indira Lakshmanan, "Finally Some Good News: Trust in News Is Up, Especially for Local Media," Poynter, https://www.poynter.org/ethics-trust/2018/finally-some-good-news-trust-in-news-is-up-especially-for-local-media/ (accessed January 17, 2019); Amy Mitchell, Jeffrey Gottfried, Elisa Shearer, and Michael Barthel, "Trust and Accuracy," Pew Research Center, http://www.journalism.org/2016/07/07/trust-and-accuracy/ (accessed January 17, 2019).

14. Josh Stearns, "Local News Is a Building Block to Rebuild Trust," Medium, https://medium.com/trust-media-and-democracy/local-news-is-a-building-block-to-rebuild-trust-fab8752f3659 (accessed January 17, 2019).

15. Fletcher and Park, "Impact of Trust."

16. Kohring and Matthes, "Trust in News Media."

17. Mayer, Davis, and Schoorman, "Integrative Model of Organizational Trust."

18. Robinson, *Networked News*, 25.

19. Robinson, 727.

20. Schudson, *Sociology of News*.

21. Gans, *News and the News Media*, 15.

22. Tuchman, *Making News*, 214.

23. Presentation by David Bornstein at Temple University, September 26, 2018.

24. Lippmann, *Stakes of Diplomacy*, 198.

25. Presentation by David Bornstein at Temple University.

26. For an example of the *Cleveland Plain Dealer*'s solutions journalism reporting, see "Lead Poisoning Is a Tough Problem but Here Are Some Solutions: Toxic Neglect," October 23, 2015, https://www.cleveland.com/healthfit/index.ssf/2015/10/yes_lead_poisoning_is_a_tough.html.

27. Presentation by David Bornstein at Temple University.

28. Communication with SJN's director of communities, May 31, 2018, and May 13, 2019.

29. Galtung, "On the Role of the Media."

30. Galtung and Fischer, "High Road, Low Road."

31. Lee and Maslog, "War or Peace Journalism?"

32. Hanitzsch, "Situating Peace Journalism."

33. Iggers, *Good News, Bad News*.

34. See, for example, this interview by the founder of the Constructive Institute in Denmark with Galtung: Ulrik Haagerup, "Academic Who Defined News Principles Says

Journalists Are Too Negative," *The Guardian*, January 18, 2019, https://www.theguardian.com/world/2019/jan/18/johan-galtung-news-principles-journalists-too-negative.

35. Rosen, "Challenge of Public Journalism," 44.
36. Massey, "Civic Journalism and Nonelite Sourcing," 395.
37. Friedland and Nichols, *Measuring Civic Journalism's Progress*, 2.
38. Kurpius, "Sources and Civic Journalism."
39. Glasser and Lee, "Repositioning the Newsroom."
40. Deuze, "What Is Journalism?"
41. Ekdale et al., "Making Change."
42. Angelica Das, "Pathways to Engagement: Understanding How Newsrooms Are Working with Communities," Democracy Fund, https://www.democracyfund.org/publications/pathways-to-engagement-understanding-how-newsrooms-are-working-with-communi (accessed January 17, 2019); Batsell, *Engaged Journalism*.
43. Lewis, Holton, and Coddington, "Reciprocal Journalism."
44. Rodriguez, "Latin American Approach."
45. Gillmor, *We the Media*, 120.
46. Rosen, "People Formerly Known as the Audience."
47. Jenkins, *Convergence Culture*.
48. Lindsay Green-Barber, "Towards a Useful Typology of Engaged Journalism," Medium, https://medium.com/the-impact-architects/towards-a-useful-typology-of-engaged-journalism-790c96c4577e (accessed January 17, 2019).
49. Lischka and Messerli, "Examining the Benefits."
50. Lewis, Holton, and Coddington, "Reciprocal Journalism," 229.
51. Belair-Gagnon, Nelson, and Lewis, "Audience Engagement," 5.
52. For a discussion of where journalists fall on a continuum from thin to thicker engagement, see Lawrence, Radcliffe, and Schmidt, "Practicing Engagement."
53. Andrew DeVigal, "The Continuum of Engagement," Medium, https://medium.com/lets-gather/the-continuum-of-engagement-89778f9d6c3a (accessed January 17, 2019).
54. For an example of how the Hearken consulting group has defined and measured engagement, see "Looking for Evidence That Audience Engagement Helps Newsrooms? Here You Go," Medium, May 3, 2018, https://medium.com/we-are-hearken/receipts-1bc3d35a88bf.
55. Nelson, "Elusive Engagement Metric"
56. Gieryn, *Cultural Boundaries of Science*.
57. Carlson, "Introduction."
58. Bourdieu, *Field of Cultural Production*.
59. Robinson, *Networked News*, 74.
60. Spivak, "Can the Subaltern Speak?"
61. Rutherford, "Third Space," 208.
62. Frankenberg, *White Women, Race Matters*, 197.
63. Schudson, "Objectivity Norm"
64. Carey, "'A Republic, If You Can Keep It,'" 220.
65. Ball-Rokeach, Kim, and Matei, "Storytelling Neighborhood"; Kim and Ball-Rokeach, "Civic Engagement."
66. I was a member of the Metamorphosis Project research group from 2014 to 2017.
67. Anderson, *Imagined Communities*.

68. Broad, Gonzalez, and Ball-Rokeach, "Intergroup Relations."
69. Ali, *Media Localism*.
70. Friedland, *Communication, Community, and Democracy*.
71. Ali, *Media Localism*, 766.
72. Ball-Rokeach, Kim, and Matei, "Storytelling Neighborhood"; Matei and Ball-Rokeach, "Watts"; Sampson, *Great American City*.
73. Broad, Gonzalez, and Ball-Rokeach, "Intergroup Relations"; Son and Ball-Rokeach, "Whole Community."
74. Palmer, *Becoming the News*.
75. Villanueva et al., "Communication Asset Mapping."
76. Villanueva et al., "Bringing Local Voices into Community Revitalization."
77. Villanueva and Wenzel, "Engaged Communication Scholar."
78. Broad, "Communication Infrastructure Theory."
79. Alhambra Source was founded by principal investigators Sandra Ball-Rokeach and Michael Parks, working with editor Daniela Gerson. The Metamorphosis research group, which I later joined, provided ongoing monitoring and research of the project and its impact on civic engagement.
80. Gerson et al., "From Audience to Reporter."
81. Chen et al., "Causing Ripples."
82. Kristen Hare, "Local Edition: How a Tiny Nonprofit Is Listening to and Working with the Community," Poynter, https://www.poynter.org/news/local-edition-how-tiny-nonprofit-listening-and-working-community-including-lawn-bowlers (accessed January 17, 2019); Phoenix Tso, "The Federal Money behind the Almansor Park Improvement Debate," Alhambra Source, https://www.alhambrasource.org/story/the-federal-money-behind-the-almansor-park-improvements-debate (accessed January 17, 2019).
83. Daniela Gerson, "4 Lessons Learned about Community Engagement from the Alhambra Source," Mediashift, http://mediashift.org/2015/09/4-lessons-learned-about-community-engagement-from-alhambra-source/ (accessed January 17, 2019).
84. Cheng, *Changs Next Door*; Wenzel, "Eating Together, Separately."

Chapter 1. Shifting Stories with Solutions Journalism

1. For a discussion on the importance of terms used to describe unrest, see Paul Bisceglio, "There's a Difference between Riots and Rebellion," UCLA Newsroom, July 13, 2015, http://newsroom.ucla.edu/stories/theres-a-difference-between-riots-and-rebellion.
2. United States National Advisory Commission on Civil Disorders, *Kerner Report*.
3. McCone and Christopher, "Violence in the City," 84.
4. McCone and Christopher, 84.
5. Three workshops were held at the University of Southern California in March 2015. Quotes from workshop participants throughout the chapter are from the first two workshops. The first brought together community organization representatives, including Sarah, Claudia, Arturo, Antoine, Will, and Brenda. The second included journalists, including Steve, Mercedes, Hector, and Imani.
6. Ball-Rokeach, Kim, and Matei, "Storytelling Neighborhood"; Matei and Ball-Rokeach. "Watts"; Sampson, *Great American City*.
7. See the introduction for more discussion of communication infrastructure theory's concept of the "storytelling network."

8. See introduction for a more detailed discussion of communication infrastructure theory; Ball-Rokeach, Kim, and Matei, "Storytelling Neighborhood"; and Kim and Ball-Rokeach, "Civic Engagement."

9. Pastor, "Keeping It Real," 34.

10. According to 2016 American Community Survey; see https://censusreporter.org/profiles/79500US0603751-los-angeles-county-south-central-la-city-south-centralwatts-puma-ca/.

11. Pastor, "Keeping It Real," 34.

12. Robinson and Culver, "When White Reporters Cover Race."

13. Robinson and Culver, "When White Reporters Cover Race."

14. Hall et al., *Policing the Crisis*.

15. Galtung and Ruge, "Structure of Foreign News."

16. As discussed below, researchers have found that television tends to disproportionately depict Black and Latinx people as lawbreakers. See Dixon and Linz, "Overrepresentation and Underrepresentation."

17. Matei and Ball-Rokeach. "Watts."

18. Broad, Gonzalez, and Ball-Rokeach, "Intergroup Relations."

19. Interview with Los Angeles Times reporter, Los Angeles, February 2015.

20. Our meeting with various journalists in preparation for our combined workshop was held at the University of Southern California in March 2015. Quotes from journalists in the following section are from this meeting. Participants included Steve, Mercedes, Hector, and Imani.

21. Our first workshop with community organization representatives was held at the University of Southern California in March 2015. Quotes from representatives are from this meeting. Participants included Sarah, Claudia, Arturo, Antoine, Will, and Brenda.

22. Soroka and McAdams, "Experimental Study."

23. Fiske, "Attention and Weight in Person Perception."

24. Hilbig, "Sad, Thus True."

25. Newhagen and Reeves, "Evening's Bad News."

26. Brader, "Striking a Responsive Chord"; Geer, *In Defense of Negativity*; Shah et al., "Political Consumerism."

27. Matsaganis, "Rediscovering the Communication Engine"; Nicholson et al., "Unintended Effects."

28. Newman et al., "Digital News Report."

29. Harcup and O'Neill, "What Is News?"

30. Boorstin, *Image*; Gandy, "Information in Health."

31. Broad, Gonzalez, and Ball-Rokeach, "Intergroup Relations."

32. For a discussion of the Latasha Harlins incident, see Angel Jennings, "How the Killing of Latasha Harlins Changed South L.A., Long before Black Lives Matter," *Los Angeles Times*, March 18, 2016, http://www.latimes.com/local/california/la-me-0318-latasha-harlins-20160318-story.html.

33. This section adapts research that informed Wenzel et al., "Engaging Stigmatized Communities."

34. This A/B story model was adapted from the Solutions Journalism Network and Engaging News model. Thanks to both SJN and Engaging News staff members for offering input on sample stories.

35. Raven, focus group discussion with African American residents (Group 1), Los Angeles, October 24, 2015. Further quotes from Raven are from this discussion.

36. For details on the 100 Days, 100 Nights incident, see "100 Days, 100 Nights: How LAPD Is Dealing with Rumors, Gangs and Fear," *Los Angeles Times*, August 9, 2015, http://homicide.latimes.com/post/100-days-100-nights-lapd-qa/.

37. Her case and others resonate with more recent findings about news avoidance and perceived negativity: Nic Newman, "Overview and Key Findings of the 2017 Report," Reuters Institute Digital News Report, http://www.digitalnewsreport.org/survey/2017/overview-key-findings-2017/ (accessed January 17, 2019).

38. Marisol, focus group discussion with Latinx residents (Group 2), Los Angeles, October 24, 2015.

39. Jamal, focus group discussion with African American residents (Group 6), Los Angeles, November 7, 2015.

40. Mayer, Davis, and Schoorman, "Integrative Model."

41. Focus group discussion with African American residents (Group 6), Los Angeles, November 7, 2015.

42. Focus group discussion with Latinx residents (Group 3), Los Angeles, October 24, 2015.

43. Dixon and Linz, "Overrepresentation and Underrepresentation."

44. Dixon, "Crime News and Racialized Beliefs."

45. Tyler, focus group discussion with African American residents (Group 5), Los Angeles, November 7, 2015.

46. For example, see "Portrayal and Perception: Two Audits of News Media Reporting on African American Men and Boys," Open Society Foundation, November 1, 2011, https://www.opensocietyfoundations.org/sites/default/files/portrayal-and-perception-20111101.pdf.

47. See "Not to Be Trusted: Dangerous Levels of Inaccuracy in TV Crime Reporting in NYC," Color of Change, March 2015, https://s3.amazonaws.com/s3.colorofchange.org/images/ColorOfChangeNewsAccuracyReportCardNYC.pdf

48. Entman and Rojecki, *Black Image in the White Mind*, 84.

49. Jamal, focus group discussion.

50. Duane, focus group discussion with African American residents (Group 6), Los Angeles, November 7, 2015.

51. Sue et al., "Racial Microaggressions in Everyday Life."

52. López, *Dog Whistle Politics*.

53. Jackson, *Racial Paranoia*, 3.

54. Manuel, focus group discussion with Latinx residents (Group 2), Los Angeles, October 24, 2015.

55. Duane, focus group discussion.

56. Focus group discussion with Latinx residents (Group 2), Los Angeles, October 24, 2015.

57. Duane, focus group discussion.

58. Jamal, focus group discussion.

59. Javier, focus group discussion with Latinx residents (Group 3), Los Angeles, October 24, 2015.

60. Tuchman, *Making News*, 214.

61. For instance, Bianca, focus group discussion with Latinx residents (Group 3), Los Angeles, October 24, 2015.

62. Duane, focus group discussion.
63. Robinson and Culver, "When White Reporters Cover Race"; Ward, "Inventing Objectivity."
64. Robinson and Culver, "When White Reporters Cover Race," 376.
65. Keanna, focus group discussion with African American residents (Group 6), Los Angeles, November 7, 2015.
66. Curry and Hammonds, "Power of Solutions Journalism."
67. Jamal, focus group discussion.
68. Mayer, Davis, and Schoorman, "Integrative Model."
69. The project did not continue due to funding and resource limitations on the university research group.

Chapter 2. Connecting Journalists and Community Members

1. WBEZ, "Curious City," WBEZ.org, https://www.wbez.org/shows/curious-city/ (accessed July 27, 2019).
2. Interview with Shawn Allee, December 5, 2016. This interview is the source of his quotes below.
3. Chris Bentley, "What Really Happens to Chicago's Blue Cart Recycling," WBEZ.org, https://www.wbez.org/shows/curious-city/what-really-happens-to-chicagos-blue-cart-recycling/42d45307-001f-48ee-a649-9a63c7cceba2 (accessed July 27, 2019).
4. Vocalo initially experimented with including content produced by listeners and later by youth radio producers. This format was later abandoned, and the station was rebranded as an "urban alternative music station" that incorporated talk content. Vocalo, "About," Volcalo.org, http://vocalo.org/about (accessed January 17, 2019).
5. Some may know Malatia as the cofounder of *This American Life*, referenced at the end of each episode.
6. As an example of Malatia's interests and influences, in 2007 he authored a nearly 16,000-word treatise on the future of public radio quoting Carey, along with John Dewey, Richard Sennett, and many others: Torey Malatia, "Potential Difference: Redesigning Public Radio for a Changing Society," Current.org, https://current.org/wp-content/uploads/archive-site/radio/radio00708vocalo-extended.pdf (accessed January 17, 2019).
7. Interview with Torey Malatia, January 17, 2019. The quotes in the next paragraph are also from this interview.
8. Jennifer Brandel, "Curious and Curiouser: Localore Project Aims to Open WBEZ's Editorial Process," Airmedia.org, https://airmedia.org/curious-and-curiouser-localore-project-aims-open-wbezs-editorial-process/ (accessed January 17, 2019).
9. Correspondence with Jennifer Brandel, May 13, 2019.
10. For a diagram of Hearken's "story cycle" model, see Hearken, https://www.wearehearken.com/hearken-overview-about/.
11. Schmidt and Lawrence, "Putting Engagement to Work."
12. Interview with Jennifer Brandel, January 17, 2017.
13. Lewis, Holton, and Coddington, "Reciprocal Journalism," 233.
14. Belair-Gagnon, Nelson, and Lewis, "Audience Engagement."
15. Jennifer Brandel, "Looking for Evidence That Audience Engagement Helps Newsrooms? Here You Go," Medium.com, https://medium.com/we-are-hearken/receipts-1bc3d35a88bf (accessed January 17, 2019).

16. Ball-Rokeach, Kim, and Matei, "Storytelling Neighborhood"; Kim and Ball-Rokeach, "Civic Engagement."

17. Carey, "Press, Public Opinion, and Public Discourse," 238.

18. For *Curious City*'s visualization of where questions had previously originated, see "Chicago Community Areas," Carto, 2016, https://curiouscity.carto.com/viz/a2be4f36-de52-11e6-b2c6-0ecd1babdde5/public_map.

19. WBEZ Curious City, "How Can Curious City Diversify the Pool of People Who Ask Questions?," Tumblr, 2016, http://wbezcuriouscity.tumblr.com/post/140362287302/how-can-curious-city-diversify-the-pool-of-people (accessed January 17, 2019).

20. Niall McCarthy, "The World's Largest Cities by Area," Statista.com, https://www.statista.com/chart/13966/the-worlds-largest-cities-by-area/ (accessed January 17, 2019).

21. City of Chicago, "City of Chicago Community Areas," Chicago.gov, http://www.cityofchicago.org/content/dam/city/depts/doit/general/GIS/Chicago_Maps/Community_Areas/Community_Areas_w_Number.pdf (accessed January 17, 2019).

22. Chicago neighborhood names and boundaries fluctuate and are contested; see "Chicago Neighborhoods," City of Chicago, http://www.cityofchicago.org/content/dam/city/depts/doit/general/GIS/Chicago_Maps/Citywide_Maps/City_Neighborhoods_1978_11x17.pdf (accessed January 17, 2019).

23. Massey and Denton, *American Apartheid*.

24. Sampson, *Great American City*, 306.

25. For a history of restrictive covenants that prevented property owners from selling or renting to African Americans around the city and in northern suburbs, see "Restrictive Covenants," Encyclopedia of Chicago, http://www.encyclopedia.chicagohistory.org/pages/1067.html (accessed January 17, 2019).

26. For a discussion of redlining's historical author and present legacy, see "A Tax on Blackness," Slate, May 13, 2015, http://www.slate.com/articles/news_and_politics/politics/2015/05/racism_in_real_estate_landlords_redlining_housing_values_and_discrimination.html.

27. Alvarez, "Community That Would Not Take 'No' for an Answer."

28. American Community Survey, "Demographic and Housing Estimates," American FactFinder, https://factfinder.census.gov/faces/tableservices/jsf/pages/productview.xhtml?src=CF (accessed November 9, 2019).

29. Nate Silver, "The Most Diverse Cities Are Often the Most Segregated," Fivethirtyeight.com, http://fivethirtyeight.com/features/the-most-diverse-cities-are-often-the-most-segregated/ (accessed January 17, 2019).

30. Lolly Bowean, "Segregation Declines in Chicago but City Still Ranks High, Census Data Show," *Chicago Tribune*, January 4, 2016, http://www.chicagotribune.com/news/ct-segregation-declines-neighborhoods-change-met-20160103-story.html.

31. Hwang and Sampson, "Divergent Pathways of Gentrification."

32. *New York Times* and Kaiser Family Foundation, "Poll of Chicago," Documentcloud.org, https://www.documentcloud.org/documents/2824824-Chicago-Trn-Final.html (accessed January 17, 2019).

33. For background on gun violence during the period of this study, see "Gun Violence in Chicago, 2016," Urban Labs, January 2017, http://urbanlabs.uchicago.edu/projects/gun-violence-in-chicago-2016.

34. Emily Van Duyn, Jay Jennings, and Natalie J. Stroud, "Chicago News Landscape," Center for Media Engagement, https://mediaengagement.org/wp-content/uploads/2018/01/CME-Chicago-News-Landscape-Report.pdf (accessed January 17, 2019).
35. Interview with Dorothy, Chicago, May 31, 2016.
36. Hall et al., *Policing the Crisis*.
37. Bennett et al., "'Video Malaise' Revisited."
38. Mayer, Davis, and Schoorman, "Integrative Model."
39. Interview with two women, Chicago, May 31, 2016.
40. Interview with Kyle, Chicago, May 31, 2016. Quotes from Kyle below are from this interview.
41. Interview with Tom, May 31, 2016. Quotes from Tom in the following two paragraphs are from this interview.
42. Interview with journalist 2, October 6, 2016.
43. Interview with journalist 2.
44. Interview with journalist 3, October 6, 2016.
45. For an example of industry discussions around transparency and trust, see "Josh Stearns Status," Twitter, December 18, 2018, https://twitter.com/jcstearns/status/1075214539577327616.
46. Interview with Tom, June 29, 2016.
47. Manny Ramos, "Cook County Black Population Continues to Decline," *Chicago Sun-Times*, June 20, 2018, https://chicago.suntimes.com/news/cook-county-black-population-continues-to-decline-census-data/; "Seeking a New Mayor, Chicago Sees Many Black Residents Voting with Their Feet," New York Times, February 25, 2019, https://www.nytimes.com/2019/02/25/us/chicago-mayoral-election.html.
48. The Listening Post Collective has put together guides for how journalists can more systematically approach listening sessions; see "Listening Post Playbook," Listening Post Collective, https://www.listeningpostcollective.org/playbook/listen (accessed January 17, 2019).
49. Interview with journalist 2.
50. Interview with journalist 4, October 7, 2016.
51. Interview with Torey Malatia.
52. Interview with resident, Chicago, May 31, 2016.
53. Lewis, Holton, and Coddington, "Reciprocal Journalism," 235.
54. Interview with Tom, May 31, 2016.
55. Interview with leader of youth organization, July 30, 2016.
56. Interview with Tom, June 29, 2016.
57. Interview with Emily, a library staffer, June 29, 2016.
58. Center for Cooperative Media, http://centerforcooperativemedia.org (accessed January 17, 2019).
59. Resolve Philadelphia, https://resolvephilly.org (accessed January 17, 2019).
60. Christine Schmidt, "Nine Local Partners in Charlotte Form a New Reporting Collaborative with Solutions Journalism Network and the Knight Foundation," Nieman Lab, https://www.niemanlab.org/2019/03/nine-local-partners-in-charlotte-form-a-new-reporting-collaborative-with-solutions-journalism-network-and-the-knight-foundation/ (accessed January 17, 2019).
61. City Bureau, https://www.citybureau.org (accessed January 17, 2019).

62. Public media collaboration with hyperlocal initiatives will be explored further in chapter 4.
63. Interview with Shawn Allee, December 5, 2016.
64. Allee and Healy, "Curious City Questions Project."
65. Eryn Carlson, "Journalism and Libraries: 'Both Exist to Support Strong, Well-Informed Communities,'" Nieman Reports, June 19, 2019, https://niemanreports.org/articles/journalism-and-libraries-both-exist-to-support-strong-well-informed-communities/.
66. A. W. Geiger, "Most Americans—Especially Millennials—Say Libraries Can Help Them Find Reliable, Trustworthy Information," Pew Research Center, http://www.pewresearch.org/fact-tank/2017/08/30/most-americans-especially-millennials-say-libraries-can-help-them-find-reliable-trustworthy-information/ (accessed January 17, 2019).
67. Interview with Torey Malatia.
68. Lewis, Holton, and Coddington, "Reciprocal Journalism," 233.
69. Belair-Gagnon, Nelson, and Lewis "Audience Engagement."
70. Community organizing strategies and how these approaches intersect with perceptions of the role of journalists will be discussed in more depth in chapter 5.
71. Spivak, "Can the Subaltern Speak?"

Chapter 3. Developing an Intervention

1. Interview with Heather, May 19, 2017. The quotes in the following paragraphs are also from this interview.
2. See chapter 2.
3. Nic Newman, "Overview and Key Findings of the 2017 Report," Reuters Institute Digital News Report, http://www.digitalnewsreport.org/survey/2017/overview-key-findings-2017/ (accessed January 17, 2019).
4. Zuckerman, "Mistrust," 4.
5. These sections adapt research that informed Wenzel, "Red State, Purple Town." This project took place in three main phases: (1) our initial research study (April–June 2017), (2) a workshop to connect stakeholders in a participatory design process (August 2017), and (3) a study of a pilot project by a hyperlocal news outlet (November 2017–February 2018). The project was done in partnership with Sam Ford, a Bowling Green–based media consultant with affiliations with MIT and Columbia's Tow Center for Digital Journalism.
6. "2016 Kentucky Presidential Election Results," Politico, http://www.politico.com/2016-election/results/map/president/kentucky/ (accessed January 17, 2019).
7. Amy Mitchell and Michael Barthel, "Americans' Attitudes about the News Media Deeply Divided along Partisan Lines," Pew Research Center, http://www.journalism.org/2017/05/10/americans-attitudes-about-the-news-media-deeply-divided-along-partisan-lines/ (accessed January 17, 2019).
8. "Partisans Differ Widely in Views of Police Officers, College Professors," Pew Research Center, http://www.people-press.org/2017/09/13/partisans-differ-widely-in-views-of-police-officers-college-professors/ (accessed January 17, 2019).
9. Bishop, *Big Sort*.
10. Johnston, Manley, and Jones, "Spatial Polarization of Presidential Voting."
11. Cramer, *Politics of Resentment*, 217.
12. Ali, *Media Localism*.

13. Friedland, "Communication, Community, and Democracy."
14. Ball-Rokeach, Kim, and Matei, "Storytelling Neighborhood"; Kim and Ball-Rokeach, "Civic Engagement."
15. Wilkin, "Exploring the Potential."
16. Chen, Ognyanova, and Zhao, "Communication and Socio-demographic Forces."
17. See chapter 1 and also Wenzel et al., "Engaging Stigmatized Communities."
18. Villanueva and Wenzel, "Engaged Communication Scholar."
19. Broad, "Communication Infrastructure Theory"; Wenzel, "Public Media and Marginalized Publics."
20. Vanessa, Focus group discussion, Bowling Green, April 11, 2017.
21. Samantha Schmidt and Lindsey Bever, "Kellyanne Conway Cites 'Bowling Green Massacre' That Never Happened to Defend Travel Ban," *Washington Post*, February 3, 2017, https://www.washingtonpost.com/news/morning-mix/wp/2017/02/03/kellyanne-conway-cites-bowling-green-massacre-that-never-happened-to-defend-travel-ban/?utm_term=.a10132e62cd4.
22. American Community Survey, "Demographic and Housing Estimates," American FactFinder, https://factfinder.census.gov/faces/tableservices/jsf/pages/productview.xhtml?src=CF (accessed October 27, 2019).
23. American Community Survey, "Poverty Status in the Past 12 Months," American FactFinder, https://factfinder.census.gov/faces/tableservices/jsf/pages/productview.xhtml?src=CF (accessed October 28, 2019).
24. For photos of the "memorial," see "Mock Vigils Held for Bowling Green 'Victims' after Trump Spokeswoman Invented Massacre to Defend Muslim Ban," *Mirror Online*, February 4, 2017, https://www.mirror.co.uk/news/world-news/mock-vigil-held-bowling-green-9758486.
25. "The Partisan Divide on Political Values Grows Even Wider," Pew Research Center, http://assets.pewresearch.org/wp-content/uploads/sites/5/2017/10/05162647/10-05-2017-Political-landscape-release.pdf (accessed January 17, 2019).
26. Allport, *Nature of Prejudice*.
27. The first phase of our case study included focus groups, story diaries, and interviews.
28. Costera Meijer, "Practicing Audience-Centred Journalism Research."
29. This included eleven women and ten men, ages between eighteen and sixty-five years, five of them people of color (African American, Asian, Latinx) and sixteen non-Latinx white.
30. See Findahl, Lagerstedt, and Aurelius, "Triangulation," regarding the value of triangulation with studies using diaries; and Denzin, *Research Act*, on how triangulation allows the strength of one method to counterbalance the weakness of another.
31. *Bowling Green Daily News*, *Ohio County Monitor*, *Ohio County Times News*, Ohio Valley ReSource, WKYU, *WKU Herald*.
32. For additional details on the breakdown of national news habits, see Wenzel, "To Verify or to Disengage."
33. For a discussion of this process in an analysis of news habits in Kentucky and three other sites, see Wenzel, "To Verify or to Disengage."
34. Sarah and William, focus group discussion, Bowling Green, April 12, 2017.
35. Interview with Christy, May 20, 2017.
36. Interview with Vanessa, May 17, 2017.

37. Interview with Tricia, May 20, 2017.
38. Nic Newman, "Reuters Institute Digital News Report 2019," Reuters Institute, https://reutersinstitute.politics.ox.ac.uk/sites/default/files/2019-06/DNR_2019_FINAL_0.pdf (accessed July 27, 2019).
39. Interview with Martha, May 19, 2017.
40. Interview with Steph, May 19, 2017.
41. Interview with William, June 3, 2017.
42. Interview with Jason, May 18, 2017.
43. Interview with Steve, May 19, 2017.
44. Interview with Steph.
45. Interview with Mark, May 17, 2017.
46. Interview with William.
47. Interview with Arun, June 3, 2017.
48. Interview with Lynn, May 19, 2017.
49. Iyengar, Sood, and Lelkes, "Affect, Not Ideology."
50. Richard Fletcher and Rasmus Kleis Nielsen, "Using Social Media Appears to Diversify Your News Diet, Not Narrow It," Nieman Lab, http://www.niemanlab.org/2017/06/using-social-media-appears-to-diversify-your-news-diet-not-narrow-it/ (accessed January 17, 2019).
51. Interview with Helen, May 19, 2017. Quotes from Helen in the following paragraph are also from this interview.
52. Interview with Dave, May 18, 2017.
53. Interview with Ehsan, May 17, 2017.
54. Interview with editor of *Ohio County Times*, April 12, 2017.
55. Interview with Dustin and Lee Bratcher, April 12, 2017.
56. Interview with Dustin Bratcher, February 2, 2018.
57. Interview with Heather, May 19, 2017.
58. Had the study included non-English-speaking participants, there would likely be more networks bounded by language and culture. An additional study of the communication needs of the substantial immigrant and refugee community in the area is needed to fully understand the region's communication infrastructures.
59. Unemployment was 6.1 percent in Ohio County versus 3.4 percent in Bowling Green, according to the Bureau of Labor Statistics, 2016.
60. Joe Karaganis and Sam Ford, "Polarization Doesn't Have to Be a Self-Fulfilling Prophecy," Slate, December 18, 2018, https://slate.com/news-and-politics/2018/12/political-polarization-bowling-green-study-kentucky-immigration.html.
61. These sections adapt research that informed Wenzel, "Engaged Journalism in Rural Communities."
62. In addition to shadowing the *Ohio County Monitor* editors and observing the community contributors and liars table activities, I conducted semi-structured interviews with the two editors, five community contributors, five liars table participants, one convenience store staffer, one public library staffer, and four participants in events at the library.
63. Surveys were distributed via the *Ohio County Monitor*'s website and Facebook page.
64. Gerson et al., "From Audience to Reporter."
65. For more explanation of the society column tradition, see "Before Facebook, Society Columns Provided News—and Community," *Columbia Journalism Review*, September 25, 2017, https://www.cjr.org/tow_center/facebook-society-columns-community.php.

66. For discussion of liars tables, see "Project Entry #7: The True Service of a Convenience Store," The Artisanal Economies Project, https://artisanaleconomiesproject.org/2017/05/18/project-entry-7-the-true-service-of-a-convenience-store/ (accessed January 17, 2019).

67. Interview with Dustin Bratcher.
68. Interview with Martha, February 4, 2018.
69. Interview with Jenny, February 2, 2018.
70. Lee Bratcher at community contributors meeting, March 25, 2018.
71. Interview with Tom, February 2, 2018.
72. Interview with Lee Bratcher, February 2, 2018.
73. Interview with Heather, February 1, 2018.
74. See chapter 2 discussion of a case example using the Hearken engagement platform.
75. Borger, van Hoof, and Sanders, "Expecting Reciprocity."
76. Interview with Walter, January 28, 2018.
77. Interview with Terry, January 28, 2018.
78. Interview with Mike, January 28, 2018.
79. Interview with Lee Bratcher.
80. Mayer, Davis, and Schoorman, "Integrative Model."
81. Interview with Jake, January 28, 2018.
82. Interview with Terry.
83. Interview with Walter.
84. Interview with Jean, February 2, 2018.
85. Interview with Tom.
86. Solutions Journalism Network, https://www.solutionsjournalism.org/who-we-are/mission (accessed January 17, 2019).
87. Interview with Jean.
88. Interview with Mike.
89. Jennifer Brandel, "Looking for Evidence That Audience Engagement Helps Newsrooms? Here You Go," Medium.com, https://medium.com/we-are-hearken/receipts-1bc3d35a88bf (accessed January 17, 2019).
90. Emily Goligoski and Stephanie Ho, "Why Your Community Members Want to Aid Your Reporting," Membership Puzzle Project, https://membershippuzzle.org/articles-overview/participation-pathways (accessed January 17, 2019).
91. The outlet was premised both on participation and on financial membership, but it ended up violating the trust of members by changing the location of its headquarters. See "Crowdfunded Journalism Startup: The Correspondent under Fire," *Columbia Journalism Review*, March 28, 2019, https://www.cjr.org/the_media_today/crowdfunding-correspondent-office.php.
92. Interview with Heather, February 1, 2018.

Chapter 4. The Process Is Portable

1. Linda Qiu, "Donald Trump Had Biggest Inaugural Crowd Ever? Metrics Don't Show It," Politifact, https://www.politifact.com/truth-o-meter/statements/2017/jan/21/sean-spicer/trump-had-biggest-inaugural-crowd-ever-metrics-don/ (accessed January 17, 2019).

2. Rebecca Sinderbrand, "How Kellyanne Conway Ushered in the Era of 'Alternative Facts,'" *Washington Post*, January 22, 2017, https://www.washingtonpost.com/news/

the-fix/wp/2017/01/22/how-kellyanne-conway-ushered-in-the-era-of-alternative-facts/?utm_term=.68980247cc3f.

3. Brandon, focus group discussion, October 19, 2017. Future quotes from Brandon are from this discussion.

4. "Just How Many People Were at the Million Man March in 1995?," *Washington Post*, https://www.washingtonpost.com/apps/g/page/national/just-how-many-people-were-at-the-million-man-march-in-1995/1841/ (accessed January 17, 2019).

5. Indira Lakshmanan, "Finally Some Good News: Trust in News Is Up, Especially for Local Media," Poynter, https://www.poynter.org/news/finally-some-good-news-trust-news-especially-local-media (accessed January 17, 2019).

6. Josh Stearns, "Local News Is a Building Block to Rebuild Trust," Medium, https://medium.com/trust-media-and-democracy/local-news-is-a-building-block-to-rebuild-trust-fab8752f3659 (accessed January 17, 2019).

7. Our initial research study was done with support from the Tow Center for Digital Journalism, with colleagues Anthony Nadler, Melissa Valle, and Marc Lamont Hill.

8. In Germantown, a community that is majority African American, sixteen participants were Black; three were white. Only two self-identified as Republican; the rest described themselves as Democrat, progressive, or independent. In majority white Montgomery County, all participants were white. Twelve identified as Democrat or progressive, five as Republican or conservative, and four as independent or "nonaffiliated."

9. At each site we ensured that at least one of the co-moderators represented the majority demographic of the group (for example, a moderator who identified as Black at the Germantown site, and one who identified as white at the Montgomery County site).

10. Matsaganis, Golden, and Scott, "Communication Infrastructure Theory."

11. Interview with Donna, December 7, 2017. Quotes from Donna in this paragraph and the next are also from this interview.

12. Interview with Celeste, November 26, 2017.

13. Focus group discussion, Germantown, November 11, 2017.

14. Celeste and Donna, focus group discussion, Germantown, November 12, 2017.

15. Mayer, Davis, and Schoorman, "Integrative Model."

16. Focus group discussion, Germantown, November 11, 2017.

17. Usher, "Putting 'Place' in the Center of Journalism Research," 49.

18. Jamal, focus group discussion, Germantown, November 11, 2017.

19. Donna and Raheem, focus group discussion, Germantown, November 12, 2017.

20. Interview with Brenda, December 8, 2017.

21. Interview with Mark, December 6, 2017.

22. Interview with Anne, December 8, 2017.

23. Emily, focus group discussion, Montgomery County, November 16, 2017.

24. This included representatives from Free Press's News Voices, the Listening Post Collective, Your Voice Ohio, and Resolve Philadelphia.

25. Germantown workshop, March 31, 2018.

26. Montgomery County workshop, April 7, 2018.

27. Montgomery County workshop, April 7, 2018.

28. Germantown workshop, March 31, 2018.

29. City Bureau, "Documenters," City Bureau, https://www.citybureau.org/documenters/ (accessed January 17, 2019).

30. Montgomery County workshop, April 7, 2018.

31. Bock, "Citizen Video Journalists."
32. Borger, van Hoof, and Sanders, "Expecting Reciprocity."
33. Germantown workshop, March 31, 2018.
34. Germantown workshop, March 31, 2018.
35. Germantown workshop, March 31, 2018.
36. Germantown workshop, March 31, 2018.
37. Germantown workshop, March 31, 2018.
38. Germantown workshop, March 31, 2018.
39. Johnson, "Citizen Journalism in the Community and the Classroom."
40. Laura Benshoff, "In Philly Suburbs, Readers See More 'Ghost Newspapers' as Hedge Funds Cut Costs," WHYY, https://whyy.org/articles/in-philly-suburbs-readers-see-more-ghost-newspapers-as-hedge-funds-cut-costs/ (accessed May 17, 2019).
41. Germantown workshop participant summarizing a group discussion, March 31, 2018.
42. In addition to myself and Marc Lamont Hill at Temple University, the project has been co-organized by Letrell Crittenden at Jefferson University, who has collaborated on research and devoted a course to the project.
43. Germantown Info Hub, "Germantown Community Conversation: Keeping Germantown Beautiful," Eventbrite, https://www.eventbrite.com/e/germantown-community-conversation-keeping-germantown-beautiful-tickets-57719460460# (accessed March 26, 2019).
44. Chris Malo, "Germantown Residents Meet with WHYY to Discuss Local Reporting," Germantown Info Hub, December 18, 2018, https://medium.com/germantown-info-hub/germantown-residents-meet-with-whyy-to-discuss-local-reporting-1edf1d2a0016.
45. For example, the Lenfest Institute for Journalism and the Independence Public Media Fund are both based in Philadelphia and have both funded projects the Germantown Info Hub has been involved with.

Chapter 5. A New Kind of Journalist?

1. In this chapter I use the real names of engaged journalism professionals with their permission.
2. The workshop was held on February 22, 2019.
3. Assman and Diakopoulos, "Negotiating Change."
4. Quotes in this section are from my interview with Jean Friedman-Rudovsky and Cassie Haynes, April 23, 2019.
5. From 2017 to the time of writing I have been sitting in as a participant observer on Resolve Philadelphia partner meetings. Temple University has been one of Resolve Philadelphia's partners.
6. Resolve Philadelphia, "About," ResolvePhilly.org, www.resolvephilly.org/about (accessed July 27, 2019).
7. Resolve Philadelphia, "The Reentry Project," ResolvePhilly.org, https://resolvephilly.org/wp-content/uploads/2019/05/The-ReEntry-ProjectUpdated.pdf (accessed July 27, 2019).
8. The Discourse, "About," The Discourse, https://www.thediscourse.ca/about (accessed July 27, 2019).
9. Quotes in this section are from my interview with Anita Li, November 9, 2018, and from personal communication with her, April 9, 2019.

10. Mayer, Davis, and Schoorman, "Integrative Model."

11. Emma Jones and Sadiya Ansari, "Even Communities in the GTA Need Better Information. We're Listening," The Discourse, https://www.thediscourse.ca/scarborough/even-communities-in-gta-need-better-information (accessed July 27, 2019).

12. See, for example, pushback the *Star* received after a columnist used this term: "Don't Call us Scarberia," *The Star*, July 11, 2013, https://www.thestar.com/opinion/letters_to_the_editors/2013/07/11/dont_call_us_scarberia.html.

13. See, for example, a Story Circle they held with residents to discuss media coverage of Scarborough: "An Evening of 'Magical Thinking': Scarborough Discourse Holds Its First Story Circle," *The Discourse*, November 29, 2018, https://www.thediscourse.ca/scarborough/scarborough-discourse-story-circle.

14. Your Voice Ohio, https://yourvoiceohio.org/who-we-are/ (accessed July 27, 2019).

15. A substitute for a more profane expression of amazement or surprise.

16. Quotes in this section are from my interview with Doug Oplinger, March 19, 2018.

17. For more background on Jefferson Center's Citizens Jury model, see "How We Work," Jefferson Center, https://jefferson-center.org/about-us/how-we-work/ (accessed July 27, 2019).

18. For an overview of recent calls for transparency to build trust, see "Transparency in Journalism Isn't a New Idea, but It's More Important Than Ever," Medium, April 10, 2019, https://medium.com/the-engaged-journalism-lab/transparency-in-journalism-isnt-a-new-idea-but-it-s-more-important-than-ever-cfed217f0a46.

19. See SJN's explanation of its philosophy regarding journalism as "watchdog": "The Best Solutions Journalism of 2018," Solutions Journalism Network, November 27, 2018, https://thewholestory.solutionsjournalism.org/the-best-solutions-journalism-of-2018-3cfdd656e6fe?mc_cid=88f631e5b4&mc_eid=d9d3144438.

20. Jesse Hardman, presentation, People Powered Publishing Conference, Chicago, November 10, 2016.

21. Hardman now helps manage a national project called the Listening Post Collective, https://www.listeningpostcollective.org.

22. Hearken, https://www.wearehearken.com/ (accessed July 27, 2019).

23. Villanueva et al., "Communication Asset Mapping."

24. Groundsource, "FAQ's," Groundsource, https://www.groundsource.co/faqs#what (accessed July 27, 2019).

25. Interview with Jesse Hardman, July 31, 2018.

26. Jesse Hardman, presentation, People Powered Publishing Conference, Chicago, November 10, 2016.

27. Listening Post Collective, "Playbook," Listening Post Collective, https://www.listeningpostcollective.org/playbook (accessed July 27, 2019).

28. Sarah Alvarez, Outlier Media, "Give the People What They Ask For: An Information Needs Inquiry to Help News Organizations Meet the Information Needs of News Consumers," unpublished background paper.

29. "Searching for News: The Flint Water Crisis," Pew Research Center, http://www.journalism.org/essay/searching-for-news/ (accessed July 27, 2019).

30. Quotes in this section are from my interview with Sarah Alvarez, August 3, 2018.

31. Larson and Csikszentmihalyi, "Experience Sampling Method."

32. Christina Schmidt, "What Kind of Information—Not Just Content—Do You Need as a News Consumer?," NiemanLab, http://www.niemanlab.org/2018/07/what-kind

-of-information-not-just-content-do-you-need-as-a-news-consumer/ (accessed July 27, 2019).

33. For more examples of text correspondences, see "By Mass Texting Local Residents, Outlier Media Connects Low-Income News Consumers to Useful, Personalized Data," Nieman Lab, March 1, 2018, http://www.niemanlab.org/2018/03/by-mass-texting-local-residents-outlier-media-connects-low-income-news-consumers-to-useful-personalized-data/.

34. Harry Backlund, "Is Your Journalism a Luxury or a Necessity?," City Bureau, https://www.citybureau.org/notebook/2019/7/17/journalism-is-a-luxury-information-is-a-necessity?fbclid=IwAR33LGW-2FWZbXTEyy46Np9GO6T1Ljm1S73ipz83EjCHam2sm4zw6KWSSOs (accessed July 27, 2019).

35. Interview with Mike Rispoli, July 2, 2018.

36. On the role of interstitial actors as connectors in local storytelling networks, see Matsaganis, Golden, and Scott, "Communication Infrastructure Theory."

37. Interview with Fiona Morgan, June 27, 2018.

38. Interview with Alicia Bell, March 28, 2019.

39. Alicia Bell, "A Public Conversation with the *Charlotte Observer*," Free Press, https://www.freepress.net/our-response/advocacy-organizing/stories-field/public-conversation-charlotte-observer (accessed July 27, 2019).

40. Interview with Fiona Morgan, June 27, 2018.

41. Matsaganis, Golden, and Scott, "Communication Infrastructure Theory."

42. For examples of Public Newsroom workshops, see "Public Newsroom Workshops," City Bureau, https://www.citybureau.org/public-newsroom-workshops (accessed July 27, 2019).

43. Interview with Bettina Chang, November 16, 2018.

44. Darryl Holliday, "What's in Your Local News Contract?," Medium, https://medium.com/city-bureau/whats-in-your-local-news-contract-a849b4497602 (accessed July 27, 2019).

45. City Bureau, "Local News Contract Declaration," Google Doc, https://docs.google.com/document/d/18QMarGsZd2OqUpqHcjNfE4WEmxgK7fRZLtY3Y5N6n9U/edit.

46. "What's in Your Local News Contract?," City Bureau, April 24, 2019, https://medium.com/city-bureau/whats-in-your-local-news-contract-a849b4497602.

47. Because jesikah maria ross does not capitalize her name, I do not capitalize it in this chapter.

48. Quotes in this section are from my interview with jesikah maria ross, June 22, 2018.

49. Impact Architects and jesikah maria ross, "Place and Privilege," Capital Public Radio, http://www.capradio.org/media/12085780/Place%20and%20Privilege%20Report%20FINAL.pdf (accessed July 27, 2019).

50. Interview with Sarah Alvarez, August 3, 2018.

51. See chapter 2.

52. Interview with Doug Oplinger, March 19, 2018.

53. Quotes in this section are from my interview with Cole Goins, June 11, 2018.

54. Interview with jesikah maria ross, June 22, 2018.

55. Quotes in this section are from my interview with Mike Rispoli, July 2, 2018.

56. Carlson, "Introduction."

57. Quotes in this section are from my interview with Doug Oplinger, March 19, 2018.

58. Quotes in this section are from my interview with jesikah maria ross, June 22, 2018.

59. She joined Capital Public Radio part time as a consultant in 2013 and full time as staff in 2015.
60. Robinson and Culver, "When White Reporters Cover Race."
61. Ward "Inventing Objectivity."
62. Robinson and Culver, "When White Reporters Cover Race," 376.
63. Interview with Fiona Morgan, June 27, 2018.
64. Interview with Cole Goins, June 11, 2018.
65. Correspondence with Fiona Morgan, May 13, 2018.
66. Quotes in this section are from my interview with Fiona Morgan, June 27, 2018.
67. Journalism That Matters, http://journalismthatmatters.org (accessed July 27, 2019).
68. The World Café, "The World Café Method," The World Café, http://www.theworldcafe.com/key-concepts-resources/world-cafe-method/# (accessed July 27, 2019).
69. For example, see "Don't Just Engage. Organize!," Free Press News Voices, https://www.freepress.net/sites/default/files/2018-07/fp_news_voices_organizing_guide.pdf (accessed July 27, 2019).
70. Quotes in this section are from my interview with Mike Rispoli, July 2, 2018.
71. Quotes in this section are from my interview with Darryl Holliday, August 14, 2018.
72. Carlson, "Introduction."
73. For example, at the time of writing, the Discourse was struggling to meet its membership funding goals despite robust community engagement efforts.
74. Mike Scutari, "Still All In: The Trump Bump to Journalism Giving Shows No Sign of Letting Up," Inside Philanthropy, https://www.insidephilanthropy.com/home/2018/2/21/journalism-grants-newsmatch (accessed July 27, 2019).
75. In 2018, 486 people attended, with 602 attending in 2019. These numbers were capped, so there may have been additional interest. Correspondence with the Knight Foundation Communications office, May 17, 2019.
76. Interview with Cassie Haynes and Jean Friedman-Rudovsky, April 23, 2019.
77. Jessica Clark and Molly de Aguiar, "Things We Don't Talk About (but Should): An Open Letter to Media Funders," Medium, https://medium.com/@MollydeAguiar/things-we-dont-talk-about-but-should-an-open-letter-to-media-funders-74bb6d9c58e (accessed July 27, 2019).
78. Interview with Molly de Aguiar, March 14, 2019.
79. Nelson, "Elusive Engagement Metric."
80. Interview with Mike Rispoli, July 2, 2018.
81. Interview with Molly de Aguiar, March 14, 2019.
82. jesikah maria ross, "Want to Start Evaluating Your Engaged Reporting? Here's What I Did," Medium, March 5, 2019, https://medium.com/@jesikahmariaross/want-to-start-evaluating-your-engaged-reporting-heres-what-i-did-f65dbb43943c?fbclid=IwAR0ii_QW1QX1yfJjnVFTtvptDvGbT6JQvVaPUZST8XH2-z8DSzaw58GapXU.
83. Dot Connector Studio, Impact Pack Media Strategy Deck, http://dotconnectorstudio.com/wp-content/uploads/2016/08/instructions-final.pdf (accessed July 27, 2019).
84. Fetterman, Kaftarian, and Wandersman, *Empowerment Evaluation*.
85. For background on the Finding Common Ground initiative, see "Announcing Finding Common Ground Awardees," Medium, March 22, 2018, https://medium.com/finding-common-ground/announcing-finding-common-ground-awardees-80ca5203742.
86. A white paper sharing this guide is currently in press.

87. Broad, "Communication Infrastructure Theory."
88. Interview with Cole Goins, June 11, 2018.

Conclusion

1. Indira Lakshmanan, "Finally Some Good News: Trust in News Is Up, Especially for Local Media," Poynter, https://www.poynter.org/news/finally-some-good-news-trust-news-especially-local-media (accessed January 17, 2019).
2. See, for example, Broad, Gonzalez, and Ball-Rokeach, "Intergroup Relations."
3. Mayer, Davis, and Schoorman, "Integrative Model."
4. See SJN's explanation of its philosophy regarding journalism as "watchdog": "The Best Solutions Journalism of 2018," Solutions Journalism Network, November 27, 2018, https://thewholestory.solutionsjournalism.org/the-best-solutions-journalism-of-2018-3cfdd656e6fe?mc_cid=88f631e5b4&mc_eid=d9d3144438.
5. Robinson, *Networked News*, 25.
6. Quote relayed in an interview with Doug Oplinger, March 19, 2018.

Appendix

1. Ball-Rokeach, Kim, and Matei, "Storytelling Neighborhood"; Kim and Ball-Rokeach, "Civic Engagement."
2. Palmer, *Becoming the News*, 15.
3. In Western Kentucky, Dr. Pete Brown co-moderated. For the Philadelphia sites, either Dr. Melissa Valle or Dr. Anthony Nadler co-moderated.
4. Lunt and Livingstone, "Rethinking the Focus Group," 92.
5. Bloor et al., *Focus Groups in Social Research*.
6. Villanueva et al., "Communication Asset Mapping."
7. McCollough, Crowell, and Napoli, "Portrait of the Online Local News Audience," 105.
8. McCollough, Crowell, and Napoli, 105.
9. Bloor et al., *Focus Groups in Social Research*.
10. Denzin, *Research Act*.
11. Prior, "Immensely Inflated News Audience."
12. Findahl, Lagerstedt, and Aurelius, "Triangulation."
13. Kvale, *InterViews*.
14. Matsaganis, Golden, and Scott, "Communication Infrastructure Theory."
15. Broad, "Communication Infrastructure Theory," 225.
16. See Lawrence et al., "Building Engagement."

Bibliography

Ali, Christopher. *Media Localism: The Policies of Place*. Urbana: University of Illinois Press, 2017.
Allee, Shawn, and Bill Healy. "Curious City Questions Project." Curious City McCormick White Paper, 2017. https://docs.google.com/document/d/1s1xgcneTlmMJKk5aq-b9Z3XL3bRItr-_jnFE-xoIjvc/pub#id.6jpkqy6p0cey.
Allport, Gordon. *The Nature of Prejudice*. Reading, MA: Addison-Wesley, 1954.
Alvarez, Rene L. "A Community That Would Not Take 'No' for an Answer: Mexican Americans, the Chicago Public Schools, and the Founding of Benito Juarez High School." *Journal of Illinois History* 17, no. 1 (2014): 78–98.
Anderson, Benedict. *Imagined Communities: Reflections on the Origin and Spread of Nationalism*. Rev. ed. London: Verso, 1991.
Assman, Karin, and Nicholas Diakopoulos. "Negotiating Change: Audience Engagement Editors as Newsroom Intermediaries." *ISOJ Journal*, 2017. http://isoj.org/research/negotiating-change-audience-engagement-editors-as-newsroom-intermediaries/.
Ball-Rokeach, Sandra J., Yong-Chan Kim, and Sorin Matei. "Storytelling Neighborhood: Paths to Belonging in Diverse Urban Environments." *Communication Research* 28, no. 4 (2001): 392–428.
Batsell, Jake. *Engaged Journalism: Connecting with Digitally Empowered News Audiences*. New York: Columbia University Press, 2015.
Belair-Gagnon, Valerie, Jacob L. Nelson, and Seth C. Lewis. "Audience Engagement, Reciprocity, and the Pursuit of Community Connectedness in Public Media Journalism." *Journalism Practice* 13, no. 5 (2018). https://doi.org/10.1080/17512786.2018.1542975.
Bennett, Stephen E., Staci L. Rhine, Richard S. Flickinger, and Linda Bennett. "'Video Malaise' Revisited: Public Trust in the Media and Government." *Press/Politics* 4, no. 4 (1999): 8–23.
Bishop Bill. *The Big Sort: Why the Clustering of Like-Minded America Is Tearing Us Apart*. New York: Houghton Mifflin Harcourt, 2008.

Bloor, Michael, Jane Frankland, Michelle Thomas, and Kate Robson. *Focus Groups in Social Research*. Thousand Oaks, CA: SAGE, 2001.

Bock, Mary A. "Citizen Video Journalists and Authority in Narrative: Reviving the Role of the Witness." *Journalism* 13, no. 5 (2012): 639–53.

Boorstin, Daniel. *The Image, or, What Happened to the American Dream?* New York: Atheneum, 1962.

Borger, Merel, Anita van Hoof, and Jose Sanders. "Expecting Reciprocity: Towards a Model of the Participants' Perspective on Participatory Journalism." *New Media and Society* 18, no. 5 (2016): 708–25.

Bourdieu, Pierre. *The Field of Cultural Production*. New York: Columbia University Press, 1993.

Brader, Ted. "Striking a Responsive Chord: How Political Ads Motivate and Persuade Voters by Appealing to Emotions." *American Journal of Political Science* 49 (2005): 999–1023.

Broad, Garrett. "Communication Infrastructure Theory and Community-Based Program Evaluation: The Case of Media Mobilizing Project and the CAP Comcast Campaign." In *The Communication Ecology of 21st Century Urban Communities*, edited by Yong-Chan Kim, Matthew Matsaganis, Holley Wilkin, and Joo-Young Jung, 220–36. New York: Peter Lang, 2018.

Broad, Garrett, Carmen Gonzalez, and Sandra Ball-Rokeach. "Intergroup Relations in South Los Angeles—Combining Communication Infrastructure and Contact Hypothesis Approaches." *International Journal of Intercultural Relations* 38 (2014): 47–59.

Broad, Garrett, Minhee Son, and Sandra Ball-Rokeach. "The Whole Community Communication Infrastructure: The Case of Los Angeles." In *The Communication Crisis in America and How to Fix It*, edited by Lew Friedland and Mark Lloyd, 107–24. New York: Palgrave Macmillan, 2016.

Carey, James. "The Press, Public Opinion, and Public Discourse: On the Edge of the Postmodern." In *James Carey: A Critical Reader*, edited by Eve Stryker Munson and Catherine A. Warren, 228–60. Minneapolis: University of Minnesota Press, 1997.

———. "'A Republic, If You Can Keep It': Liberty and Public Life in the Age of Glasnost." In *James Carey: A Critical Reader*, edited by Eve Stryker Munson and Catherine A. Warren, 207–27. Minneapolis: University of Minnesota Press, 1997.

Carlson, Matt. "Introduction: The Many Boundaries of Journalism." In *Boundaries of Journalism: Professionalism, Practices and Participation*, edited by Matt Carlson and Seth C. Lewis, 1–18. New York: Routledge, 2015.

Chen, Nien-Tsu (Nancy), Katherine Ognyanova, Chi Zhang, Cynthia Wang, Sandra Ball-Rokeach, and Michael Parks. "Causing Ripples in Local Power Relations: The Meso-level Influence of a Hyperlocal News Website." *Journalism Studies* 18, no. 6 (2017): 710–31.

Chen, Nien-Tsu (Nancy), Katherine Ognyanova, and Nan Zhao. "Communication and Socio-demographic Forces Shaping Civic Engagement Patterns in a Multiethnic City." In *Communication and Community*, edited by Patricia Moy, 207–32. New York: Hampton Press, 2013.

Cheng, Wendy. *The Changs Next Door to the Díazes: Remapping Race in Suburban California*. Minneapolis: University of Minnesota Press, 2013.

Costera Meijer, Irene. "Practicing Audience-Centred Journalism Research." In *The SAGE Handbook of Digital Journalism*, edited by Tamara Witschge, C. W. Anderson, David Domingo, and Alfred Hermida, 546–61. Los Angeles: SAGE, 2016.

Cramer, Katherine J. *The Politics of Resentment: Rural Consciousness in Wisconsin and the Rise of Scott Walker*. Chicago: University of Chicago Press, 2016.

Curry, Alexander L., and Keith Hammonds. "The Power of Solutions Journalism." *Solutions Journalism Network and Engaging News Project*, 2014. http://solutionsjournalism.org/wp-content/uploads/2014/06/ENP_SJN-report.pdf.

Denzin, Norman K. *The Research Act: A Theoretical Introduction to Sociological Methods*. New York: McGraw-Hill, 1978.

Deuze, Mark. "What Is Journalism? Professional Identity and Ideology of Journalists Reconsidered." *Journalism* 6, no. 4 (2005): 442–64.

Dixon, Travis L. "Crime News and Racialized Beliefs: Understanding the Relationship between Local News Viewing and Perceptions of African Americans and Crime." *Journal of Communication* 58 (2008): 106–25.

Dixon, Travis L., and Daniel Linz. "Overrepresentation and Underrepresentation of African Americans and Latinos as Lawbreakers on Television News." *Journal of Communication* 50 (2000): 131–54.

Ekdale, Brian, Jane Singer, Melissa Tully, and Shawn Harmsen. "Making Change: Diffusion of Technological, Relational, and Cultural Innovation in the Newsroom." *Journalism and Mass Communication Quarterly* 92, no. 4 (2015): 938–58.

Entman, Robert, and Andrew Rojecki. *The Black Image in the White Mind: Media and Race in America*. Chicago: University of Chicago Press, 2000.

Fetterman, David, Shakeh Kaftarian, and Abraham Wandersman. *Empowerment Evaluation*. Los Angeles: SAGE, 2015.

Findahl, Olle, Christina Lagerstedt, and Andreas Aurelius. "Triangulation as a Way to Validate and Deepen the Knowledge about User Behavior: A Comparison between Questionnaires, Diaries and Traffic Measurements." In *Audience Research Methodologies: Between Innovation and Consolidation*, edited by Geoffroy Patriarche, Helena Bilandzic, Jakob Linaa Jensen, and Jelena Jurisic, 54–70. New York: Routledge, 2013.

Fiske, Susan. "Attention and Weight in Person Perception: The Impact of Negative and Extreme Behavior." *Journal of Personality and Social Psychology* 38, no. 6 (1980): 889–906.

Fletcher, Richard, and Sora Park. "The Impact of Trust in the News Media on Online News Consumption and Participation." *Digital Journalism* 5, no. 10 (November 2017): 1281–99. https://doi.org/10.1080/21670811.2017.1279979.

Frankenberg, Ruth. *White Women, Race Matters*. Minneapolis: University of Minnesota Press, 1993. https://www.upress.umn.edu/book-division/books/white-women-race-matters.

Friedland, Lewis. "Communication, Community, and Democracy: Toward a Theory of the Communicatively Integrated Community." *Communication Research* 28, no. 4 (August 2001): 358–91. https://doi.org/10.1177/009365001028004002.

Friedland, Lewis, and Sandy Nichols. *Measuring Civic Journalism's Progress: A Report across a Decade of Activity*. A study conducted for the Pew Center for Civic Journalism, September 2002.

Galtung, Johan. "On the Role of the Media in Worldwide Security and Peace." In *Peace and Communication*, edited by Tapio Varis, 249–66. San Jose, Costa Rica: Universidad para La Paz, 1986.

Galtung, Johan, and Dietrich Fischer. "High Road, Low Road: Charting the Course for Peace Journalism." In *Johan Galtung: Pioneer of Peace Research*, edited by Johan Galtung and Dietrich Fischer, 95–102. Switzerland: Springer, 2013.

Galtung, Johan, and Mari Holmboe Ruge. "The Structure of Foreign News: The Presentation of the Congo, Cuba and Cyprus Crises in Four Norwegian Newspapers." *Journal of Peace Research* 2, no. 1 (March 1965): 64–90. https://doi.org/10.1177/002234336500200104.

Gandy, Oscar. "Information in Health: Subsidized News." *Media, Culture and Society* 2 (1980): 103–15.

Gans, Herbert J. "News and the News Media in the Digital Age: Implications for Democracy." *Daedalus* 139, no. 2 (April 2010): 8–17. https://doi.org/10.1162/daed.2010.139.2.8.

Geer, John G. *In Defense of Negativity: Attack Ads in Presidential Campaigns*. Chicago: University of Chicago Press, 2006. https://www.press.uchicago.edu/ucp/books/book/chicago/I/bo3680300.html.

Gerson, Daniela, Nien-Tsu Nancy Chen, Andrea Wenzel, Sandra Ball-Rokeach, and Michael Parks. "From Audience to Reporter." *Journalism Practice* 11, nos. 2–3 (March 2017): 336–54. https://doi.org/10.1080/17512786.2016.1216800.

Gieryn, Thomas. *Cultural Boundaries of Science*. Chicago: University of Chicago Press, 2001. https://www.press.uchicago.edu/ucp/books/book/chicago/C/bo3642202.html.

Gillmor, Dan. *We the Media: Grassroots Journalism by the People for the People*. Sebastopol, CA: O'Reilly Media, 2004.

Glasser, Theodore L., and Francis L. F. Lee. "Repositioning the Newsroom: The American Experience with 'Public Journalism.'" In *Political Journalism: New Challenges, New Practices*, edited by Raymond Kuhn and Erik Neveu, 203–24. London: Routledge, 2007. https://doi.org/10.4324/9780203167564-20.

Hall, Stuart, Chas Critcher, Tony Jefferson, John Clarke, and Brian Roberts. *Policing the Crisis: Mugging, the State, and Law and Order*. London: Palgrave, 1978.

Hanitzsch, Thomas. "Situating Peace Journalism in Journalism Studies: A Critical Appraisal." *Conflict and Communication Online* 6, no. 2 (2007): 1–9.

Hanitzsch, Thomas, Arjen Van Dalen, and Nina Steindl. "Caught in the Nexus: A Comparative and Longitudinal Analysis of Public Trust in the Press." *International Journal of Press/Politics* 23, no. 1 (January 2018): 3–23. https://doi.org/10.1177/1940161217740695.

Harcup, Tony, and Deirdre O'Neill. "What Is News? Galtung and Ruge Revisited." *Journalism Studies* 2, no. 2 (January 2001): 261–80. https://doi.org/10.1080/14616700118449.

Hilbig, Benjamin E. "Sad, Thus True: Negativity Bias in Judgments of Truth." *Journal of Experimental Social Psychology* 45, no. 4 (2009): 983–86. https://doi.org/10.1016/j.jesp.2009.04.012.

Hwang, Jackelyn, and Robert J. Sampson. "Divergent Pathways of Gentrification: Racial Inequality and the Social Order of Renewal in Chicago Neighborhoods." *American Sociological Review* 79, no. 4 (August 2014): 726–51. https://doi.org/10.1177/0003122414535774.

Iggers, Jeremy. *Good News, Bad News: Journalism Ethics and the Public Interest*. Boulder: Perseus, 1999.

Iyengar, Shanto, Gaurav Sood, and Yphtach Lelkes. "Affect, Not Ideology: A Social Identity Perspective on Polarization." *Public Opinion Quarterly* 76, no. 3 (2012): 405–31.

Jackson, John. *Racial Paranoia: The Unintended Consequences of Political Correctness*. New York: Civitas Books, 2009.

Jenkins, Henry. *Convergence Culture: Where Old and New Media Collide*. Rev. ed. New York: NYU Press, 2008.

Johnson, Kirsten. "Citizen Journalism in the Community and the Classroom." In *Public Journalism 2.0: The Promise and Reality of a Citizen-Engaged Press*, edited by Jack Rosenberry and Burton St. John III, 99–112. New York: Routledge, 2010.

Johnston, Ron, David Manley, and Kelvyn Jones. "Spatial Polarization of Presidential Voting in the United States, 1992–2012: The 'Big Sort' Revisited." *Annals of the American Association of Geographers* 106, no. 5 (September 2016): 1047–62. https://doi.org/10.1080/24694452.2016.1191991.

Kim, Yong-Chan, and Sandra J. Ball-Rokeach. "Civic Engagement from a Communication Infrastructure Perspective." *Communication Theory* 16, no. 2 (2006): 173–97. https://doi.org/10.1111/j.1468-2885.2006.00267.x.

Kohring, Matthias, and Jörg Matthes. "Trust in News Media: Development and Validation of a Multidimensional Scale." *Communication Research* 34, no. 2 (April 2007): 231–52. https://doi.org/10.1177/0093650206298071.

Konieczna, Magda. *Journalism without Profit: Making News When the Market Fails*. Oxford: Oxford University Press, 2018.

Kurpius, David D. "Sources and Civic Journalism: Changing Patterns of Reporting?" *Journalism and Mass Communication Quarterly* 79, no. 4 (December 2002): 853–66. https://doi.org/10.1177/107769900207900406.

Kvale, Steinar. *InterViews: An Introduction to Qualitative Research Interviewing*. Los Angeles: SAGE, 1996.

Ladd, Jonathan M. *Why Americans Hate the Media and How It Matters*. Princeton: Princeton University Press, 2011.

Larson, Reed, and Mihaly Csikszentmihalyi. "The Experience Sampling Method." *New Directions for Methodology of Social and Behavioral Science* 15 (1983): 41–56.

Lawrence, Regina R., Eric Gordon, Andrew DeVigal, Caroline Mellor, and Jonathan Ladd. "Building Engagement: Supporting the Practice of Relational Journalism." Agora Journalism Center Report. Accessed June 3, 2019. https://dl.orangedox.com/building-engagement.

Lawrence, Regina R., Damian Radcliffe, and Thomas Schmidt. "Practicing Engagement: Participatory Journalism in the Web 2.0 Era." *Journalism Practice* 12, no. 10 (2017): 1220–40.

Lee, Seow Ting, and Crispin C. Maslog. "War or Peace Journalism? Asian Newspaper Coverage of Conflicts." *Journal of Communication* 55, no. 2 (2005): 311–29. https://doi.org/10.1111/j.1460-2466.2005.tb02674.x.

Lewis, Seth C., Avery E. Holton, and Mark Coddington. "Reciprocal Journalism." *Journalism Practice* 8, no. 2 (March 2014): 229–41. https://doi.org/10.1080/17512786.2013.859840.

Lippmann, Walter. *The Stakes of Diplomacy*. New York: Henry Holt, 1915.

Lischka, Juliane A., and Michael Messerli. "Examining the Benefits of Audience Integration: Does Sharing of or Commenting on Online News Enhance the Loyalty of Online Readers?" *Digital Journalism* 4, no. 5 (2016): 597–620.

López, Ian Haney. *Dog Whistle Politics: How Coded Racial Appeals Have Reinvented Racism and Wrecked the Middle Class*. Reprint, Oxford: Oxford University Press, 2015.

Lunt, Peter, and Sonia Livingstone. "Rethinking the Focus Group in Media and Communications Research." *Journal of Communication* 46, no. 2 (June 1996): 79–98. https://doi.org/10.1111/j.1460-2466.1996.tb01475.x.

Massey, Brian L. "Civic Journalism and Nonelite Sourcing: Making Routine Newswork of Community Connectedness." *Journalism and Mass Communication Quarterly* 75, no. 2 (June 1998): 394–407. https://doi.org/10.1177/107769909807500213.

Massey, Douglas S., and Nancy A. Denton. *American Apartheid: Segregation and the Making of the Underclass.* Reprint, Cambridge, MA: Harvard University Press, 1993.

Matei, Sorin Adam, and Sandra Ball-Rokeach. "Watts, the 1965 Los Angeles Riots, and the Communicative Construction of the Fear Epicenter of Los Angeles." *Communication Monographs* 72, no. 3 (September 2005): 301–23. https://doi.org/10.1080/03637750500206557.

Matsaganis, Matthew D. "Rediscovering the Communication Engine of Neighborhood Effects: How the Interaction of Residents and Community Institutions Impacts Health Literacy and How It Can Be Leveraged to Improve Health Care Access." PhD diss., University of Southern California, 2008.

Matsaganis, Matthew D., Annis G. Golden, and Muriel E. Scott. "Communication Infrastructure Theory and Reproductive Health Disparities: Enhancing Storytelling Network Integration by Developing Interstitial Actors." *International Journal of Communication* 8 (2014): 1495–1515.

Mayer, Roger C., James H. Davis, and F. David Schoorman. "An Integrative Model of Organizational Trust." *Academy of Management Review* 20, no. 3 (1995): 709–34. https://doi.org/10.2307/258792.

McCollough, Kathleen, Jessica K. Crowell, and Philip M. Napoli. "Portrait of the Online Local News Audience." *Digital Journalism* 5, no. 1 (January 2017): 100–118. https://doi.org/10.1080/21670811.2016.1152160.

McCone, John A., and W. M. Christopher. "Violence in the City: An End or a Beginning?" A Report by the Governor's Commission on the Los Angeles Riots, 1965.

Nelson, Jacob L. "The Elusive Engagement Metric." *Digital Journalism* 6, no. 4 (April 2018): 528–44. https://doi.org/10.1080/21670811.2018.1445000.

Newhagen, John E., and Byron Reeves. "The Evening's Bad News: Effects of Compelling Negative Television News Images on Memory." *Journal of Communication* 42, no. 2 (1992): 25–41. https://doi.org/10.1111/j.1460-2466.1992.tb00776.x.

Newman, Nic, Richard Fletcher, Antonis Kalogeropoulos, David A. L. Levy, and Rasmus Kleis Nielsen. "Reuters Institute Digital News Report 2017," 2017, 136. https://reutersinstitute.politics.ox.ac.uk/sites/default/files/Digital%20News%20Report%202017%20web_0.pdf.

Nicholson, Robert A., Matthew W. Kreuter, Christina Lapka, Rachel Wellborn, Eddie M. Clark, Vetta Sanders-Thompson, Heather M. Jacobsen, and Chris Casey. "Unintended Effects of Emphasizing Disparities in Cancer Communication to African-Americans." *Cancer Epidemiology, Biomarkers and Prevention : A Publication of the American Association for Cancer Research* 17, no. 11 (November 2008): 2946–53. https://doi.org/10.1158/1055-9965.EPI-08-0101.

Palmer, Ruth. *Becoming the News: How Ordinary People Respond to the Media Spotlight.* New York: Columbia University Press, 2017.

Pastor, Manuel. "Keeping It Real: Demographic Change, Economic Conflict, and Interethnic Organizing for Social Justice in Los Angeles." In *Black and Brown in Los Angeles: Beyond Conflict and Coalition*, 33–66. Berkeley: University of California Press, 2014.

Prior, Markus. "The Immensely Inflated News Audience: Assessing Bias in Self-Reported News Exposure." *Public Opinion Quarterly* 73, no. 1 (January 2009): 130–43. https://doi.org/10.1093/poq/nfp002.

Robinson, Sue. *Networked News, Racial Divides: How Power and Privilege Shape Public Discourse in Progressive Communities*. Cambridge: Cambridge University Press, 2017. https://www.amazon.com/Networked-News-Racial-Divides-Communication/dp/1108412327.

Robinson, Sue, and Kathleen Bartzen Culver. "When White Reporters Cover Race: News Media, Objectivity and Community (Dis)Trust." *Journalism: Theory, Practice and Criticism* 20, no. 3 (2019): 375–91.

Rodriguez, Clemencia. "A Latin American Approach to Citizen Journalism." In *Citizen Journalism: Global Perspectives*, vol. 2, edited by Einar Thorsen and Stuart Allan, 199–210. New York: Peter Lang, 2014.

Rosen, Jay. "The Challenge of Public Journalism." In *The Idea of Public Journalism*, edited by Theodore L. Glasser, 20–48. New York: Guilford Press, 1999.

———. "The People Formerly Known as the Audience." *PressThink* (blog), June 27, 2006. http://archive.pressthink.org/2006/06/27/ppl_frmr.html.

Rutherford, Jonathan. "The Third Space: Interview with Homi Bhabha." In *Identity: Community, Culture, Difference*, edited by Jonathan Rutherford, 207–21. London: Lawrence and Wishart, 1990.

Saito, Leland T. *Race and Politics: Asian Americans, Latinos, and Whites in a Los Angeles Suburb*. Urbana: University of Illinois Press, 1998.

Sampson, Robert J. *Great American City: Chicago and the Enduring Neighborhood Effect*. Reprint, Chicago: University of Chicago Press, 2013.

Schmidt, Thomas, and Regina R. Lawrence. "Putting Engagement to Work: How News Organizations Are Pursuing 'Public-Powered Journalism.'" Agora Journalism Center Report, 2018, https://dl.orangedox.com/putting-engagement-to-work.

Schudson, Michael. "The Objectivity Norm in American Journalism." *Journalism* 2, no. 2 (August 2001): 149–70. https://doi.org/10.1177/146488490100200201.

———. *The Sociology of News*. 2nd ed. New York: W. W. Norton, 2011.

Schudson, Michael, and Susan E. Tift. "American Journalism in Historical Perspective." In *The Press*, edited by Geneva Overholser and Kathleen Hall Jamieson, 17–47. New York: Oxford University Press, 2005.

Shah, Dhavan V., Douglas M. McLeod, Eunkyung Kim, Sun Young Lee, Melissa R. Gotlieb, Shirley S. Ho, and Hilde Breivik. "Political Consumerism: How Communication and Consumption Orientations Drive 'Lifestyle Politics.'" *Annals of the American Academy of Political and Social Science* 611, no. 1 (May 2007): 217–35. https://doi.org/10.1177/0002716206298714.

Son, Minhee, and Sandra Ball-Rokeach. "The Whole Community Communication Infrastructure: The Case of Los Angeles." In *The Communication Crisis in America and How to Fix It*, edited by Mark Lloyd and Lewis Friedland, 107–24. New York: Palgrave Macmillan, 2016.

Soroka, Stuart, and Stephen McAdams. "An Experimental Study of the Differential Effects of Positive versus Negative News Content." Paper presented at the Elections, Public Opinion and Parties Annual Conference, University of Essex, Colchester, UK, September 10–12, 2010, http://patrick-fournier.com/d/cours11–6607.pdf.

Spivak, Gayatri Chakravorty. "Can the Subaltern Speak?" In *Marxism and the Interpretation of Culture*, edited by Cary Nelson and Lawrence Grossberg, 271–313. London: Macmillan, 1988.

Sue, Derald Wing, Christina M. Capodilupo, Gina C. Torino, Jennifer M. Bucceri, Aisha M. B. Holder, Kevin L. Nadal, and Marta Esquilin. "Racial Microaggressions in Everyday Life: Implications for Clinical Practice." *American Psychologist* 62, no. 4 (2007): 271–86. https://doi.org/10.1037/0003-066X.62.4.271.

Tuchman, Gaye. *Making News: A Study in the Construction of Reality*. Later Printing ed. New York: Free Press, 1980.

United States National Advisory Commission on Civil Disorders. *The Kerner Report: The 1968 Report of the National Advisory Commission on Civil Disorders*. 1st Pantheon ed. New York: Pantheon Books, 1988.

Usher, Nikki. "Putting 'Place' in the Center of Journalism Research: A Way Forward to Understand Challenges to Trust and Knowledge in News." *Journalism and Communication Monographs* 21, no. 2 (2019): 84–146.

Villanueva, George, Garrett Broad, Carmen Gonzalez, Sandra Ball-Rokeach, and Sheila Murphy. "Communication Asset Mapping: An Ecological Field Application toward Building Healthy Communities." *International Journal of Communication* 10 (January 2016): 2704–24.

Villanueva, George, Carmen Gonzalez, Minhee Son, Evelyn Moreno, Wenlin Liu, and Sandra Ball-Rokeach. "Bringing Local Voices into Community Revitalization: Engaged Communication Research in Urban Planning." *Journal of Applied Communication Research* 45, no. 5 (October 2017): 474–94. https://doi.org/10.1080/00909882.2017.1382711.

Villanueva, George, and Andrea Wenzel. "The Engaged Communication Scholar: Designing CIT-Informed Engaged Research in Diverse Communities." In *The Communication Ecology of 21st Century Urban Communities*, edited by Yong-Chan Kim, Matthew Matsaganis, Holley Wilkin, and Joo-Young Jung, 167–84. New York: Peter Lang, 2018.

Wall, Melissa. "Citizen Journalism." *Digital Journalism* 3, no. 6 (November 2015): 797–813. https://doi.org/10.1080/21670811.2014.1002513.

Ward, Stephen J. "Inventing Objectivity: New Philosophical Foundations." In *Journalism Ethics: A Philosophical Approach*, edited by Christopher Meyers, 137–52. New York: Oxford University Press, 2010.

Wenzel, Andrea. "Eating Together, Separately: Intergroup Communication and Food in a Multiethnic Community." *International Journal of Communication* 10 (January 2016): 22.

———. "Engaged Journalism in Rural Communities." *Journalism Practice* 13, no. 6 (December 2018): 708–22. https://doi.org/10.1080/17512786.2018.1562360.

———. "Public Media and Marginalized Publics." *Digital Journalism* 7, no. 1 (January 2019): 146–63. https://doi.org/10.1080/21670811.2017.1398594.

———. "Red State, Purple Town: Polarized Communities and Local Journalism in Rural and Small-Town Kentucky." *Journalism*, published online June 25, 2018, 1–17. https://doi.org/10.1177/1464884918783949.

———. "To Verify or to Disengage: Coping with 'Fake News' and Ambiguity." *International Journal of Communication* 13 (April 2019): 19.

Wenzel, Andrea, Daniela Gerson, Evelyn Moreno, Minhee Son, and Breanna Morrison Hawkins. "Engaging Stigmatized Communities through Solutions Journalism: Residents of South Los Angeles Respond." *Journalism* 19, no. 5 (May 2018): 649–67. https://doi.org/10.1177/1464884917703125.

Wilkin, Holley A. "Exploring the Potential of Communication Infrastructure Theory for Informing Efforts to Reduce Health Disparities." *Journal of Communication* 63, no. 1 (2013): 181–200. https://doi.org/10.1111/jcom.12006.

Zuckerman, Ethan. "Mistrust, Efficacy and the New Civics—A Whitepaper for the Knight Foundation." August 17, 2017. http://www.ethanzuckerman.com/blog/2017/08/17/mistrust-efficacy-and-the-new-civics-a-whitepaper-for-the-knight-foundation/.

Index

accountability journalism, 18, 117
advocacy journalism, 8
Agora Journalism Center, 12, 154
Alhambra Source, 17–18
Ali, Christopher, 16
Alinsky, Saul, 149
Allee, Shawn, 47–48, 64–65, 69, 70, 73
Allport, Gordon, 79
Alvarez, Sarah, 135–138, 143, 144
American Community Survey, 53–54
audience, 11–12, 72–74

Backlund, Harry, 137
Ball-Rokeach, Sandra, 15, 27
Beaver Dam, Kentucky, shared community stories in, 2–4
Belair-Gagnon, Valerie, 51, 72
Bell, Alicia, 139
Bishop, Bill, 77
Bornstein, David, 8, 9
boundary-work, 12–15
Bourdieu, Pierre, 13
Bowling Green, Kentucky, 78–79. *See also* polarization
Brandel, Jennifer, 50–52
Bratcher, Dustin, 92, 98, 102
Bratcher, Lee, 92, 98, 102

Broad, Garrett, 155, 170
Brown, Michael, 24

"Can the Subaltern Speak?" (Spivak), 14
Capital Public Radio, 141–143, 147, 151, 154
Carey, James, 14, 49, 52
Carlson, Matt, 13
Center for Investigative Reporting, 144
Chang, Bettina, 140
Charlotte Observer, 139
Chicago Matters, 49
citizen journalism, 10–11, 93–96; community contributors and (*see* community contributors); citizen reporters and, 115
City Bureau, 140–141, 150–151
civic journalism, 10–11
Clark, Jessica, 153
Cleveland Plain Dealer, 9
CNN, 81, 82
Coddington, Mark, 51, 63, 72
communication infrastructure theory (CIT), 4, 21, 24, 52, 62–63, 74, 165–166; assessing the storytelling network and, 167–169; evaluating interventions and, 155, 170–171; insights for local journalism from, 15–18, 155, 164; polarization and, 88, 104; process model and, 167–171; value of qualitative inquiry and, 166

community-centered journalism: competencies for (*see* competencies); funding for, 151–156; need for, 1–4, 158–164; overview of, 18–22; partnerships for, 63–66
community-centered journalists, 125–127; connected to community organizations, 143–146; learning skills and unlearning norms, 156–157; navigating newsrooms and journalism roles, 146–151; responsibilities of, 162–163
community-centered process model, 160, 167–171
community contributors, 17, 92–96, 98–103, 115; citizen journalism and (*see* citizen journalism)
community organizations, connecting journalists to, 143–146; partnerships with, 63–66
community reporters, 115. *See also* citizen journalism; community contributors
competencies, 125–127; in accessing funds and assessing impact, 151–156; community-centered convenings, 138–143; community-centered platforms and assessments, 133–138; community-centered solutions journalism, 127–133; for connecting journalists to community organizations, 143–146; learning skills and unlearning norms, 156–157; navigating newsrooms and journalism roles, 146–151
convenings, community-centered, 138–143
Conway, Kellyanne, 78
Cramer, Katherine, 77
crime coverage in Germantown, 108–110
Cronkite, Walter, 82
Crowell, Jessica K., 168
Culver, Kathleen, 148
Curious City, 47–48, 143; community partnerships and, 63–66; conclusions on outreach by, 68–69; face-to-face outreach by, 53–63; hyperlocal and ethnic media partnerships and, 66–67; libraries and, 65–66; links with audience, 72–74; offline engagement by, 70–72; participatory news cycle and, 48–52; question experiment of, 52–69; social medial marketing by, 67–68

Davis, James, 7
de Aguiar, Molly, 153
De Correspondent, 103
Democracy Fund, 11
DeVigal, Andrew, 12, 154
digital engagement, 12
direct reciprocity, 51
Discourse, the, 129–131
Drudge Report, 81

engaged journalism, 4, 5, 11–12, 13–15, 152, 158, 162–163; offline, 70–72
Entman, Robert, 40
ethnic media, 66–67

Facebook, 40, 67–68, 78, 85, 131
Fairness Doctrine, 6
field theory, 13
Finding Common Ground, 154
focus groups, 167–168
Ford, Sam, 80, 92
Fox News, 81
Frankenberg, Ruth, 14
Friedland, Lewis, 10, 16
Friedman-Rudovsky, Jean, 128–129
funding, project, 151–156

Galtung, Johan, 10
Gans, Herbert, 8
"Gapminder Test" (online quiz), 8
Germantown, Philadelphia: crime coverage in, 108–110; narratives about communities in, 116–117; neighborhood information hub in, 117–121; portable, not scalable, interventions in, 122–124; storytelling network intervention in, 113–117; trust in media in, 110–111
Gieryn, Thomas, 13
Goins, Cole, 144, 157
Gordon, Eric, 154
Green-Barber, Lindsay, 11

Hardman, Jesse, 133–135
Harlins, Latasha, 32
Hearken company, 51–52, 72

Hidden Hunger project, 145
Holliday, Darryl, 141, 150–151
Holton, Avery E., 63, 72
hyperlocal media, 66–67, 114–115; as portable, not scalable, 122–124

interviews, 168

journalism: accountability, 18, 117; advocacy, 8; boundary-work in, 12–15; citizen, 10–11, 93–96; engaged, 4, 5, 11–12, 13–15, 70–72, 152, 158, 162–163; frustration with, 2–3; hyperlocal, 66–67, 114–115; local, 6–7, 15–18, 111–112, 168–169; parachute, 27, 33, 61, 89, 106; participatory, 11; peace, 9–11; people-powered, 11; public, 9–11; reciprocal, 11; social, 11; solutions, 4, 5, 8–9, 14–15, 19–20, 36–44, 109, 127–133, 158, 162–163; trust in, 6–7, 80–83, 106, 110–111, 161–162; watchdog, 9; Wenzel as participant observer of, 4–6. *See also* community-centered journalism
Journalism that Matters, 149
journalists, community-centered, 125–127; connected to community organizations, 143–146; learning skills and unlearning norms, 156–157; navigating newsrooms and journalism roles, 146–151; responsibilities of, 162–163

Kentucky: polarization in (*see* polarization); storytelling networks in (*see* storytelling networks)
Kerner Commission, 23
Knight Media Forum, 152
Konieczna, Magda, 6
Korean Times, 32

Ladd, Jonathan, 6
Lawrence, Regina, 51, 154
Lewis, Seth C., 63, 72
Li, Anita, 129–131
liars tables, 96–98
Lippmann, Walter, 9
Listening Post Collective, 133–135
local journalism: absence of, 111–112; communication infrastructure theory (CIT) and, 15–18; interviews with, 168–169; "trust" in, 6–7
Los Angeles Times, 28, 29, 37

Malatia, Torey, 49–50, 71–72
Matei, Sorin Adam, 27
Mayer, Roger, 7
McCollough, Kathleen, 168
McCone Commission, 23
McCormick Foundation, 52
Metamorphosis Project, 15, 19, 24, 27, 36, 44
microaggression, 41
Million Man March, 105
Montgomery County, PA, 111–113; narratives about communities in, 116–117; storytelling network intervention in, 113–117
Morgan, Fiona, 139, 149
MSNBC, 82

Napoli, Philip M., 168
narratives about communities, 116–117
national media mistrust, 80–83
National Public Radio (NPR), 5, 73
negative news, 37–41
neighborhood information hubs, 117–121
Nelson, Jacob, 51, 72
news deserts, 112–113
News Voices, 138–139, 145, 147, 148–149, 150, 153
New York Times, 8, 9, 54, 82
Nichols, Sandra, 10

offline engagement, 70–72
Ohio County, KY, 78–79; reimagining community traditions in, 92–93; strengthening the storytelling network of, 98–102. *See also* polarization
Ohio County Monitor, 92, 152, 154; liars tables tour of, 96–98; paths forward and process models for, 102–104; society columns of, 93–96; strengthening the storytelling network and, 98–102
Oplinger, Doug, 131–133, 144, 146–147, 162, 163
Outlier Media, 135–138, 143, 155

Palmer, Ruth, 17
parachute journalism, 27, 33, 61, 89, 106
participatory design process, 169–170
participatory journalism, 11, 48–52
Pastor, Manuel, 26
peace journalism, 9–11
people-powered journalism, 11
Philadelphia Inquirer, 116
piloting of interventions, 170–171
pitch process, 28–31
place identity, 77–78
polarization, 75–76; assessing the storytelling network and, 79–90; in Bowling Green and Ohio County, KY, 78–79; community groups and spaces and, 85–86; interpersonal networks and, 83–85; local media and, 86–88; national media mistrust and, 80–83; paths forward and process models for, 102–104; in purple places, 76–78; reimagining community traditions in Ohio County and, 92–93; reimagining liars tables as listening posts and, 96–98; reimagining society columns as citizen journalism and, 93–96; storytelling network interventions for, 90–98; storytelling networks, place, and community issues in, 88–90; strengthening the Ohio County storytelling network and, 98–102
process model, 122–124, 126, 159–160, 167–171
public journalism, 9–11

qualitative inquiry, value of, 166

reciprocal journalism, 11
Report for America, 9
Resolve Philadelphia, 127–129, 151, 152
Rispoli, Mike, 138–139, 145, 149–150, 153
Robinson, Sue, 7, 148
Rojecki, Andrew, 40
Rosen, Jay, 10
Rosenberg, Tina, 8
ross, jesikah maria, 141–143, 145, 147–148, 154

Sampson, Robert, 53
Schmidt, Thomas, 51

Schoorman, F. David, 7
social journalism, 11
social media marketing, 67–68
society columns, 93–96
solutions journalism, 4, 5, 8–9, 14–15, 19–20, 109, 158, 162–163; community-centered, 127–133; the Discourse and, 129–131; Resolve Philadelphia and, 127–129; in South LA, 36–46; Your Voice Ohio, 131–133
Solutions Journalism Network (SJN), 8–9, 34, 100, 163
South LA: bad news in, 37–41; connecting local media and community groups in, 28–36; intervention in local storytelling network 28–36; reading solutions journalism in, 36–44; representation of Black and Brown communities in, 31–33; solutions storytelling in, 42–44; storytelling network in, 25–27, 42–46; Watts Rebellion in, 23–25, 34–35
Spivak, Gayatri Chakravorty, 13–14
story diaries, 168
storytelling networks, 4, 15–18, 20, 21–22, 24, 62, 167–169; absence of local news and, 111–112; alternative sources in suburban news desert and, 112–113; community groups and spaces for, 85–86; community reporters in, 115; covering crime at expense of community and, 108–110; hyperlocal communication assets for, 114–115; intervention projects for, 90–98, 113–117, 122–124; in Kentucky, 88–90, 98–102; local interpersonal, 83–85; local media, 86–88; narratives about community in, 116–117; neighborhood information hub in, 117–121; in Philadelphia region, 107–113; place and community issues in, 88–90; polarization and, 79–90; role of trust in, 110–111, 161–162; of South LA, 25–27, 44–46. See also *Curious City*
sustained reciprocity, 63

Time (magazine), 105
triangulation, 169
Trump, Donald, 21, 54, 75, 77, 78, 97, 105, 107, 152

trust in media, 6–7, 80–83, 106, 110–111; trustworthiness factors, 161–162
Tuchman, Gaye, 43
Twitter, 78

Walmart, 85
Ward, Stephen, 148
watchdog journalism, 9
Watts Rebellion, 23–25, 34–35. *See also* South LA

Watts Revisited project, 36–37
WBEZ, 5, 49–51, 60, 61, 65, 67, 73; offline engagement by, 71–72; social media marketing and, 68
WHYY, 119–120, 149

Your Voice Ohio, 131–133, 144, 146–147, 151, 162, 163

Zuckerman, Ethan, 76

ANDREA WENZEL is an assistant professor of journalism at Temple University.

The University of Illinois Press
is a founding member of the
Association of University Presses.

―――――――――――――

University of Illinois Press
1325 South Oak Street
Champaign, IL 61820-6903
www.press.uillinois.edu